FRIDA KAHLO

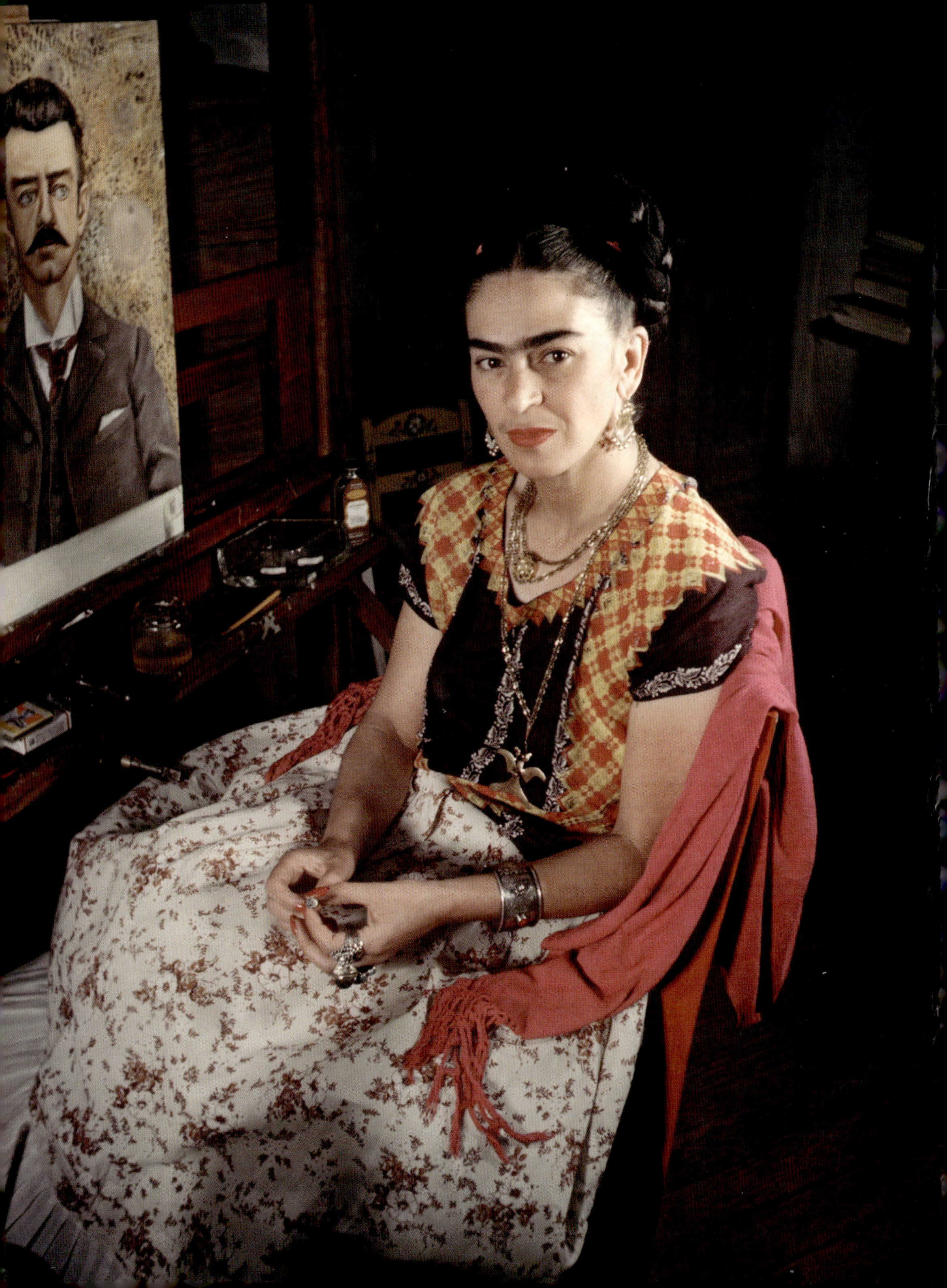

FRIDA KAHLO

THE GISÈLE FREUND PHOTOGRAPHS

WITH TEXTS BY GÉRARD DE CORTANZE,
GISÈLE FREUND, AND LORRAINE AUDRIC

Abrams, New York

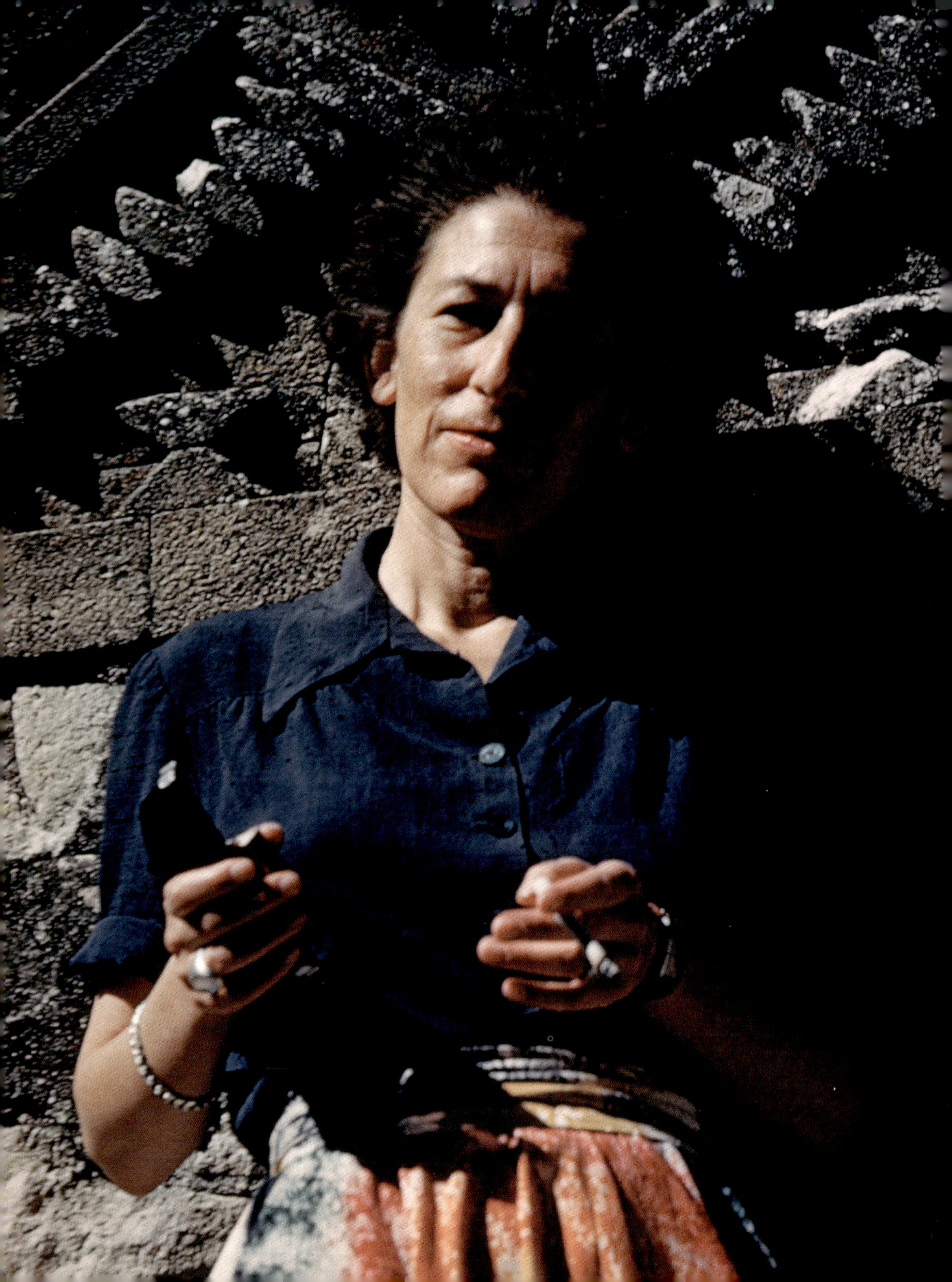

Previous page: Frida Kahlo at home, 1951.
Opposite: Gisèle Freund, anonymous portrait, Mexico, 1951.

1

FRIDA AND DIEGO'S WORLD IN GISÈLE FREUND'S CAMERA

BY GÉRARD DE CORTANZE

"The world of photojournalism consists of telling a story with nothing but images. It is no longer a matter of gathering a few photographs to illustrate a subject, but of organizing a certain number of photos around a central symbolic image, which summarizes every element of the story that the additional photos tell in detail."

Gisèle Freund.[1]

At the outbreak of World War II, German-born Gisèle Freund was thirty-two years old and had been French by marriage since 1936. Having sought refuge in unoccupied France in the tiny village of Saint-Sozy, near Souillac, Freund received a timely letter from Victoria Ocampo, "extravagantly rich and powerful, friend to writers, lover of France and its culture, and publisher of the famous magazine *Sur*,"[2] inviting her to come live in Argentina. With her exit visa in hand, Gisèle Freund took a ship from Bilbao, Spain, survived a tumultuous crossing, and landed in Buenos Aires, where the French intellectual Roger Caillois was waiting for her, not on the dock but in the comfort of his car.

The young woman was setting foot for the first time not only in the land of Borges, but also in South America. This artist, who had photographed the "bruised bodies of comrades battered by Hitlerians,"[3] felt uneasy in this "wealthy setting where everyone was scheming"[4] and quickly told the beautiful Victoria that she was not there "to photograph the ladies of high society."[5] And so her Argentine friend opened every door for her, and Freund soon found herself en route to photograph Tierra del Fuego, a hellish region where convicts were sent because of its impossible remoteness. Starting out from Buenos Aires, she also traveled to other South American nations: Uruguay, Chile, Ecuador. In each country, she shot photo stories that were then published by the press: "Previously I had practiced the portrait, but to know the American continent I had only one choice: to become a *photojournalist*."[6]

Returning to France in 1946, Freund made a series of photo stories about craftsmen, worked for the cultural department of the Ministry of Foreign Affairs, and–most important–became one of the inaugural members of the Magnum Photos agency cofounded by Robert Capa and Henri Cartier-Bresson in 1947.

1. *Le Monde et ma caméra [The World in My Camera]*, Denoël, 1970. 2. *Gisèle Freund, portrait: Entretiens avec Rauda Jamis [Gisèle Freund, Portrait: Conversations with Rauda Jamis]*, Des femmes/Antoinette Fouque, 1991. 3. *Le Monde et ma caméra*. 4. *Gisèle Freund, portrait*. 5. *Le Monde et ma caméra*. 6. Ibid.

Freund was one of the first women to join Magnum. The agency's members divided the world among themselves. Freund was naturally entrusted with covering South America, though Cartier-Bresson remarked that she took a little too much interest in art, notably the pre-Columbian, which she photographed extensively.

"I fell wildly in love with Mexico and a Mexican man. What a country! Everything there is beautiful, from the most ancient artistic relics to the slightest craft object picked up at the markets. Without overlooking the landscape and, of course, the people."

Among her first stories in South America, a 1950 commission from *Life* magazine proved decisive: The assignment was nothing less than a trip to Argentina to take a series of photos of the presidential couple Eva and Juan Domingo Perón. Señora Perón, nicknamed the *bataclana* ("chorus girl") by her enemies, liked jewelry, beautiful dresses, fur coats, and shoes, accumulating hundreds of pairs. The general, elegant and svelte in a uniform sparkling with decorations, had a red face covered in acne. Gisèle Freund photographed what she saw. After the shoot was completed, she was summoned to the Ministry of Information to have her negatives inspected.

Gisèle Freund never went to that appointment. Instead, she fled to Uruguay. The story's publication set off a diplomatic incident between Buenos Aires and Washington. *Life* was banned in Argentina, Gisèle Freund's American visa was not renewed, and

Magnum, which was beginning to have problems with McCarthyism, used this as an excuse to stop working with her.

After a brief return to Paris, Gisèle Freund accepted the writer Alfonso Reyes's invitation to travel to Mexico City to give a lecture at the Colegio de México. She planned to stay a few weeks, take some photos, and go home. Yet her Mexican journey would only come to an end in 1952: "I fell wildly in love with Mexico and a Mexican man. What a country! Everything there is beautiful, from the most ancient artistic relics to the slightest craft object picked up at the markets. Without overlooking the landscape and, of course, the people. Nothing in Mexico is mediocre or insignificant. This country of violent contrasts totally captivates the traveler. Mexico touched me deeply. There, I often burst into tears through mere contact with nature."[7]

Over these two years, the Mexican government put a chauffeured car at her disposal to take her wherever she wished, allowing her to crisscross the country in every direction: "Some areas were still inaccessible and the roads often in very bad shape. The car was sometimes stopped by tree trunks lying across the road and crude little ambushes to rob us. Not to mention the endless breakdowns that compromised each trip and those days the chauffeur refused to drive because of mechanical problems, masking his fear of traveling farther in technical incompetence."[8] She visited the Mayan sites in Yucatán, crossed the Isthmus of Tehuantepec, went to Lake Pátzcuaro and to the coast of Michoacán, traveled among the Tzotzil Indians, and photographed farmers, villagers, children, and women, notably the famous Tehuanas, whom she had passionately described in "Femmes Mexicaines" ["Mexican Women"], a text written in Buenos Aires in 1950 and unpublished to this day: "The charm of Mexican women is probably due to the mixture of Indian and Spanish blood, which gives them such a peculiar and–if I may say so–romantic character. Most of them are svelte, move gracefully, and have the olive skin and smooth black hair of their Indian ancestors. Mexican women also hold their country's traditions dear. Every woman wears a *rebozo,* a large scarf draped over the shoulders in even folds. In hot areas, it is made of light, silky fabric, while on the colder high plateaus it is often made of wool–vividly colorful, sometimes striped, but nearly always of a single color. Mexican women love jewelry. Since the Aztec era, Mexican craftsmen have excelled in the minor arts of gold and silver, and this country, rich with mines of these precious metals, provides them with all the raw materials. In Mexico, one also finds

7. *Gisèle Freund, portrait.* 8. Ibid.

numerous semiprecious stones such as jade and amethyst, which are those most often used in jewelry. The Tehuana of the Isthmus of Tehuantepec, reputed to be among the most beautiful women in Mexico, love gold pieces and filigreed jewelry above all else, and one sees humble peasant women and market vendors covered in jewels that would make women all over the world envious."[9]

She became fascinated with ancient Mexican art–Olmec, Toltec, Mayan, Aztec–as well as the frescoes of the muralists painting "for the people": José Clemente Orozco, David Alfaro Siqueiros, and . . . Diego Rivera.

> "This country of violent contrasts totally captivates the traveler. Mexico touched me deeply. There, I often burst into tears through mere contact with nature."

Gisèle Freund arrived in Mexico with several letters of introduction. One was from her Argentine friend María Rosa Oliver to Frida Kahlo and her husband, Diego Rivera. The fashionable couple of the moment–known to all, a two-headed eagle, a living artistic and political icon–had recently celebrated the tenth anniversary of their remarriage. Frida and Diego were photographed in "formal" garb for the first time by the press: a veil and crown for the bride, and a Spanish-style male mantle (*capa*) and wide-brimmed hat (*chambergo*) for Diego. "In Mexico, their fame is tremendous, and Diego's is greater than that of most movie stars. When heavy, paunchy Diego goes into a restaurant wearing a loose jacket, he always takes a vague look around with his gloomy eyes. The waitress rarely fails to ask him for an autograph, and there is often a female tourist around to photograph him. If she is young and beautiful, Diego consents to pose, and even to kiss her hand. But if she is older and ordinary-looking, he will pretend not to speak English and will remain absorbed in his meal."[10]

Shortly before Freund's arrival in Mexico, the Palace of Fine Arts held a sprawling retrospective of Rivera's visual art: "The entire Palace of Fine Arts was rearranged for a gigantic exhibition: The occasion was to celebrate fifty years of the painter's work. Rivera paintings

9. "Femmes Mexicaines" ["Mexican Women"] (1950), unpublished, Gisèle Freund collection, IMEC. 10. "Diego Rivera construit sa tombe" ["Diego Rivera Builds His Tomb"] (1955), unpublished, Gisèle Freund collection, IMEC.

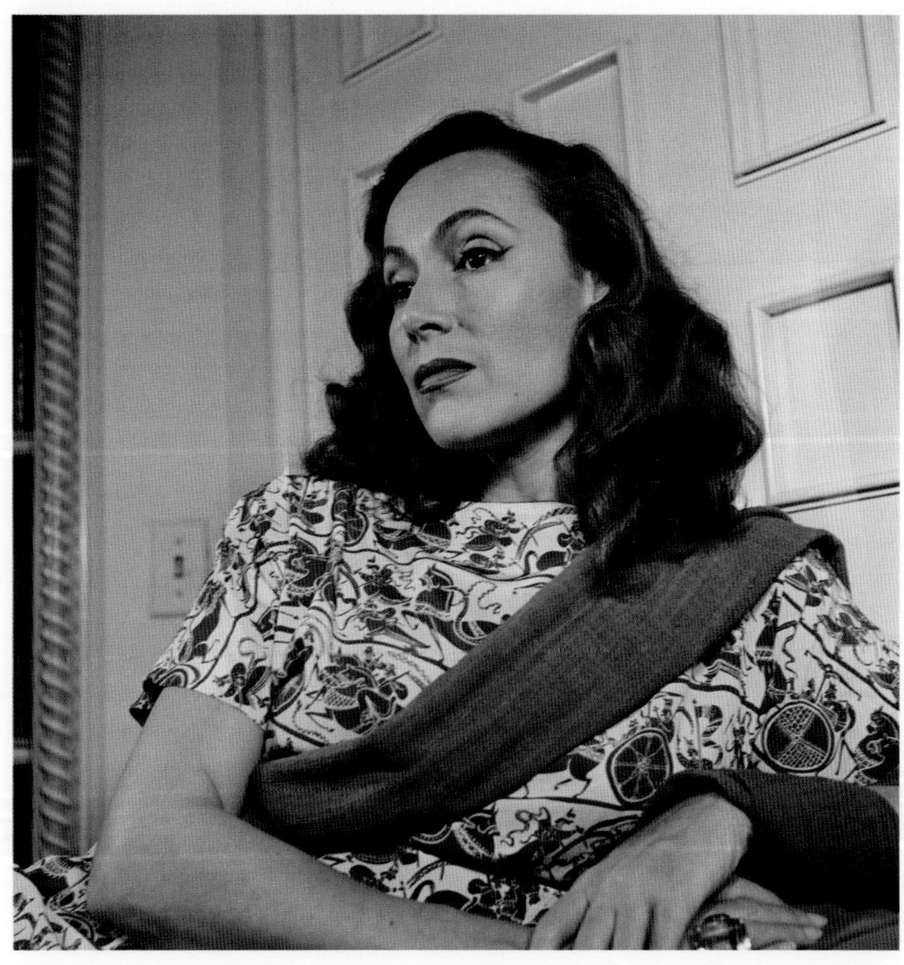

Dolores del Rio at home, Mexico, 1951. The actress was among the famous personalities photographed by Gisèle Freund during her stay in Mexico.

were shipped from all over the world, from museums and private collections, showing the different phases of his artistic evolution: works of his youth, neo-impressionist paintings made in Paris before World War I, cubist works, then the paintings showing his rediscovery of Mexico from 1921 to the present day. The exhibition was up for several months and the number of visitors was estimated at more than one million."[11]

Diego immediately took the photographer under his wing, promising to show her Mexico and take her to all the festivals, of which he knew the locations and exact dates, from the most traditional to the most celebrated: votive, ritual, local.[12] He drew her into the heart of the supernatural world, took her to remote, dangerous areas, put her in contact with Indians who continued to refuse to submit to the central government instituted by the revolution, and allowed her to witness pagan rituals held in Catholic churches. "He took me to incredible places. I have many pictures of what would now be called Mexican folklore. They captivated France and, later, all of Europe,"[13] she told Kahlo biographer Rauda Jamis in 1991. Most important, he opened the doors to his "pyramid" of San Pablo Tepetlapa, which he was building in utter secrecy to store his own work and his collection of pre-Cortesian art, a kind of museum to his own glory where he hoped to have his and Frida's ashes interred: "And now, stone by stone, Diego is completing his pyramid, the most extraordinary combination of museum and tomb that the world has ever seen. Like the Mayan and Aztec pyramids that inspired him, this monument dominates the rolling valley. Inside, all the rooms are decorated with mosaics created by Diego himself and based on authentic pre-Columbian drawings. Countless niches will house his collection of pre-Columbian sculptures from Mexico, consisting of over ten thousand priceless pieces. Here, Diego wants his ashes to rest beside Frida's. When looking at this enormous mausoleum, which Diego will leave to the Mexican people along with his collections, one is tempted to ask whether the painter has attempted to ensure that his glory will weather the centuries."[14]

How did Freund see Diego Rivera? She answered that question in her book *Le Monde et ma caméra [The World in My Camera]*: "At sixty-eight, he weighed more than one hundred and twenty kilos [265 pounds] and seemed endowed with extraordinary physical vigor and nearly superhuman endurance. I often saw him painting in public buildings, perched on a

11. "Diego Rivera construit sa tombe." 12. See pages 108–09 in *Gisèle Freund, portrait.* 13. Ibid. 14. "Diego Rivera construit sa tombe."

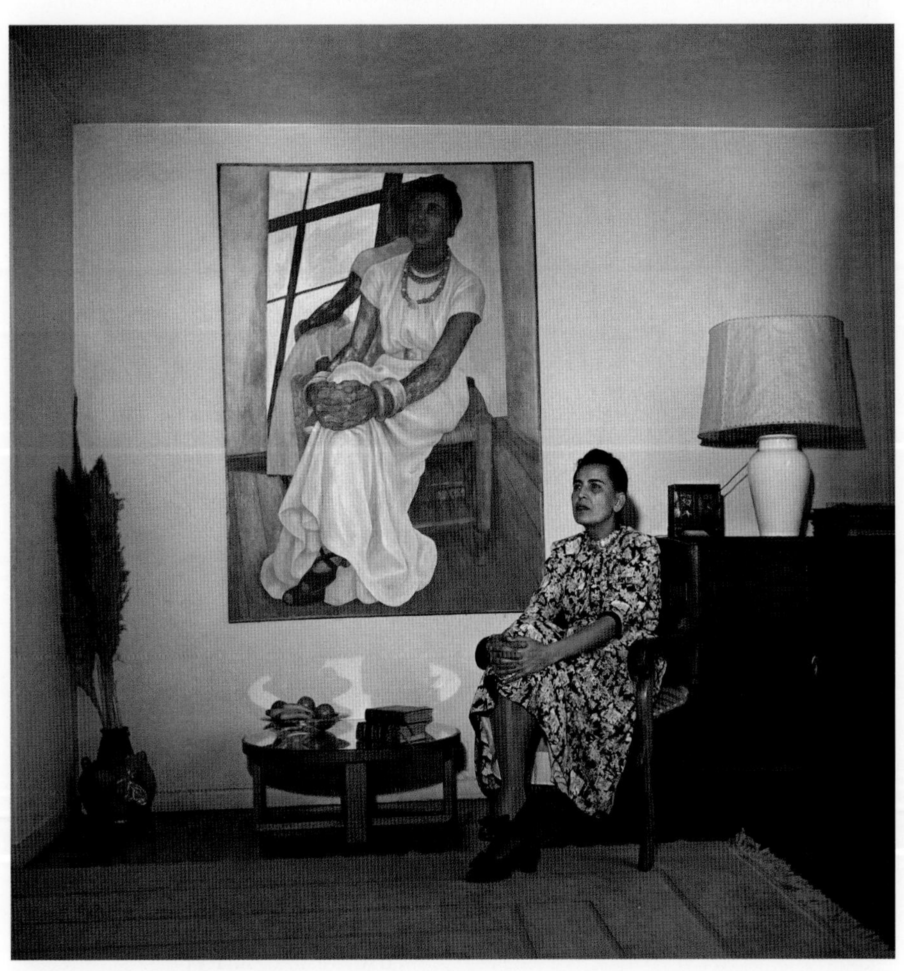

Lupe Marín, Diego Rivera's second wife,
in front of her portrait by Diego Rivera, Mexico, 1951.

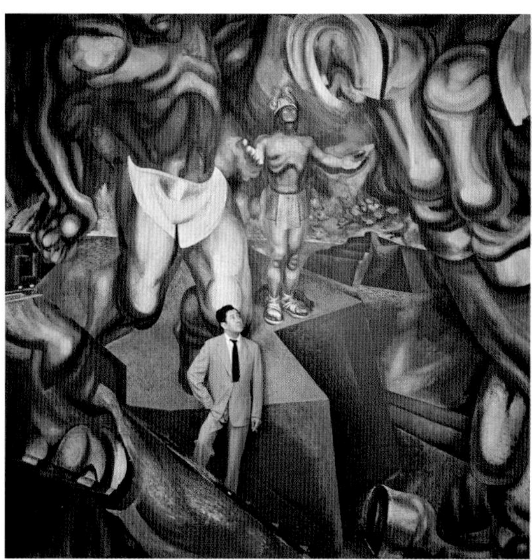

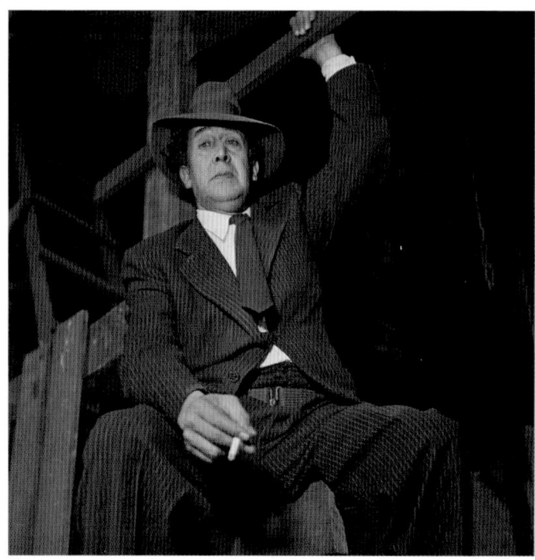

David Alfaro Siqueiros, Mexico City, 1951.
Top, in front of one of his frescoes; above, right, and following double-page spread, in his studio.

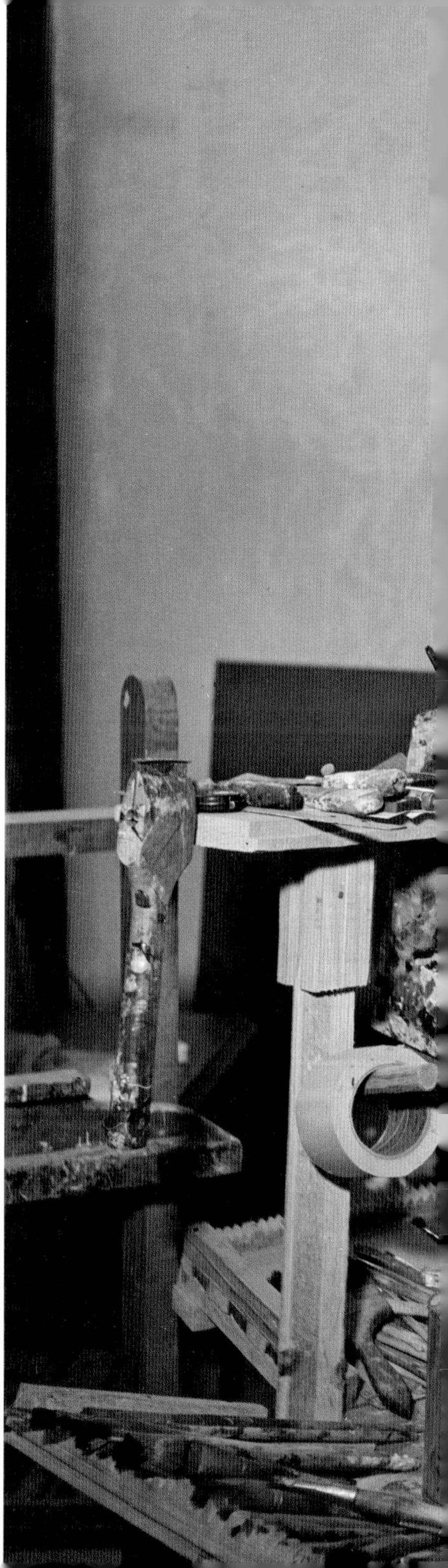

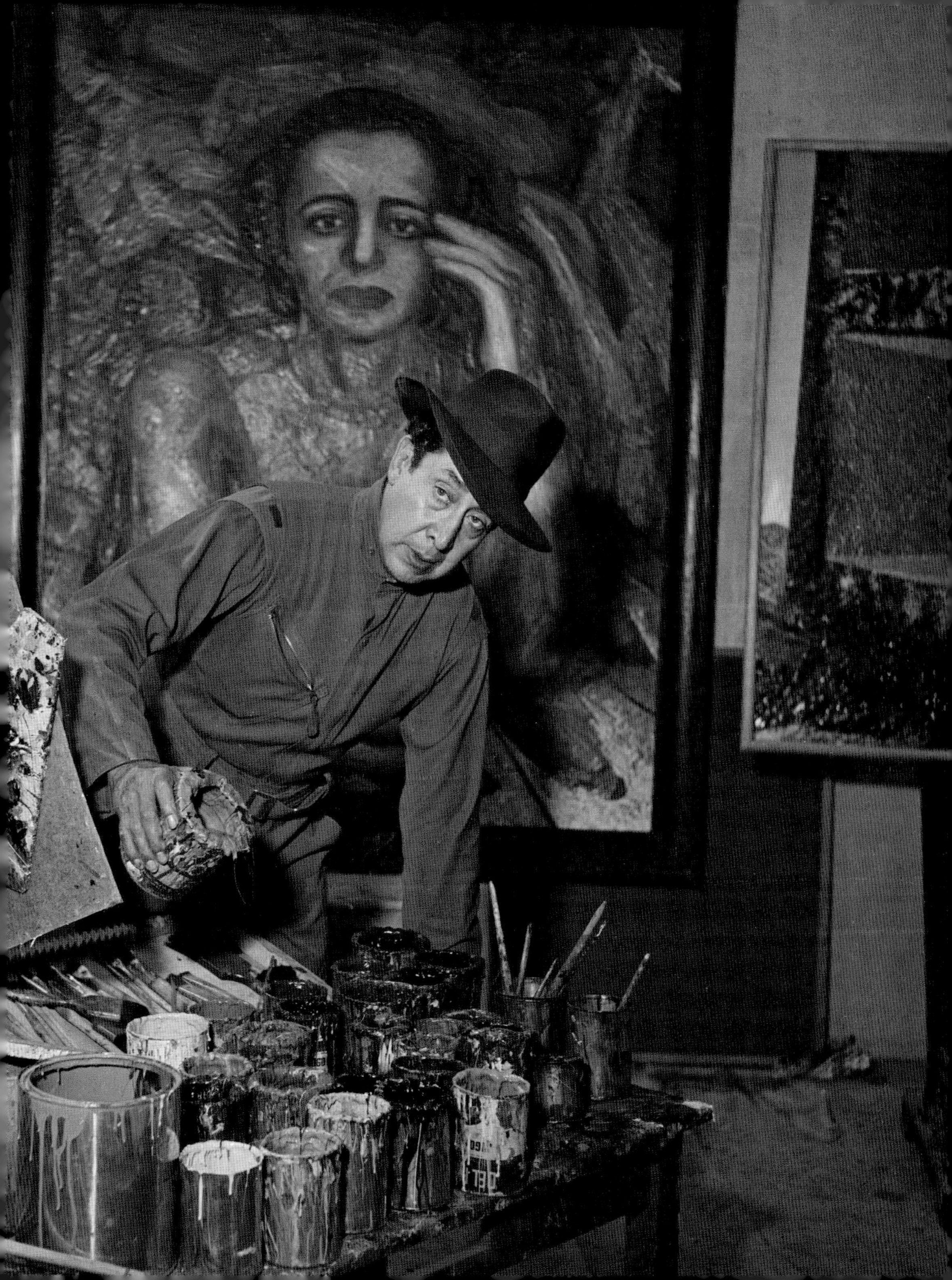

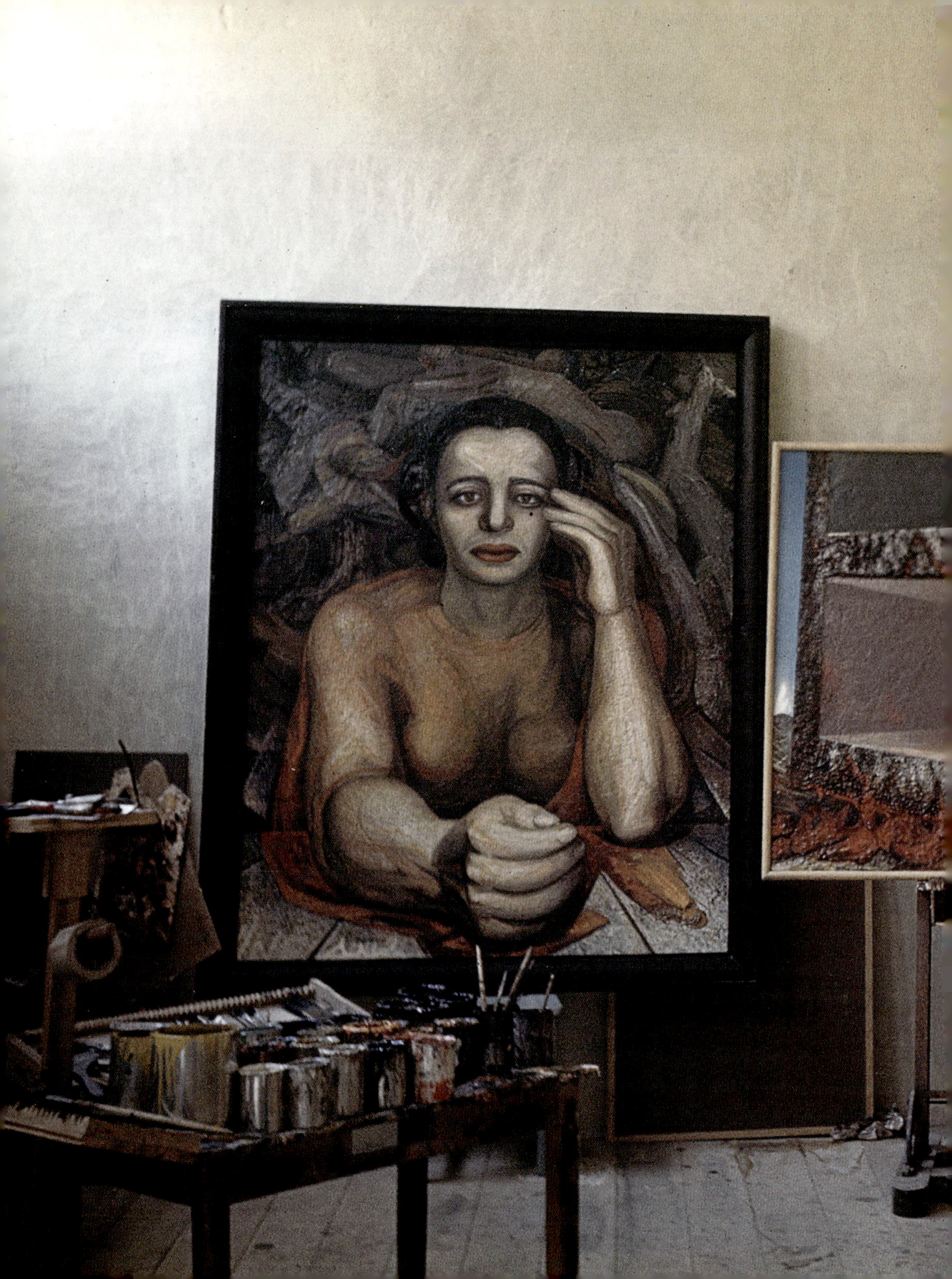

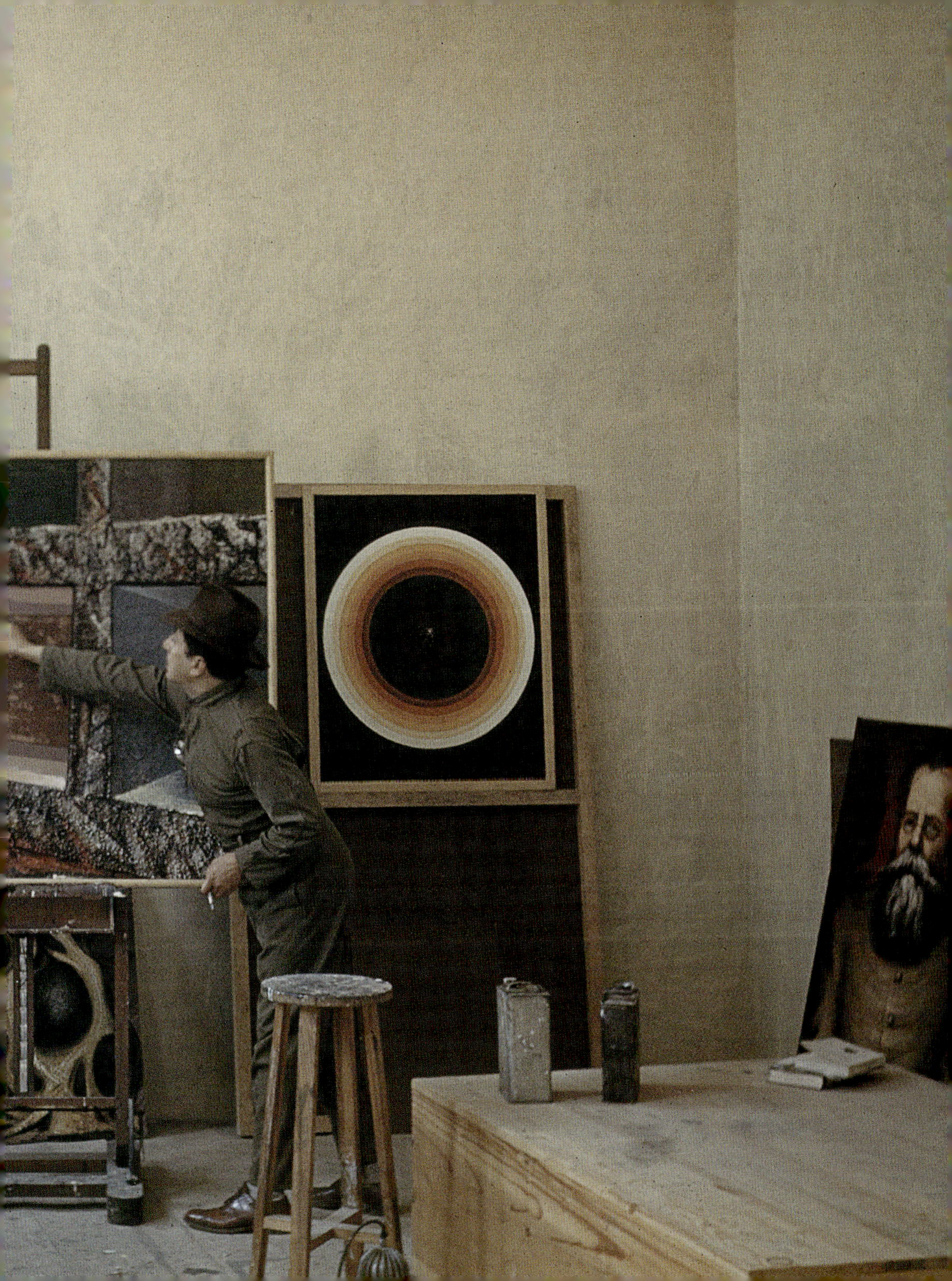

scaffold like a weighty eagle. He told me he got up every morning at six. An hour later, he was already at work, stopping only at midnight. And when he wasn't working, the ebullient torrent of his energy led him to commit unpredictable acts. In his private life, he was a prodigious liar, provoking countless scandals. He was a real headache for the government, never restraining himself from expressing his political opinions in the form of Marxist slogans on monumental frescoes, which led foreigners to mistakenly believe that Mexico was a revolutionary country."

In short, Gisèle Freund was under his spell. She praised his inexhaustible inventiveness and devastating humor, was amused by his extramarital conquests (at the time, the papers were full of his stormy love affair with the actress María Félix), and expressed admiration for how open and available "the most famous man in Mexico" was.[15] She wrote: "Throughout his long and eventful career, Diego Rivera has been the government's 'bête noire,' and yet even his enemies agree that without him Mexico would not be so appealing. Like the beaches of Acapulco, the floating gardens of Xochimilco, and the marvels of Monte Albán, the great artist is one of the country's leading attractions. This explains why the conservative government allows him to decorate public buildings with monumental frescoes covered in Marxist slogans. Tourists admire his bright colors. In general, they do not understand Spanish, but even

15. *Gisèle Freund, portrait.*

if they can read it, Diego's political ideas only elicit amused shrugs in official circles, because they believe that the dog barks more loudly than it bites."[16]

What about Frida? "A heroic, nearly legendary figure, she sits in her wheelchair year after year facing her easel and painting terrifying canvases in the surrealist manner. Strangely beautiful, she has a lively intelligence and a caustic wit," Gisèle Freund wrote in *Le Monde et ma caméra*. She elaborated on her impressions in her conversations with Rauda Jamis: "She was a formidable being, but in great distress. In the last years of her life, she was constantly swallowing a wide assortment of pills. Not only because of the physical pain due to her terrible tram accident, but also because she was a deeply conflicted being. She loved men, but did not turn away from women. She would shower you with gifts large and small, ranging from a charm, a tiny brass ex-voto, or a good luck stone to pre-Columbian pottery, as well as the heavy jewelry that she was crazy about. She was always writing to all the people she loved and I received many letters from her which are now lost. One day she told me: *I don't want to live a long time. I am really suffering too much.*" Freund also noted that the couple was always violently, cruelly arguing, that they were both capable of saying horrible things to each other, and that "being around them at those times was like torture or heroism."[17]

The years 1950 to 1952 were critical ones for the two painters. Frida spent most of 1950 in the American British Cowdray Hospital, undergoing several operations on her spinal column. She consulted up to five doctors, all of whom advised that her crushed right foot be amputated, and she wrote to Dr. Leo Eloesser that the "only variation is the level at which the amputation should be done."[18] She received subcutaneous injections of helium-hydrogen gas and oxygen, was constantly pricked with needles and stuffed with pills, and had to wear corsets made of plaster. Though she had to take Chloromycetin every three hours and was the first person in Mexico to try Terramycine, she never stopped painting. Her bedroom was turned into a permanent reception hall, decorated with sugar skulls, a scattering of paint cans, brushes, drawings tacked to the walls, chandeliers, and a Soviet flag. Nurses, doctors, and friends gathered there to eat the victuals brought by her sister Cristina, watch films projected by Diego, and drink and sing. Frida, who felt "as useless as a sewer grate,"[19] drew and wrote in her journal, painted the self-portrait *The Circle*, and returned to a canvas begun years earlier and left unfinished: *Portrait*

16. "Diego Rivera construit sa tombe." 17. Ibid. 18. *Frida Kahlo par Frida Kahlo, lettres 1922–1954 [Frida Kahlo by Frida Kahlo, Letters 1922–1954]*, Points/Seuil, 2009. 19. Ibid.

of Frida's Family, also known as *My Family*. In 1951, she began painting *Portrait of My Father, Viva la Vida and the Dr. Juan Farill, Self-Portrait with the Portrait of Doctor Farill, Glances, Still Life,* and *Weeping Coconuts,* also known as *Coconut Tears*. The following year proved less fruitful, with Kahlo primarily devoting herself to *Living Nature* and the famous *Congress of Peoples for Peace*.

As for Diego, while the gradual decline of Frida's health demanded "qualities he [did] not have,"[20] he publicly defended the cause of the Soviet Union, supported a peace conference in Stockholm, and after twenty-nine years of off-and-on work, returned in 1951 to the National Palace project. The following year, he painted *The Nightmare of War and the Dream of Peace* with the hope of being reinstated to the Mexican Communist Party, from which he had been expelled in 1929 due to his work for the government. The fresco depicts Stalin and Mao Zedong as pacifist heroes and shows Frida in her wheelchair. The government immediately banned it from being exhibited, sparking a demonstration during which two people were shot by the police. For the fourth time, the Mexican Communist Party rejected the painter's request for readmission.

While she did not witness all these events at the couple's side, Gisèle Freund was never far away. She visited them often. All these details provide the necessary context to understand the photos Freund took. She was right there, in the privacy of their home, La Casa Azul [the Blue House]. Speaking with Rivera biographer Patrick Marnham, American Communist Party cofounder Ella Wolfe, a neighbor of La Casa Azul, described their home life as entirely unique: "I did not know anyone who kept as strange a house as the Riveras. Monkeys came in through the window at lunchtime. They jumped on the table, stole food, and went off. And then there were seven hairless Xolotl dogs, named after the members of the Politburo. The funniest thing was that they came when you called them. Rivera could be very kind or very harsh. We were lucky because he was always pleasant to us. He spent most of his time telling us stories, marvelous stories. There was something hypnotic about him. Even when you knew that what he was telling you was pure fiction, you couldn't help but listen to him."[21]

Gisèle Freund photographed the world but was never more at ease than when she photographed private life. She liked to be disconcerted by the atmosphere surrounding the man or woman whose portrait she took. She also liked to photograph, in her own words, the "shock of the surprise that subsists in us"[22]–for example, the author André Gide startled in

20. Patrick Marnham, *Dreaming with His Eyes Open: A Life of Diego Rivera,* Knopf, 1998. 21. Ibid. 22. *Le Monde et ma caméra.*

his monastic room at the far end of his sumptuous and spacious apartment on rue Vaneau. In short, she constantly sought out an individual's geography: "I always preferred photographing a person in his private space, among his own belongings. The model feels that he is in a familiar world, which relaxes him and makes the task easier. And the décor of a home reflects the person who inhabits it. Catching someone next to the trinket he cherishes makes the photo more expressive."[23]

"I felt that the moment was approaching when Mexico would devour me. It is a country where the contrasts are so stark that they are beyond human."

By 1952, Diego had begun to age rapidly and looked like a tired old man. Frida was going through a terrible ordeal. Diego stuck to his mission, trying to represent ideas, while Frida tried harder than ever to paint her private life. Gisèle Freund caught all this through her lens, knowing all the while that an image never reproduces reality; it remains an image, covering over reality, giving a counterfeit vision of the world.[24] Thus, in her photos there is always more than first meets the eye. Freund's work presents a man posing in his studio–who is undergoing radiotherapy for cancer of the penis–and a woman walking in her garden–who is working twice as hard as ever not only to be able to buy herself the drugs she needs to survive, but also to help Diego, who has no more money. The man is planning a new series of frescoes that will

23. *Le Monde et ma caméra*. 24. *Gisèle Freund, portrait*.

never be realized, and the woman paints a canvas on which we see her offer her heart-palette to the doctor treating her.

Gisèle Freund always said that faces were her passion and that she never mixed her photojournalism with her work as a portraitist, just as she always refused to retouch photos–even her portrait of François Mitterrand, president of the French Republic, was not retouched.

"In Mexico, violence, even if it were due to an excess of beauty, was in danger of overpowering me. I feared I would be carried away by this excess."

In 1952, Gisèle Freund photographed Frida Kahlo in a deteriorating state, doped on painkillers, creating paintings that, according to Dr. Velasco y Polo, "reveal states of excitement similar to those brought on by drug addiction."[25] And yet Kahlo had a tremendous desire to live. She wrote as much in her diary: "I do not feel pain. I am only drunk with . . . fatigue, and, as can be expected, very often in a state of despair. A despair that cannot be described in words. Yet I want to live and I have started painting again."[26]

Gisèle Freund also photographed a Frida Kahlo who, having rejoined the Mexican Communist Party in 1949 after having left it in 1929 subsequent to Rivera's expulsion, was deeply concerned with the revolutionary reach of her painting and its actual impact on the reality of her time: "I want to transform it into something useful, because so far I have only used this means of expression to create a frank expression of myself, which was sadly completely inadequate to serve the Party. I have to fight with all my strength so that the positive things that I can still accomplish will also be useful to the revolution."[27] She added: "This is my only real reason to live." In her diary, one also finds the words: "I myself am a Communist being."

The woman whom Gisèle Freund photographed at her easel, in her garden, near her personal belongings, and in the company of her doctor, later ferociously attacked the legacy of Trotsky, despite the fact that she had once madly loved him. As Hayden Herrera notes in her biography of Frida Kahlo, the artist inserted militant inscriptions, hastily traced peace doves,

25. Quoted by Hayden Herrera in *Frida: A Biography of Frida Kahlo*, HarperCollins, 1983. 26. *Diary of Frida Kahlo*, Abradale/Abrams, 1995. 27. Quoted by Raquel Tibol in *Frida Kahlo: Über ihr Leben und Werk nebst Aufzeichnungen und Briefen [About Her Life and Work, with Notes and Letters]*, Verlag Neue Kritik, 1980.

and included revolutionary references in her graphic works: She "politicized" them. She politicized paintings whose lines were increasingly chaotic, agitated, wild–as if her artwork were in a permanent struggle with political thought. So, unlike other authors, I will not write that Frida Kahlo was a "fervent Stalinist" in the last years of her life. Yes, a drawing in her diary entitled *Marxism Will Give Health to the Sick* shows a sanctified Karl Marx coming down from the heavens to heal her. Yes, the final canvas left on her easel was an unfinished portrait of Stalin. What of it? Everything in her life and work demonstrates a total love of freedom, freedom to create, love, and live, a profound love of people, a tolerance, a gentleness that Gisèle Freund's photos successfully captured.

On December 8, 1952, after Gisèle Freund had returned to Europe, and a report of her all-too-frequent visits to Diego and Frida were causing her trouble with the FBI, Frida Kahlo and her students participated in the redecoration of the frescoes of La Rosita bar, taking advantage of the occasion to celebrate Diego Rivera's sixty-fifth birthday and the traditional Christmas *Posadas*.[28] It was three parties in one, during which Frida abandoned her crutches and wheelchair and crossed the street followed by a joyous crowd, calling out: "No more corset! Never again! It doesn't matter what happens! Never again!" This was the woman whom Gisèle Freund photographed. The very same woman who died of a probable analgesic overdose less than two years later, a week after her forty-seventh birthday.

It is said that when Frida's ashes came out of the crematorium, Diego took a handful of them and ate them. This was the man whom Gisèle Freund photographed. The very same man who married Emma Hurtado, his art dealer, barely twelve months after Frida's death, then left her for Frida's friend Dolores Olmedo.

Many years later, when she was asked why she returned to France–the country where she spent the most years of her life–in 1952, Gisèle Freund offered a key to the mystery while simultaneously shedding new light on her photos: "I felt that the moment was approaching when Mexico would devour me. It is a country where the contrasts are so stark that they are beyond human. Suddenly, France and Europe seemed to me to be on a human scale. In Mexico, violence, even if it were due to an excess of beauty, was in danger of overpowering me. I feared I would be carried away by this excess."[29]

28. Editor's Note: *Las Posadas* is a nine-day religious celebration preceding Christmas. 29. *Gisèle Freund, portrait.*

2

FRIDA KAHLO

BY GISÈLE FREUND[1]

Diego Rivera with Gisèle Freund in front of his temple (now the Anahuacalli Museum), San Pablo Tepetlapa, Mexico, 1951.

1. Editor's Note: Previously unpublished text, written during Freund's time in Mexico, between 1950 and 1952, Gisèle Freund collection, IMEC.

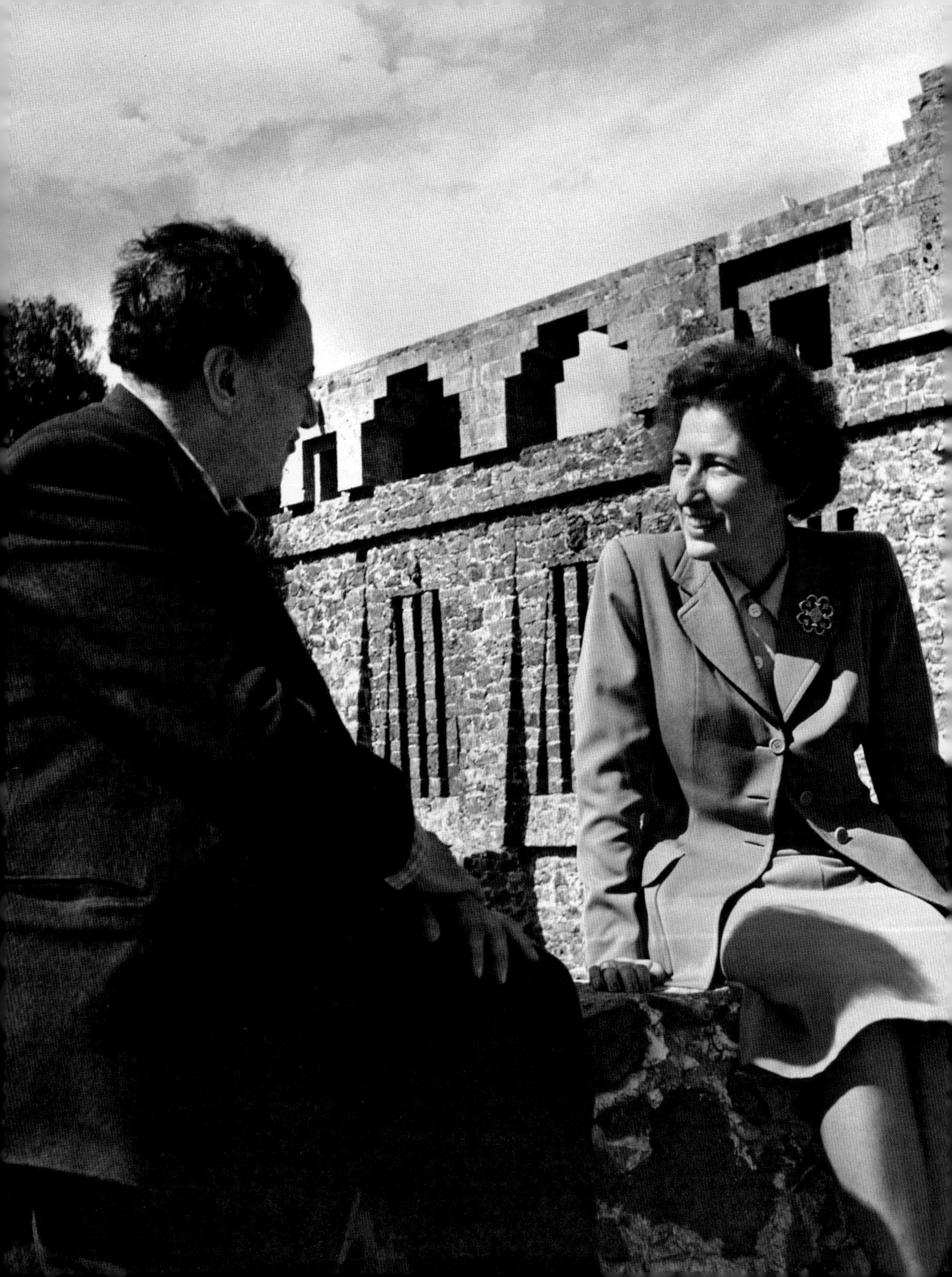

Coyoacán is a suburb of Mexico City. Some twenty minutes from the capital of Mexico, one already has the feeling of being in the heart of the countryside. The colonial houses are low and the streets muddy. Here, in a house painted blue, lives Frida Kahlo.

"She looks like an Aztec princess. Smooth black hair covers her shoulders. She wears many gold Indian necklaces and a red silk serape over her frail shoulders . . . Frida Kahlo welcomes us with a wide smile."

After we ring the doorbell, an Indian with a large sombrero on his head cautiously opens the door and asks for our names. The door is closed again and a certain amount of time passes before we are allowed inside. Suddenly, we seem to be living in another world. We enter a garden full of trees and tropical flowers. Cactuses wrap around statues and pre-Cortesian sculptures. A fountain flows into a small ornamental pool in which ducks bathe. Pigeons fly in the air and we notice their many nests in large terra-cotta vases decorating the tops of the walls.

We ascend a few stone steps to a small patio. We find a thin and fragile young woman lying on a chaise lounge, dressed in long, silky, colorful skirts. She looks like an Aztec princess. Smooth black hair covers her shoulders. She wears many gold Indian necklaces and a red silk serape over her frail shoulders. Every one of her fingers bears enormous rings with finely carved precious stones. From her olive face, dark black eyes look out from beneath large thick eyebrows; her full mouth is carefully painted.

Frida Kahlo welcomes us with a wide smile. She smokes, she laughs, she speaks with a warm, melodious voice. Her entire personality radiates a lively intelligence, a profoundly human spirit, and an exuberant vitality. She hates anything snobbish, anything fake, anything conventional and affected.

She was born in 1910[2] with the Mexican Revolution. Her father was a German photographer, her mother Mexican. The father was an atheist, the mother a believer. Frida was a devilish little girl. She preferred having boys as playmates to girls her own age. By the age of eight, she was watching bullfights and liked to walk in the markets and talk with the common people. At eleven, she wanted to become a doctor.

In 1926, at the age of sixteen, while trying to take a bus, she was caught between a tram and the arriving bus.[3] A few minutes later, she was taken away unconscious, bathed in a pool of blood. Her spinal column was shattered, her right foot and several bones broken. From the day of this horrible accident, her personality changed completely. She became more feminine, more profound . . . and she began to paint.

"I started painting," she tells us, "because I was bored of always being in bed; since I was young, the accident did not take on such a tragic form. I felt sufficient energy to do anything, instead of studying medicine. And without even realizing it, I began to paint."

2. Editor's Note: Frida Kahlo was actually born in 1907 (the date on her birth certificate), but later claimed to have been born in 1910.
3. Editor's Note: In actuality, the bus she had boarded was hit by a tram.

Frida Kahlo is one of the most powerful and moving painters in Mexico. Her art was born of her physical tragedy. Her father would bring her a paint box and the invalid would start drawing lines. First they were small realistic paintings: roses, horses, children. Then the intimate tragedy of her damaged body made her revolt against these quiet forms and she began to paint strange things, solely inspired by her fantasy. She became a surrealist and her painting expressed the constant concerns of her subconscious, existing somewhere between depressing nocturnal forces and the beautiful daytime forces of earth and sex.

"I started painting," she tells us, "because I was bored of always being in bed."

"I really do not know if my paintings are surrealist," she says, "but I know that they are the frankest expression of myself, without ever taking into consideration anyone's judgement or prejudice. I have painted very little and without the slightest desire for glory or ambition, but before all else, out of the

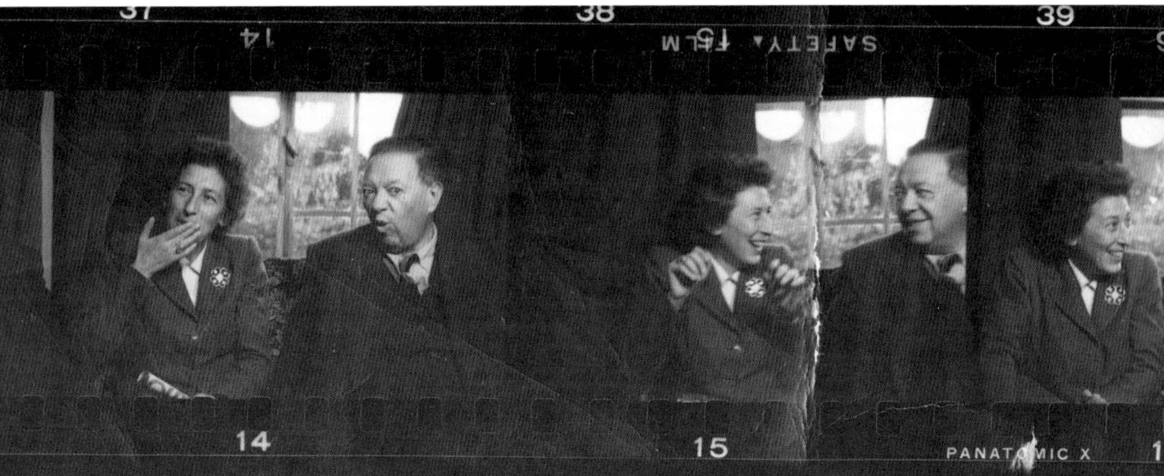

conviction that I enjoy it, and then to be able to make my living with my work. I am trying, as much as I can, to always be myself, with the bitter consciousness that many lives would not suffice to paint as I desire, and all that I desire."

Most of Frida Kahlo's paintings are self-portraits. They reflect her tragic inner duality, born of the terrible drama of her life, the unceasing struggle between her passionate nature, her love of life and all her joys, and her paralyzed, painful, and fragile body.

Diego Rivera is the contradictory, telluric, and inspired man to whom she is married. He has the head of a pre-Cortesian god. With his unsettling, mocking presence, he brings her his struggles and his life's problems.

Frida Kahlo lives in isolation in her house in Coyoacán. Surrounded by her dogs, her birds, and her flowers, she listens to the murmur of the water, the sound of the wind making the leaves tremble, and the thousand inner voices that give her courage and creative power.

Diego Rivera and Gisèle Freund, Mexico, c. 1954.

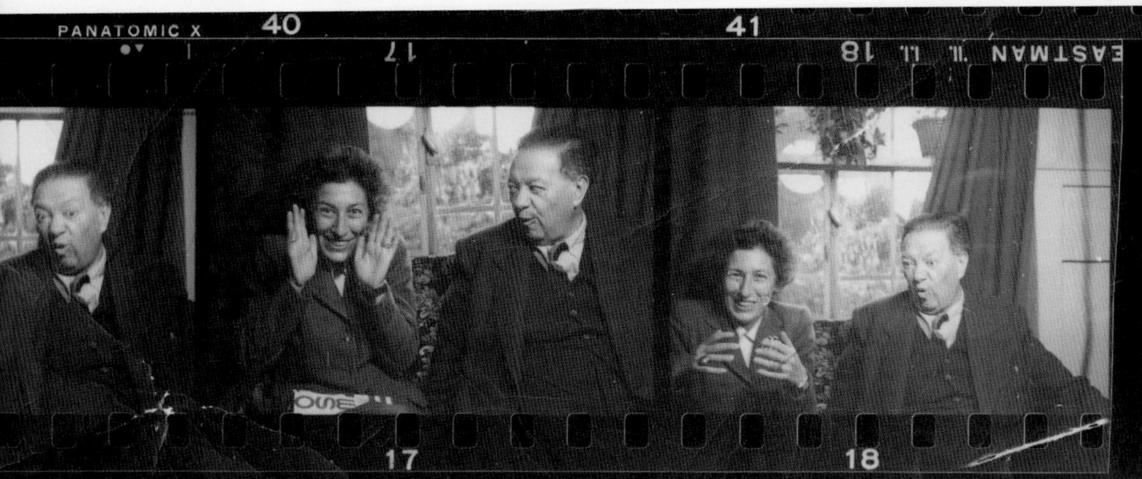

3

GISÈLE FREUND'S PHOTOS

MORE THAN ONE HUNDRED RARE OR PREVIOUSLY UNPUBLISHED IMAGES

Frida Kahlo in the garden of her house,
La Casa Azul, in Coyoacán, Mexico City, 1951.

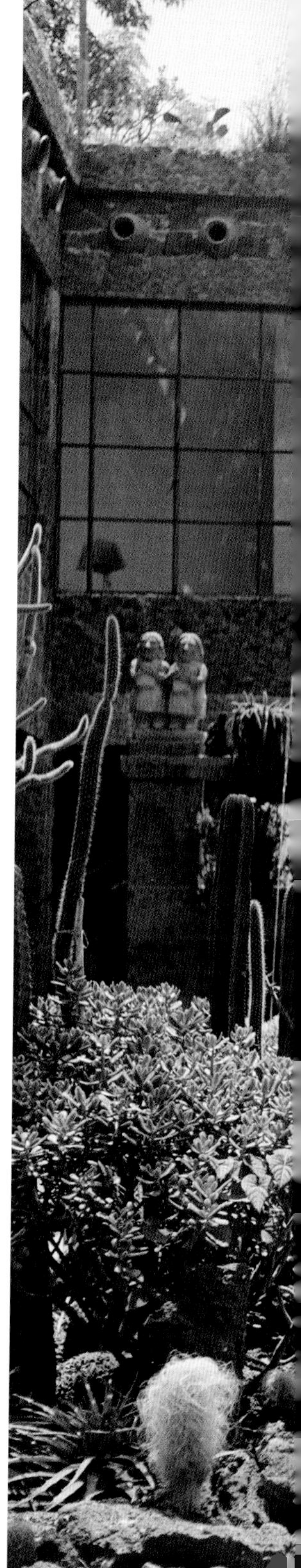

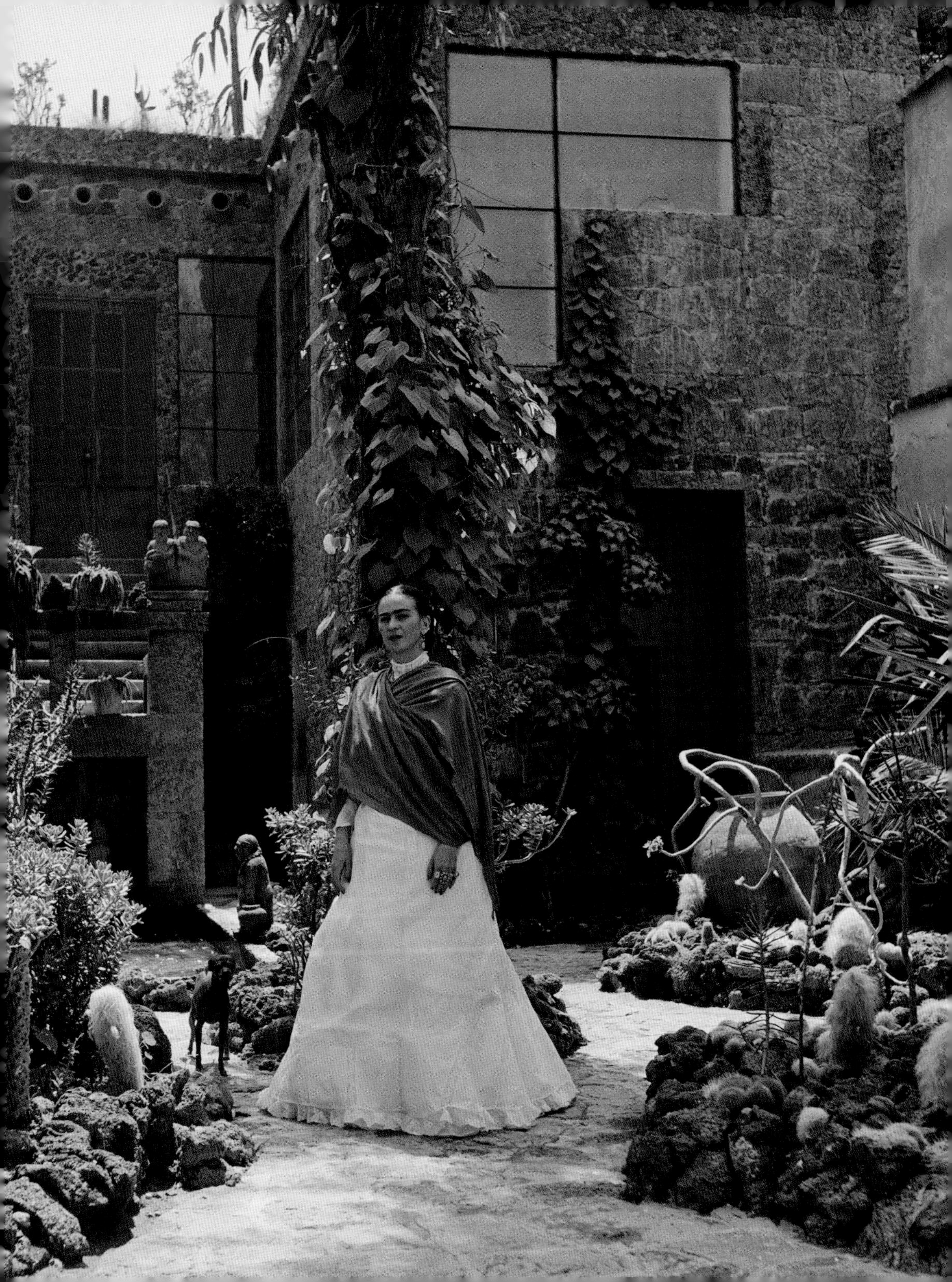

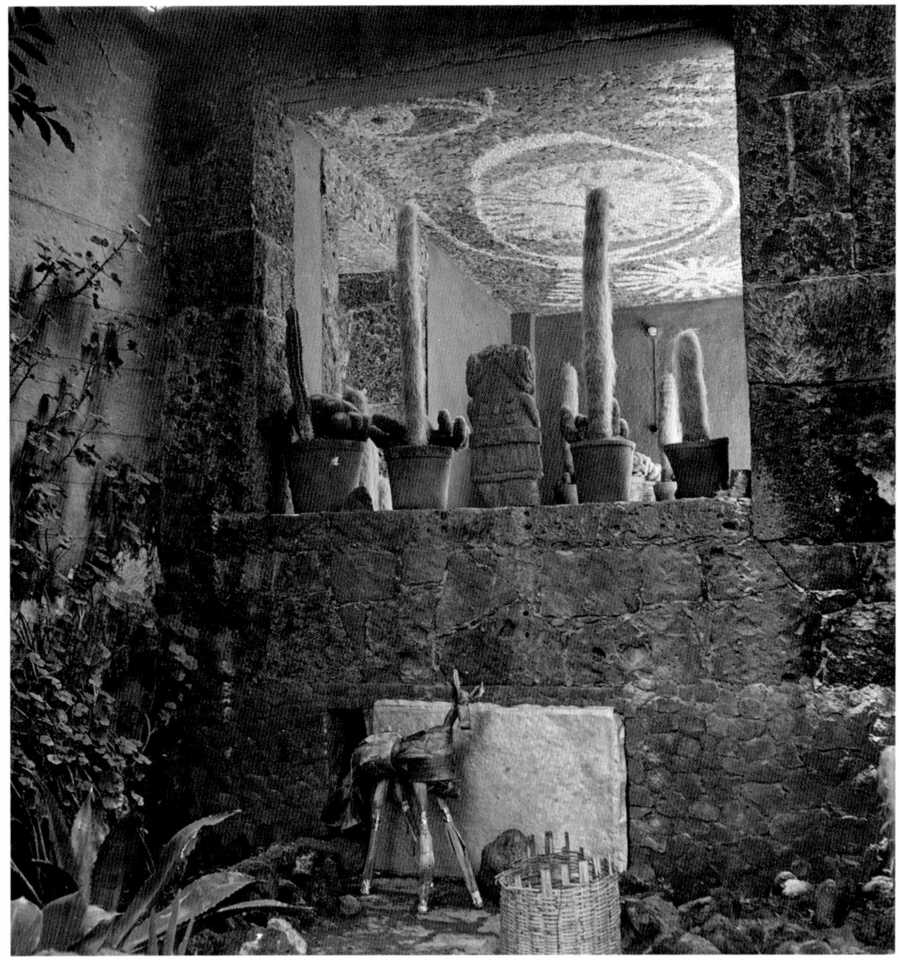

Exterior view of the house, and Frida Kahlo in front of *Portrait of My Father*.

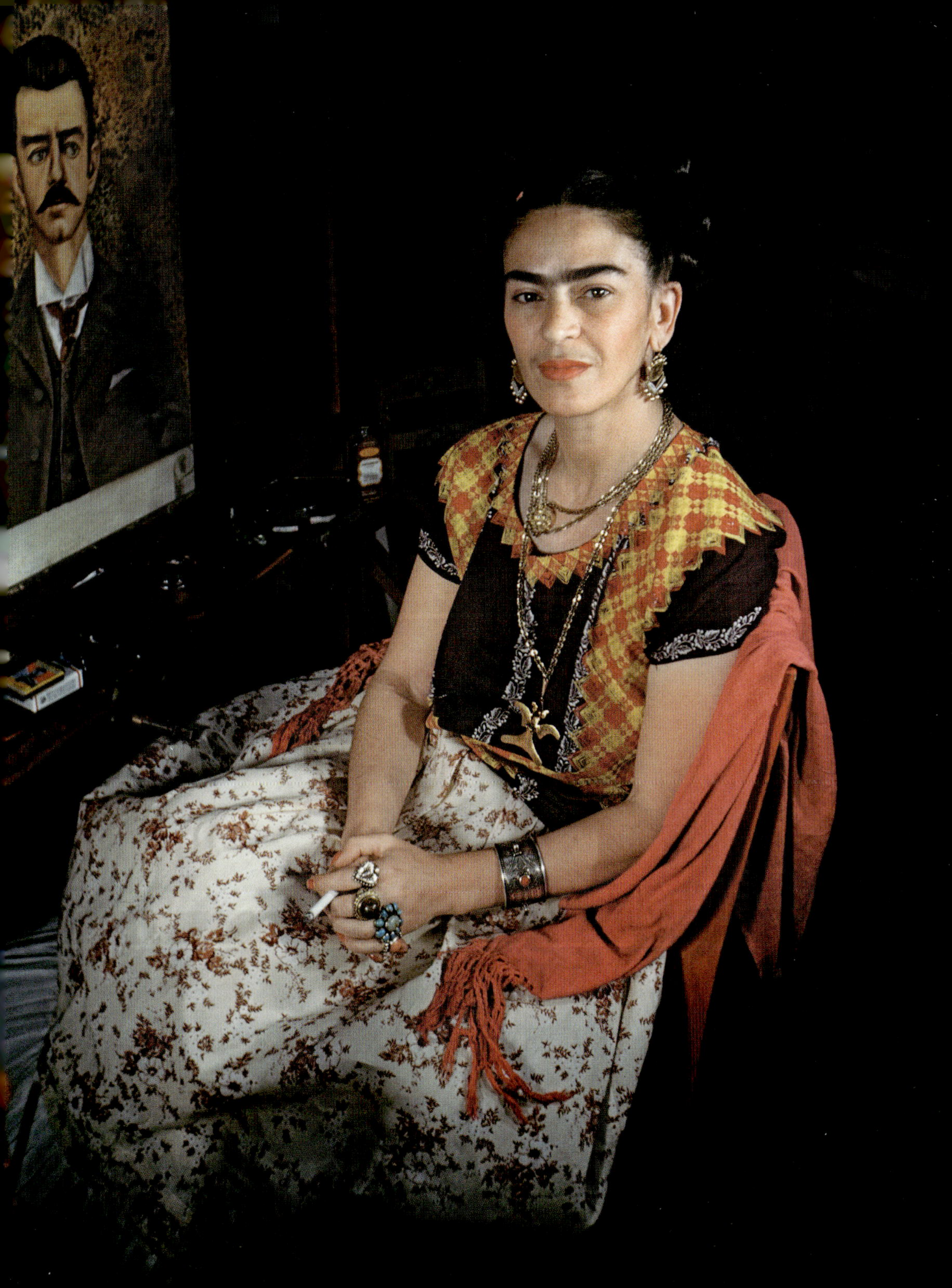

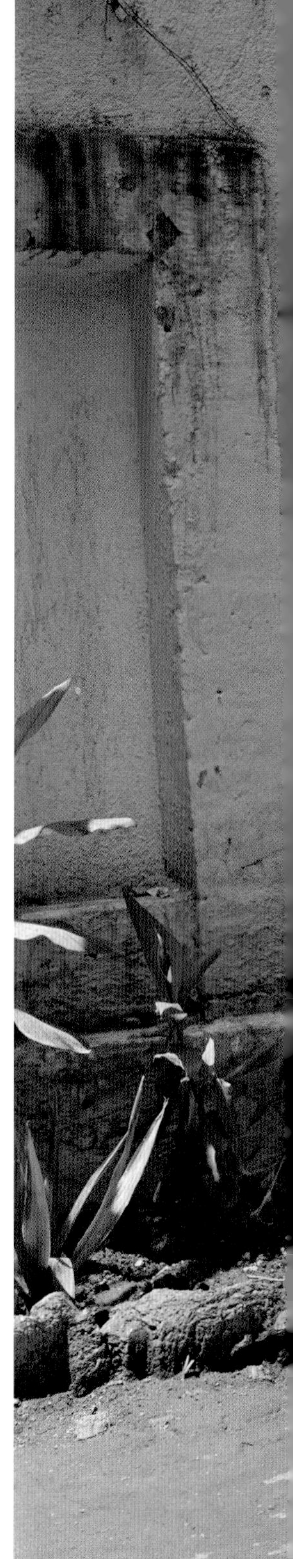

Frida Kahlo with her dogs in Coyoacán, Mexico City, 1951.

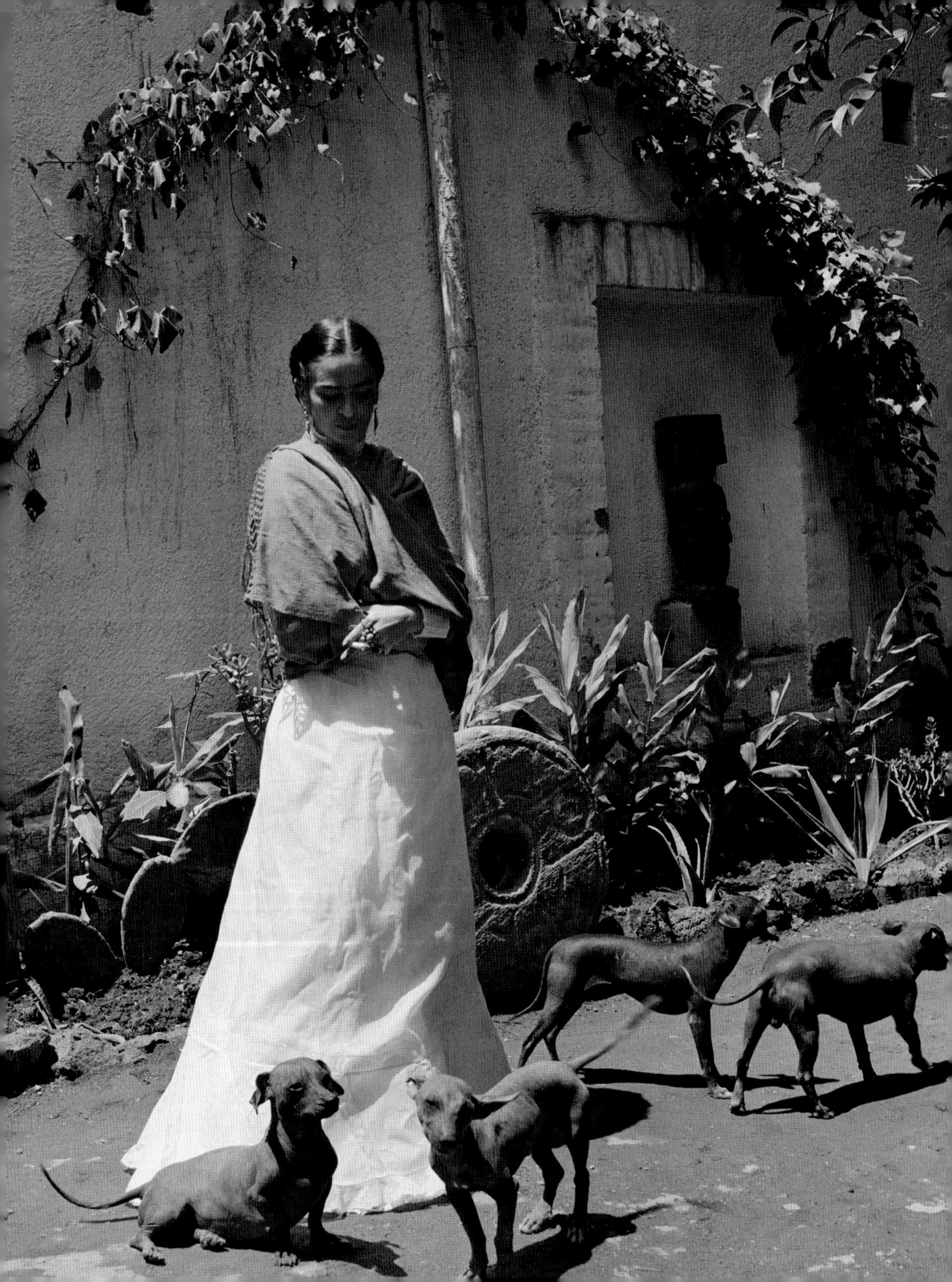

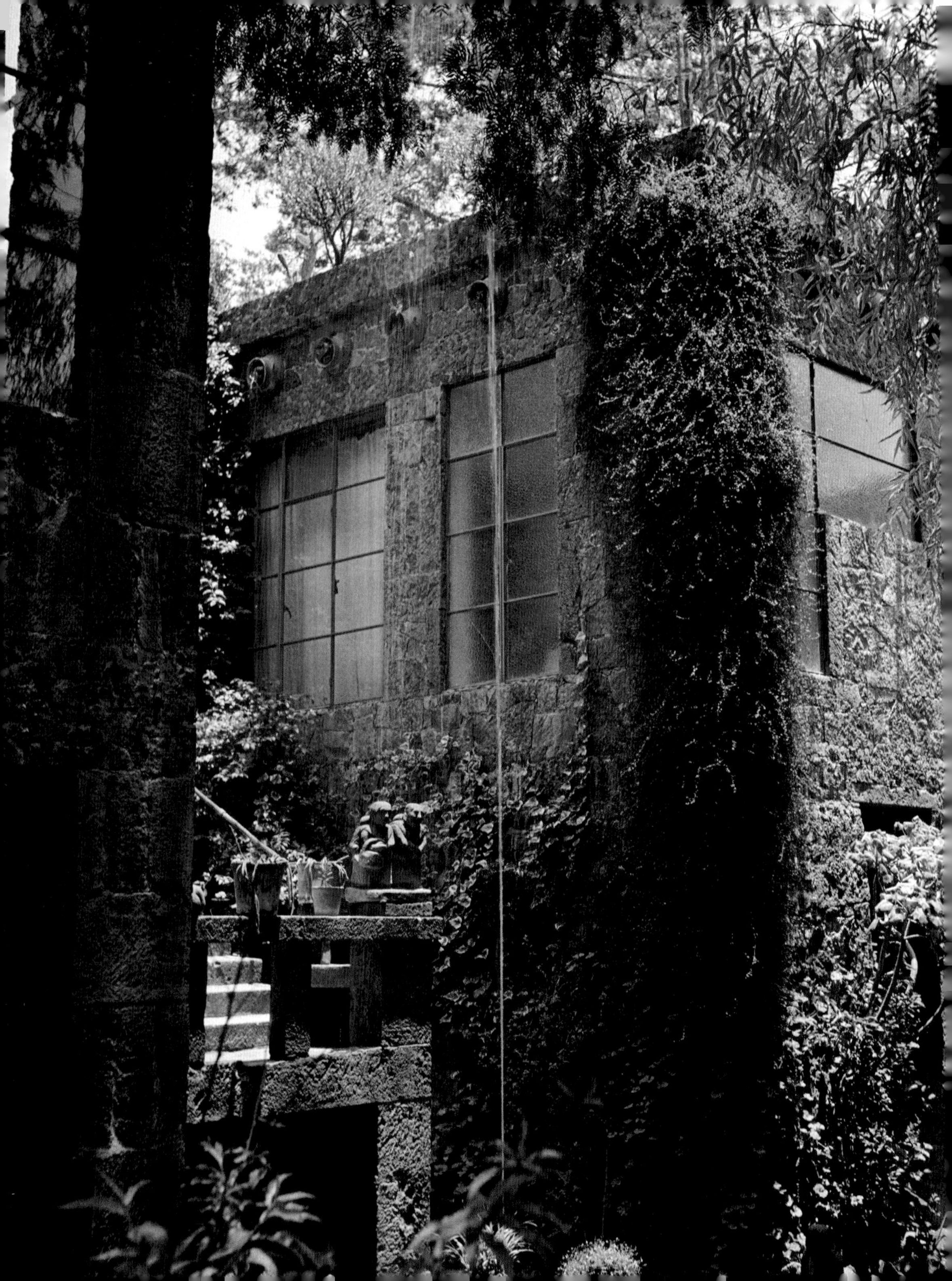

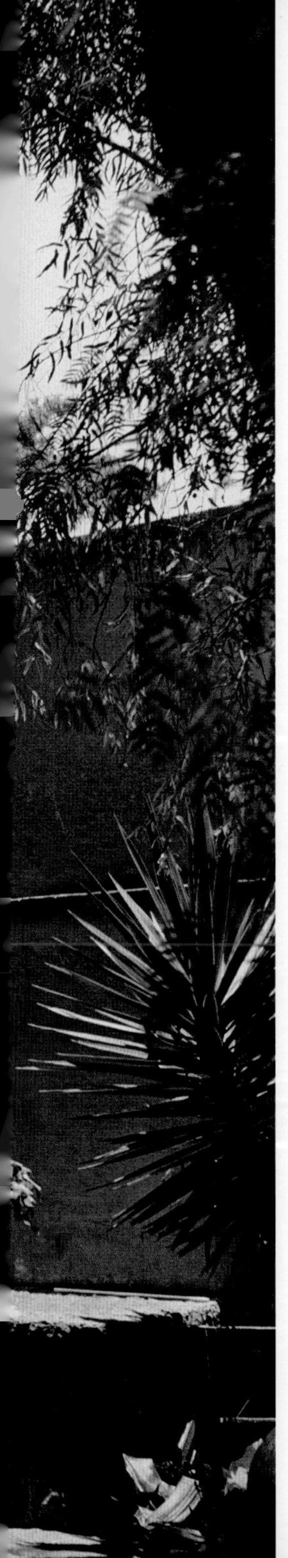

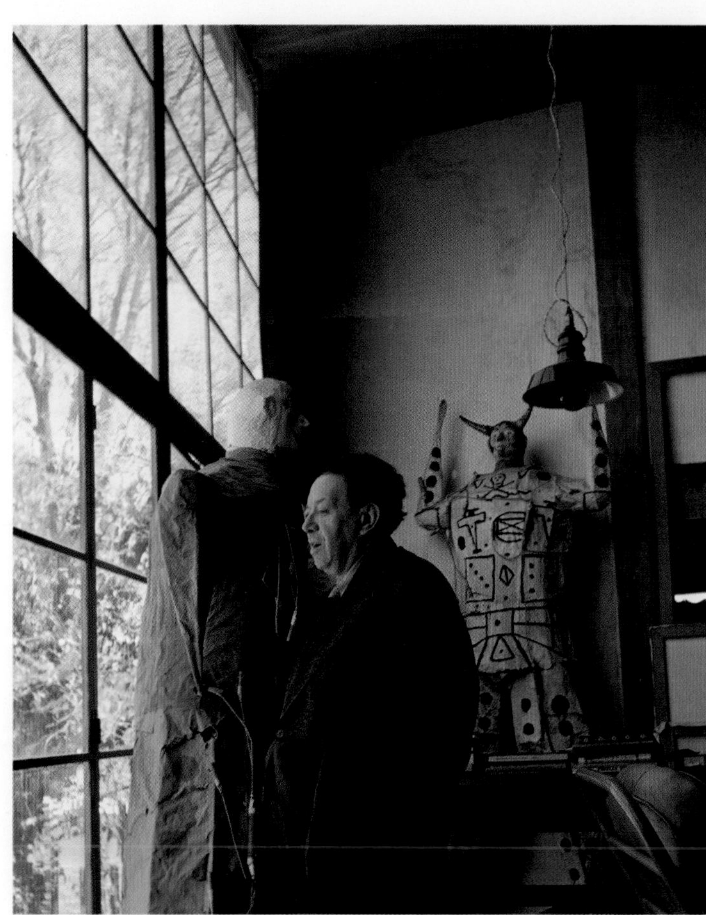

Exterior view of the house, and Diego Rivera in his studio, 1951.

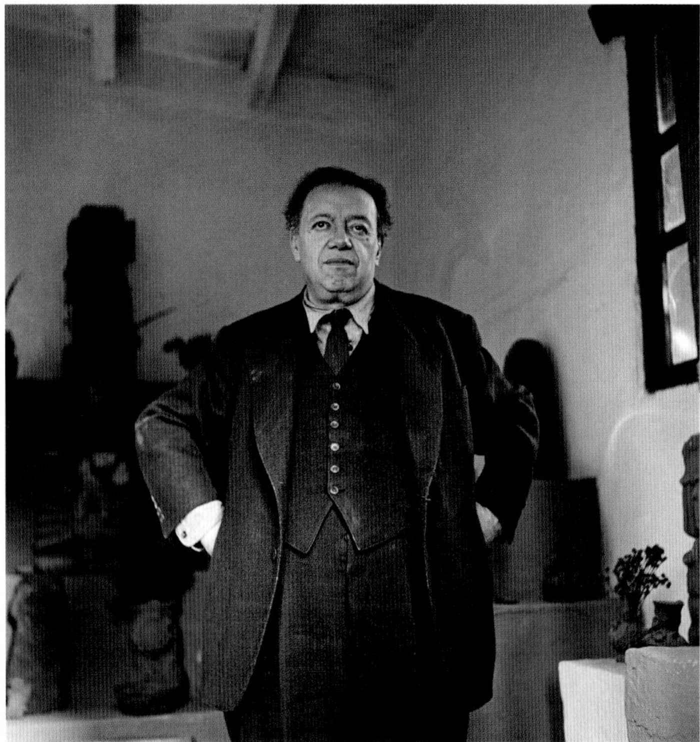

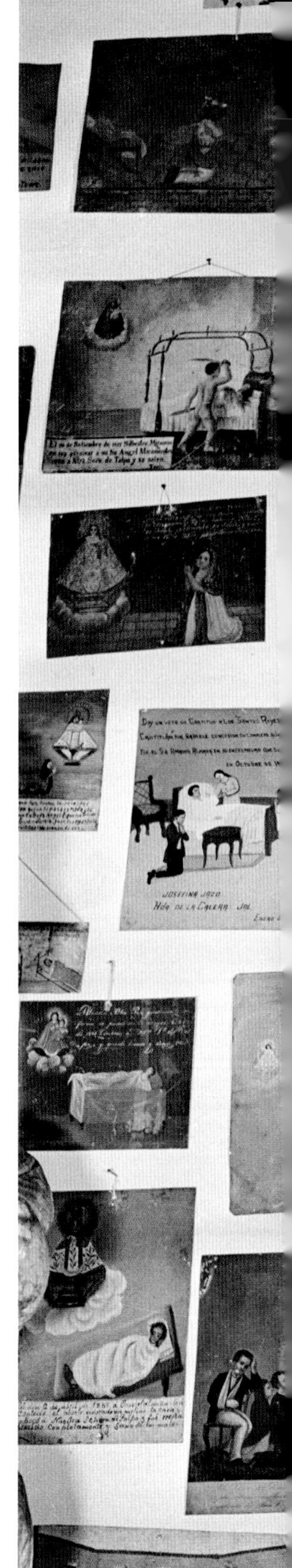

Right, ex-voto on one of the house's interior walls, and above, Diego Rivera in front of his collection. "While waiting to install his vast collection of . . . pre-Columbian art, Diego Rivera stores them in his house's small storage spaces, on trees, and in sheds built in his garden" (Gisèle Freund caption for the photo story "Découverte d'une ville précortésienne près de Mexico City" ["Discovery of a Pre-Cortesian City Near Mexico City"], 1951).

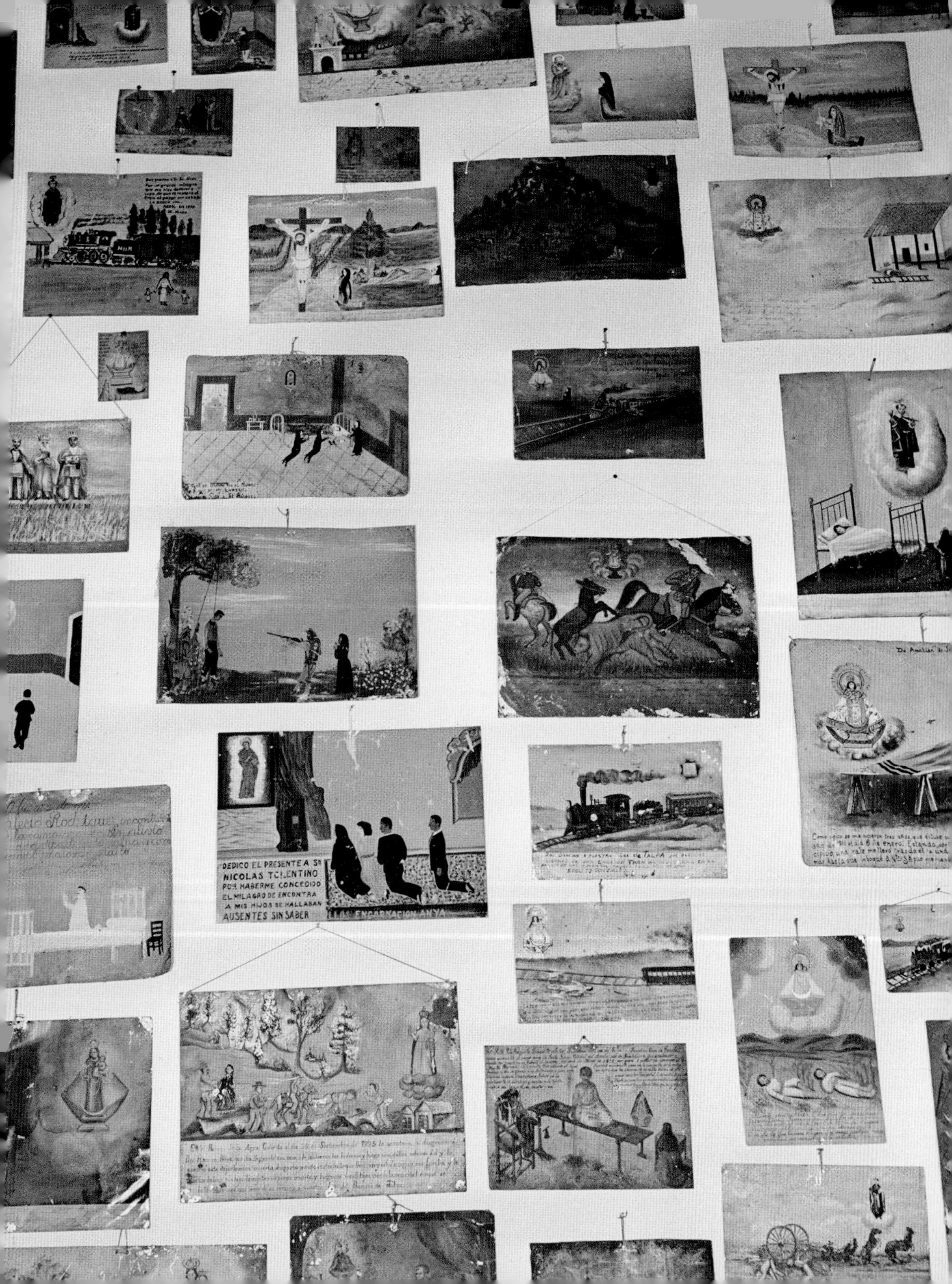
DEDICO EL PRESENTE A Sn
NICOLAS TOLENTINO
POR HABERME CONCEDIDO
EL MILAGRO DE ENCONTRA
A MIS HIJOS SE HALLABAN
AUSENTES SIN SABER

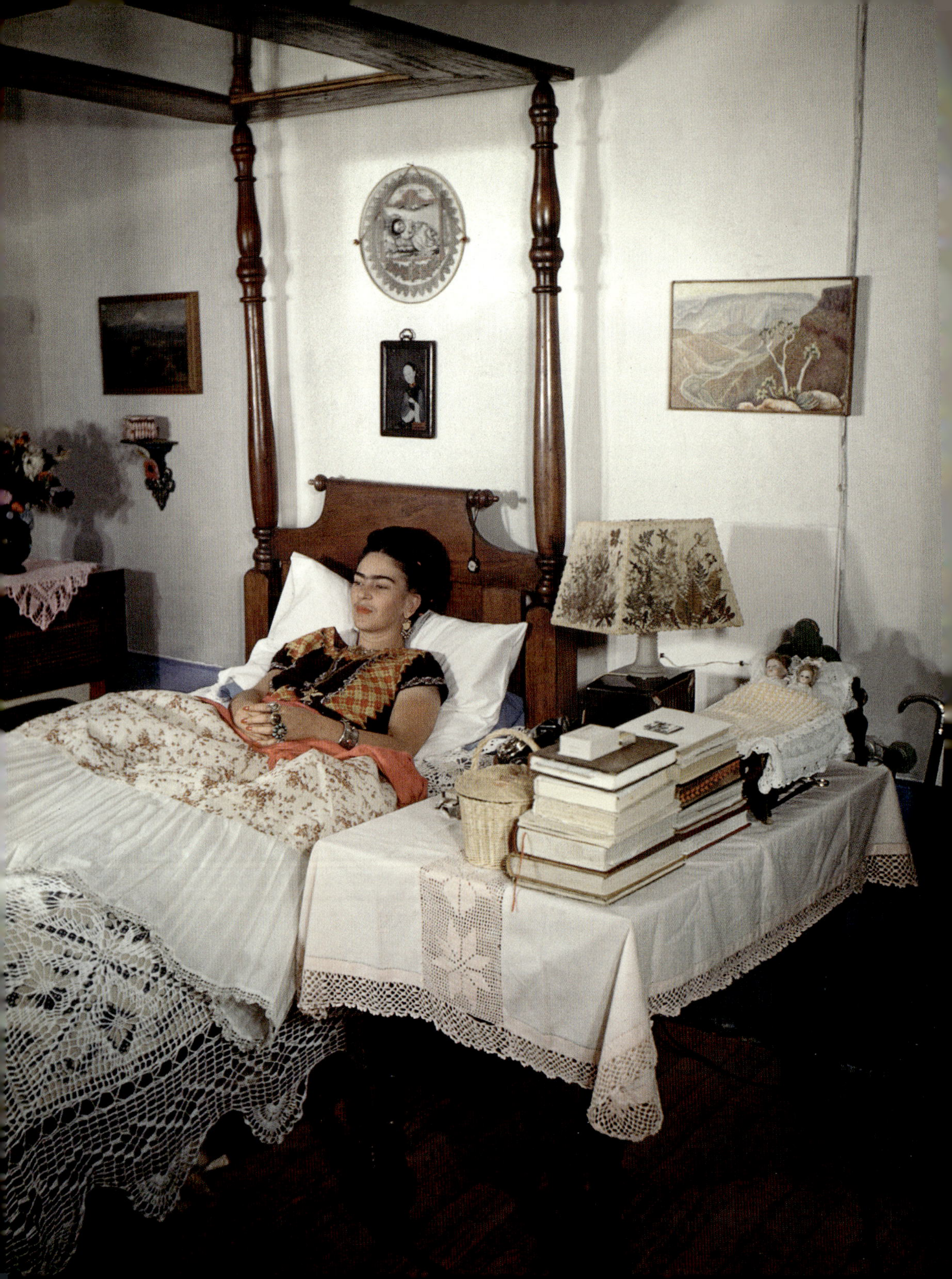

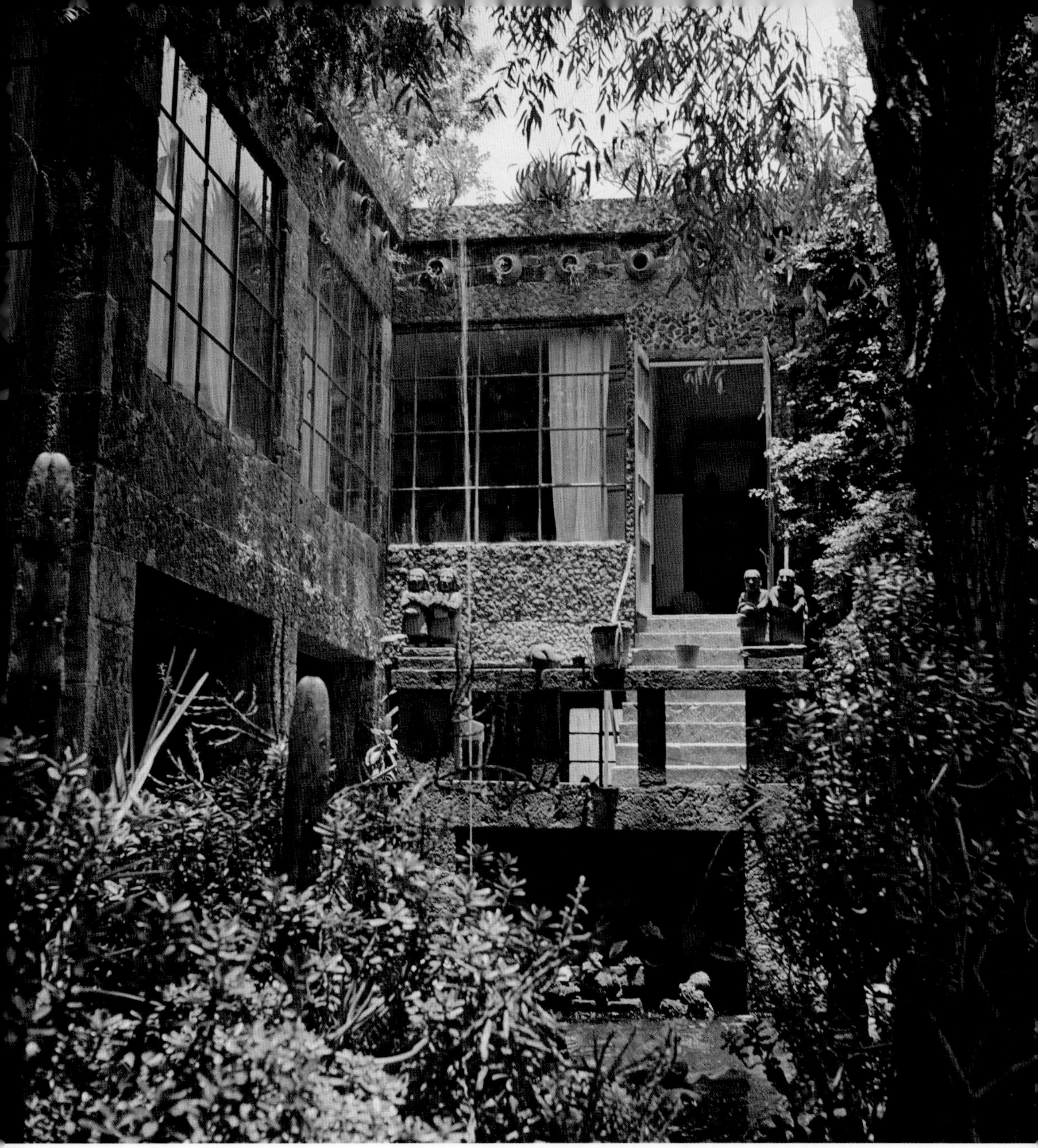

Frida Kahlo in her bedroom, and exterior view of the house. "Injured in an accident, this heroic, nearly legendary figure had a strange and irresistible beauty, which she had inherited from a Mexican mother and a German father" (Gisèle Freund caption found on the back of a press print, 1951).

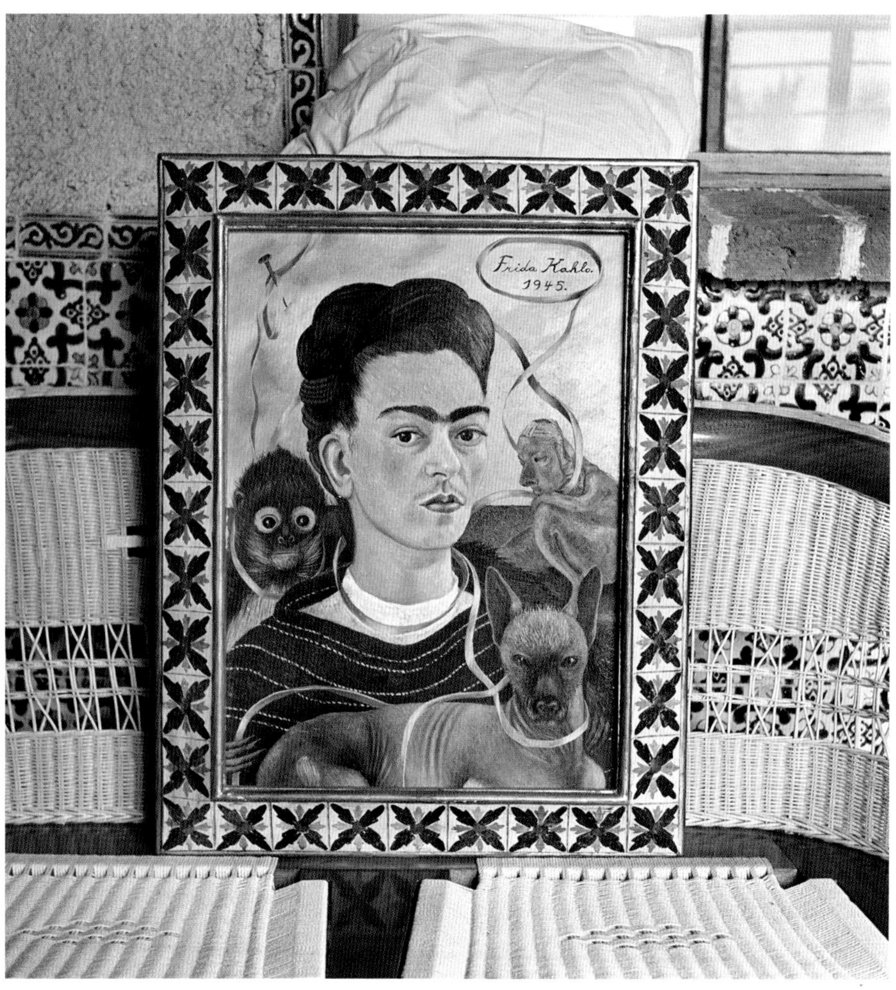

Self-Portrait with Small Monkey, Frida Kahlo painting photographed in her home, 1951.

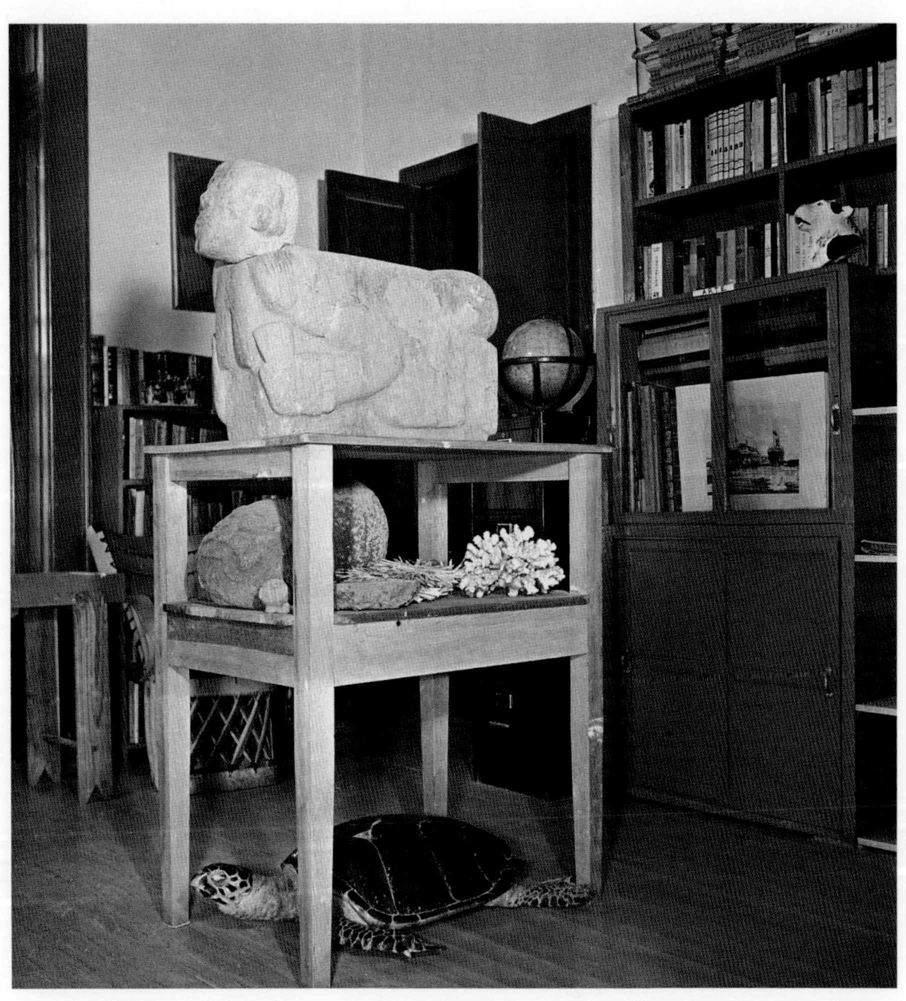

Interior view of the house, 1951.

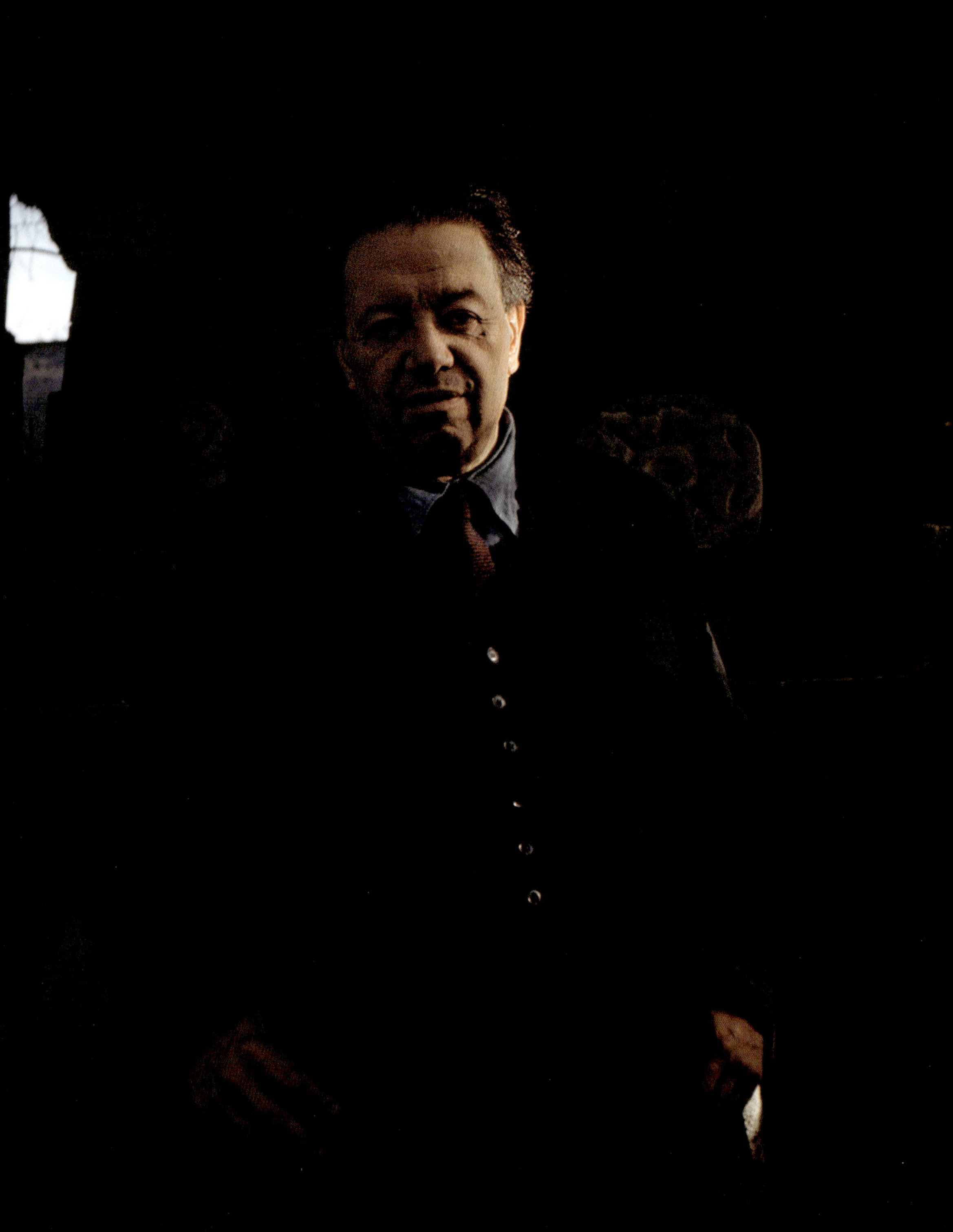

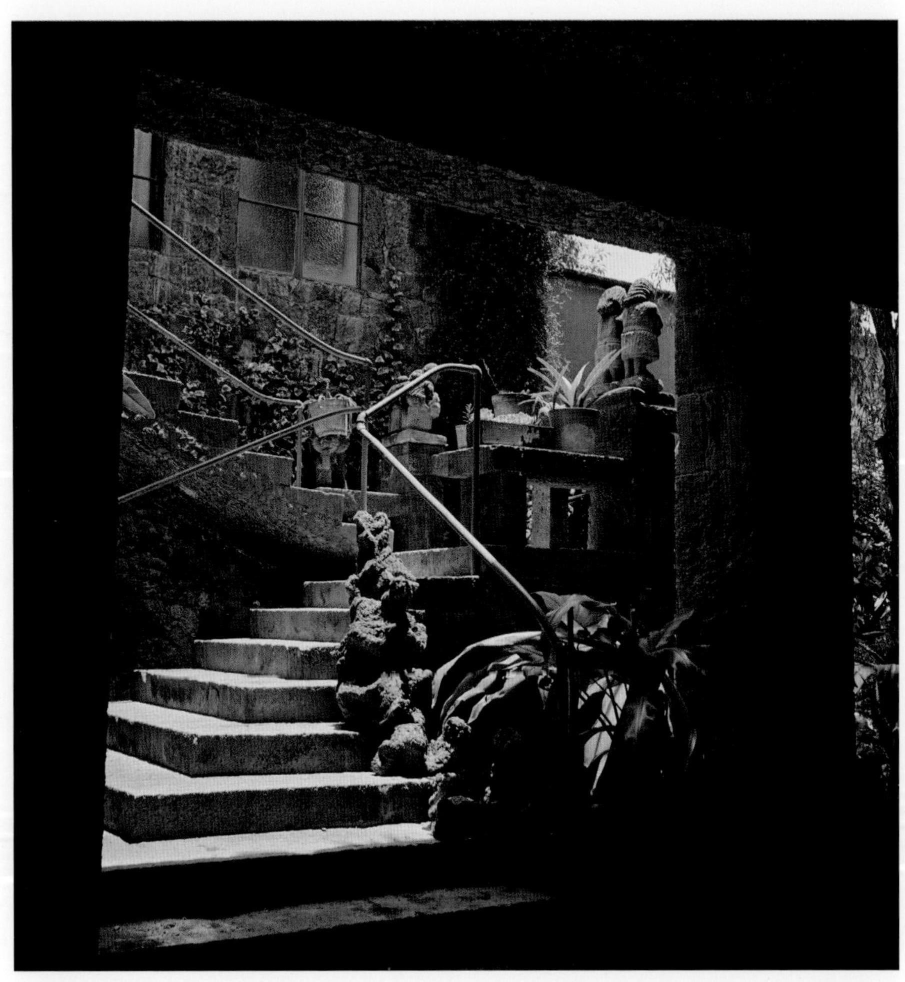

Diego Rivera in one of the house's sheds, and view of an exterior staircase, 1951.

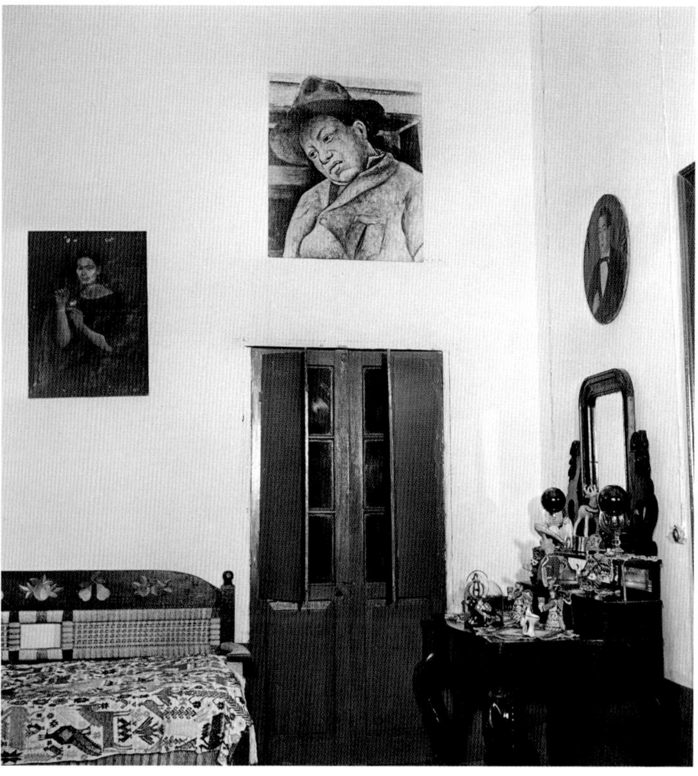

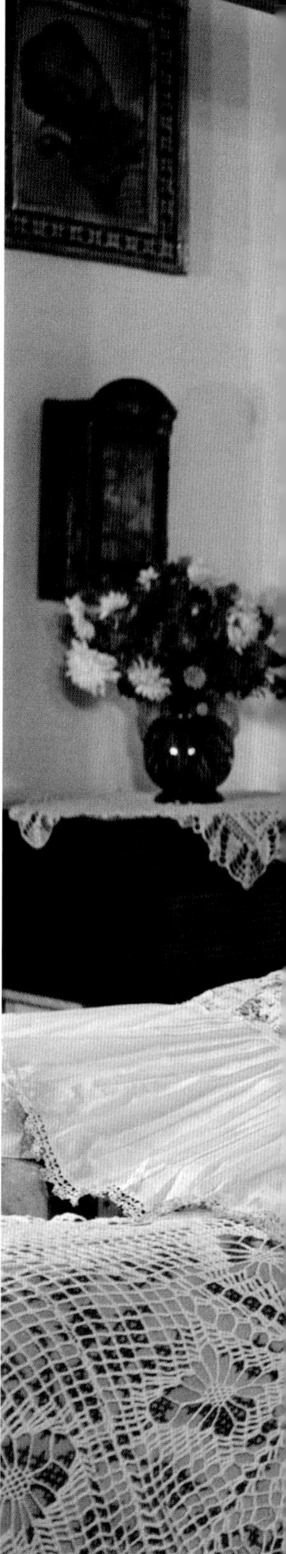

Interior view of the house, and Frida lying on her bed, 1951.

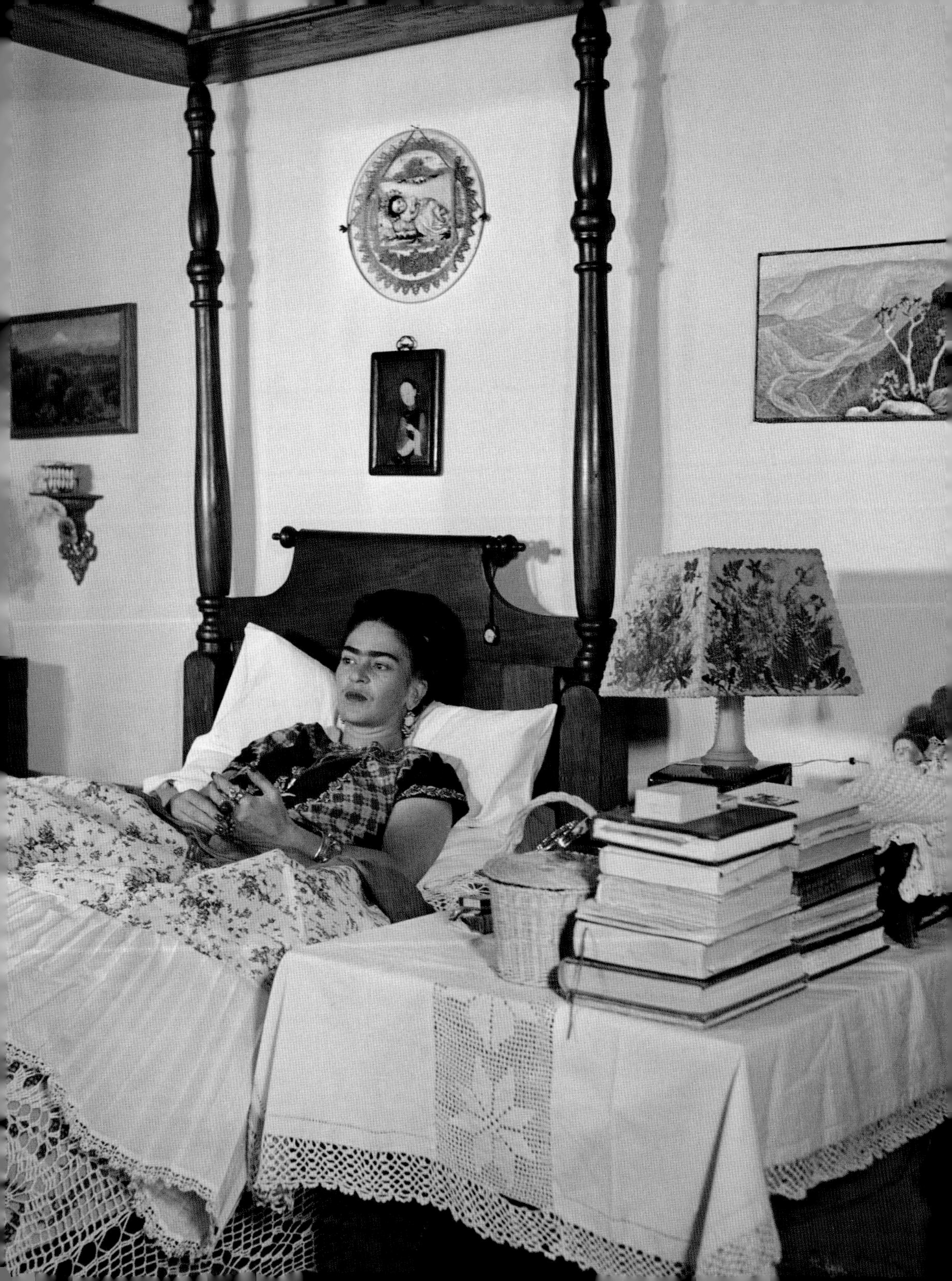

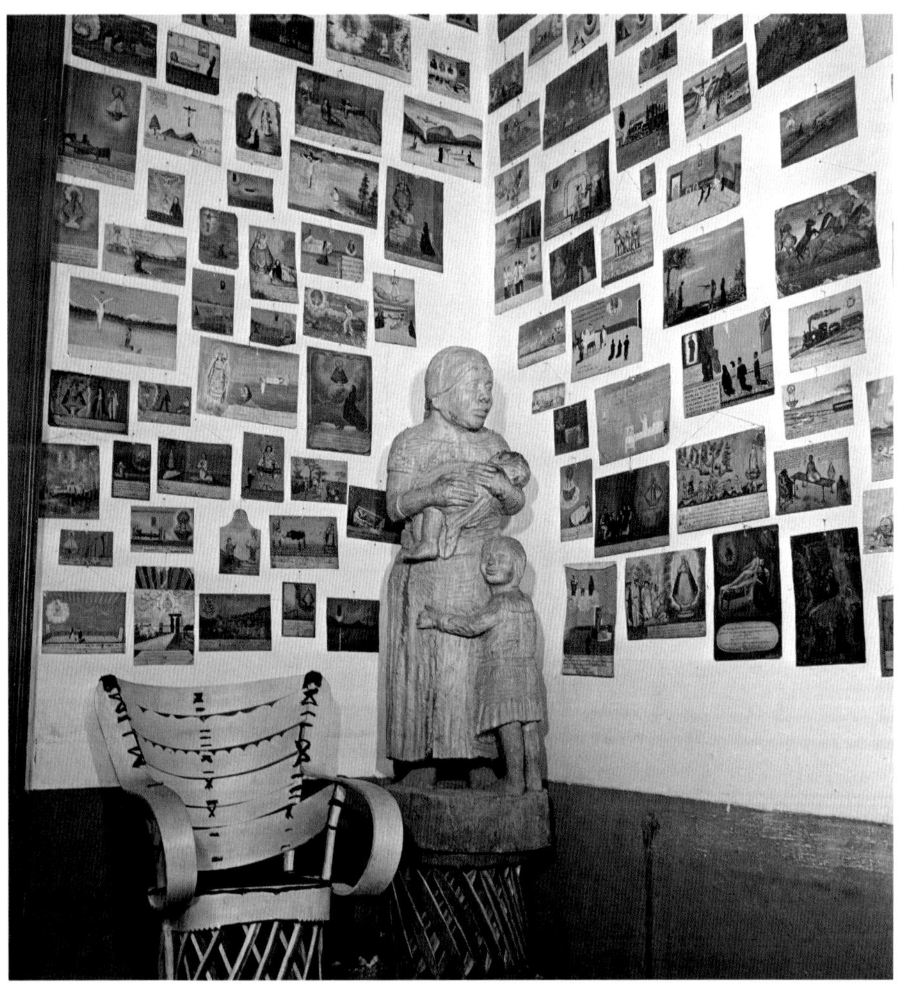

Ex-votos on interior walls of the house, 1951.

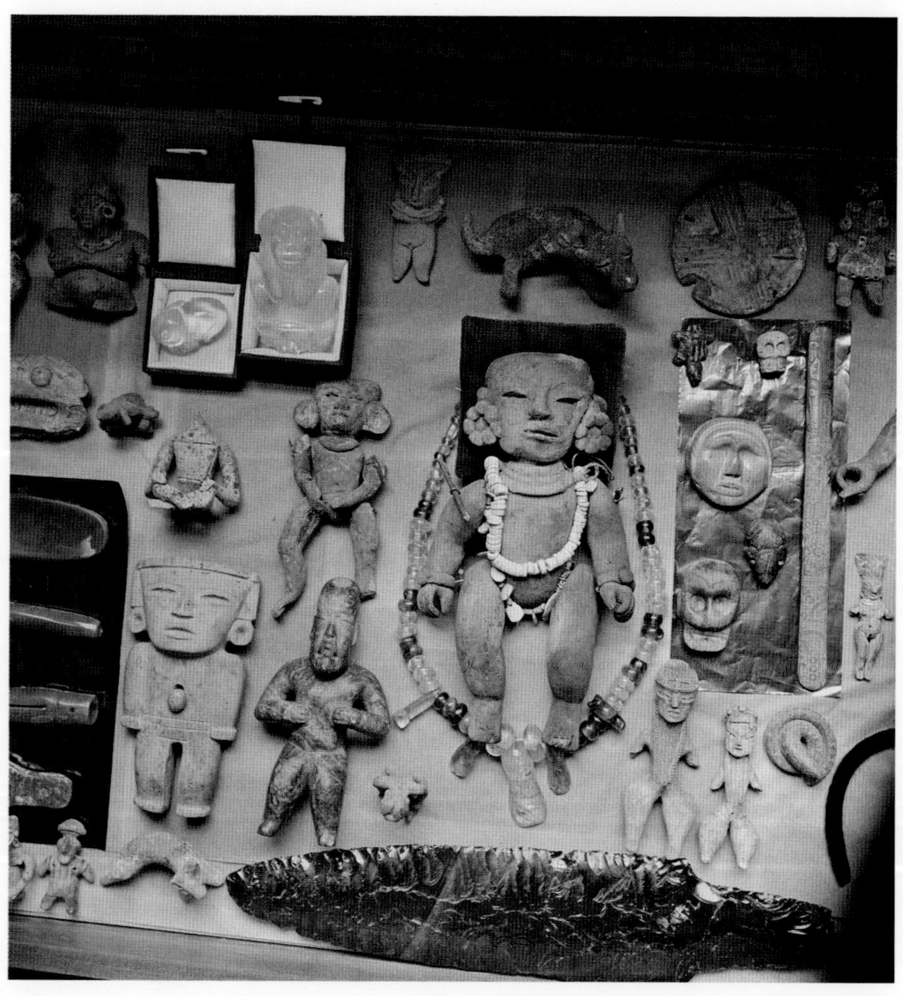

Interior view of the house, 1951. "Pre-Cortesian figures on the wall of a room in Frida's house in 1951" (Gisèle Freund caption found on the back of a press print).

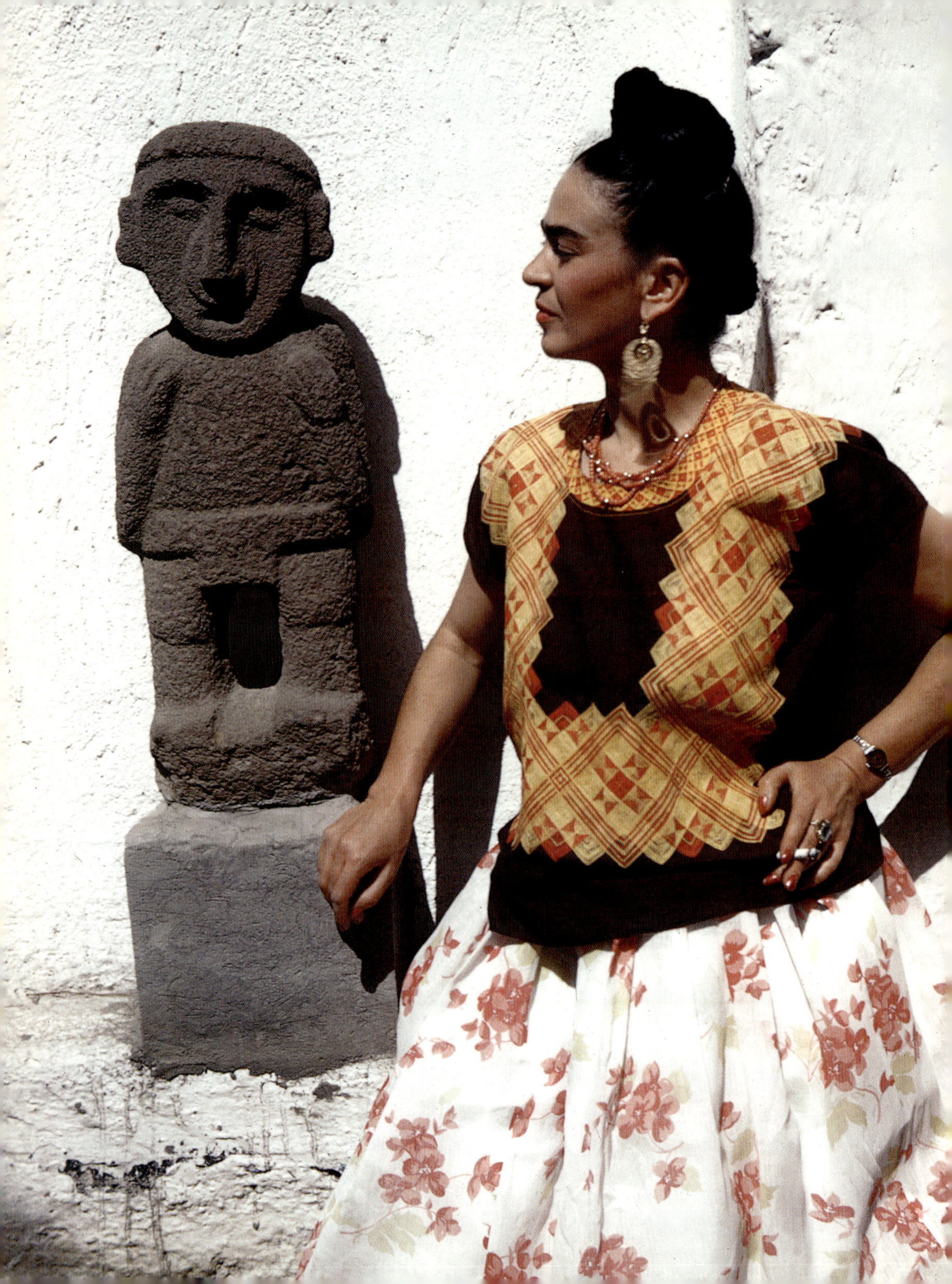

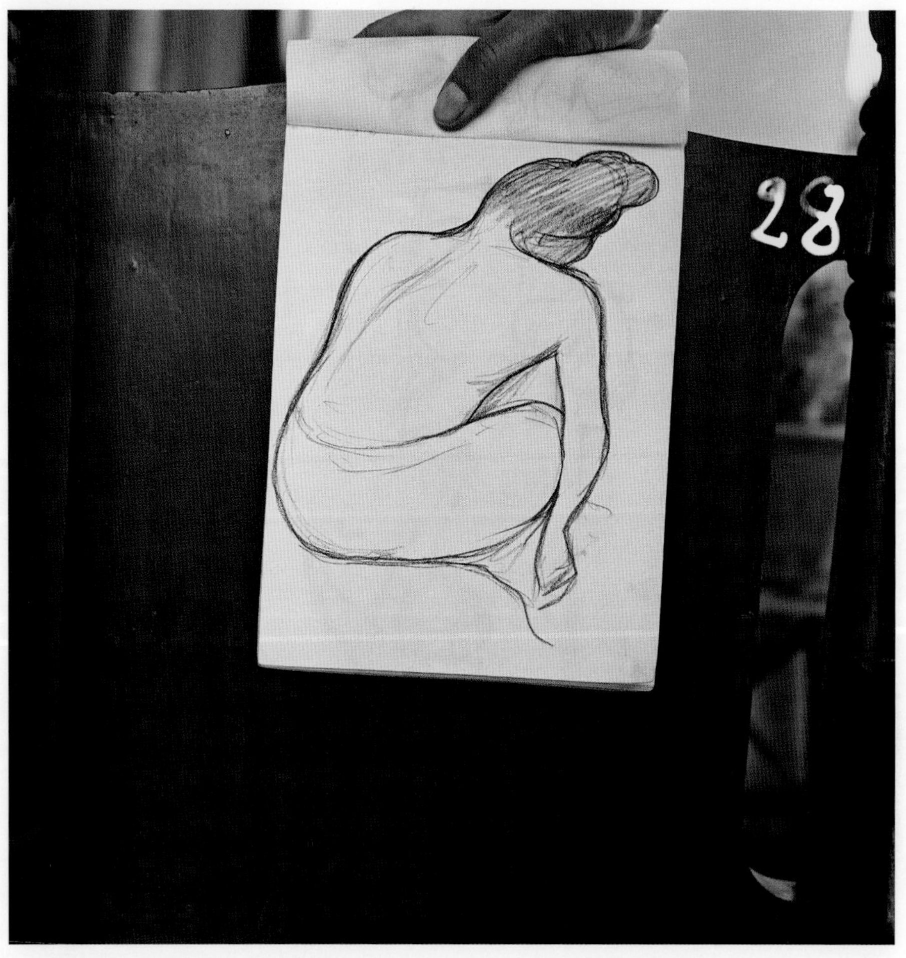

Frida Kahlo in the garden of her house, and sketch drawn by Diego Rivera during a trip to Tehuantepec, Mexico, 1951. "Reproduction of charcoal drawings from Rivera's sketchbook. Before beginning his mural paintings, Rivera takes trips to small Mexican villages to observe and make sketches of people, which he then uses in his mural paintings" (Gisèle Freund caption from the photo story "Mexican Painters at Work").

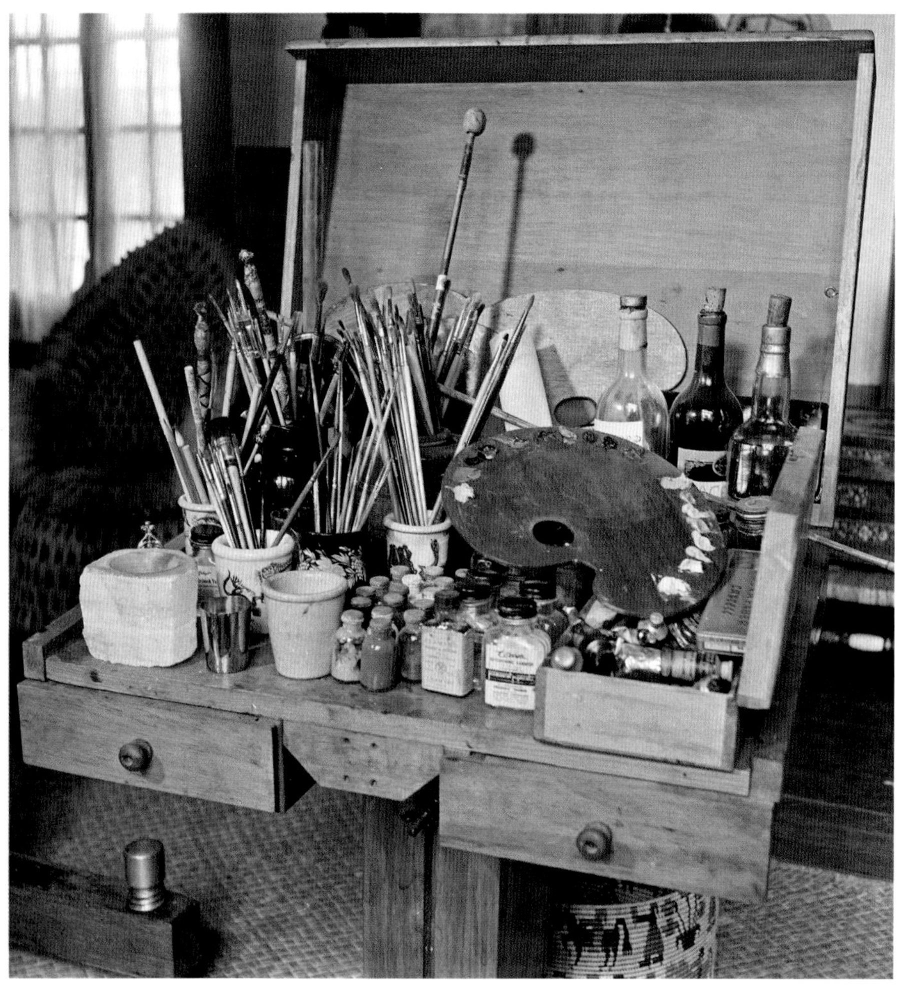

Frida Kahlo's paint box, 1951.
She developed her own recipes for creating special colors.

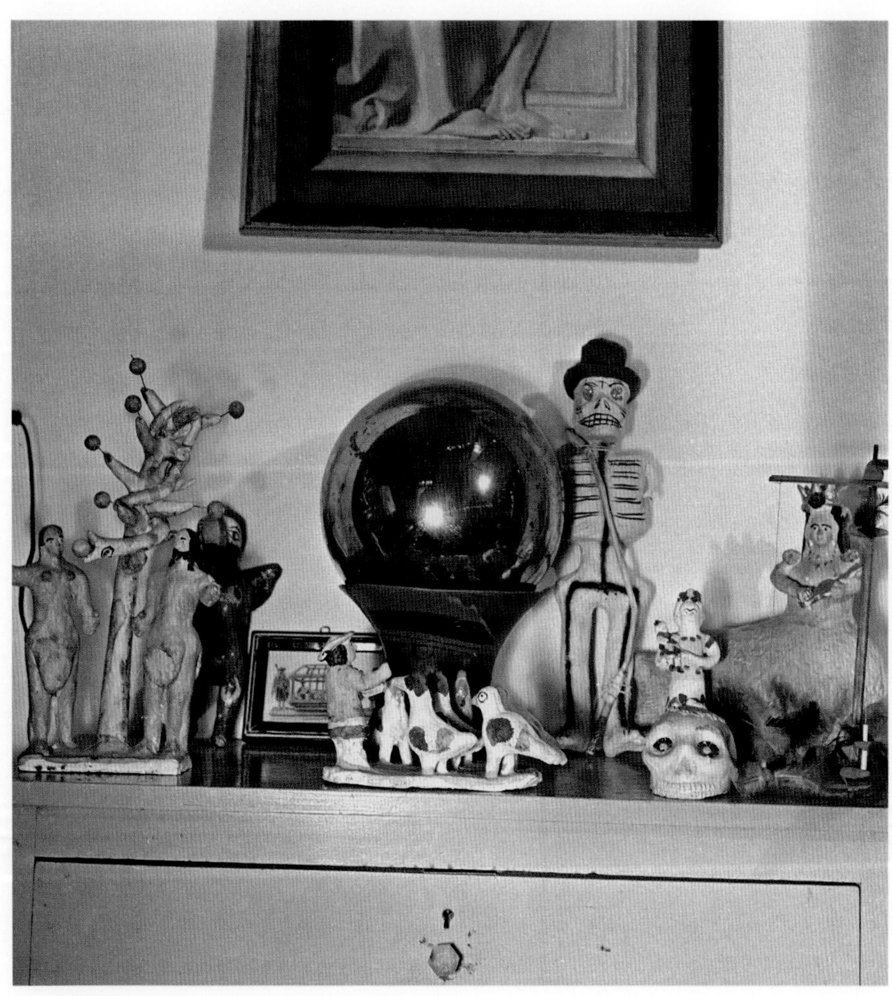

A sugar skull, skeleton, and other objects related to the Day of the Dead in La Casa Azul, 1951.

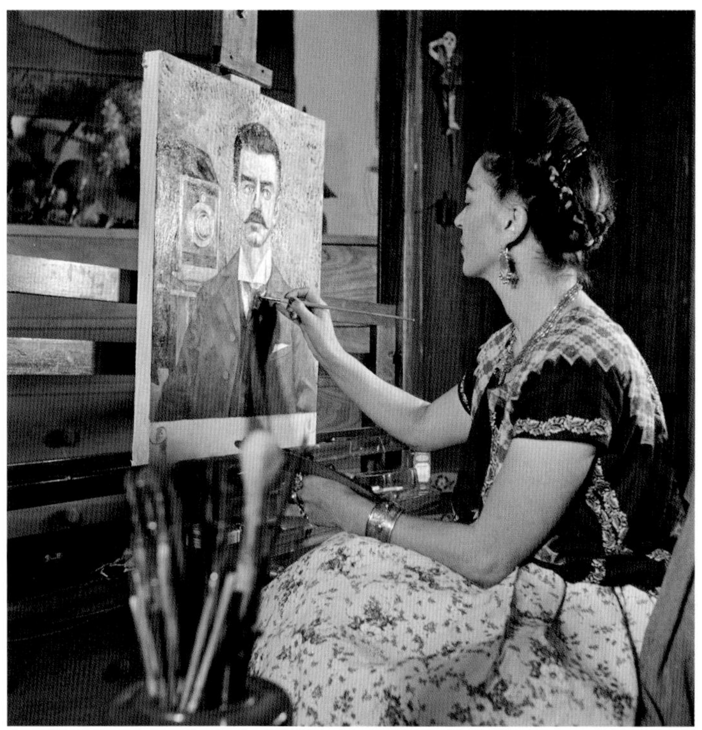

Frida Kahlo working on *Portrait of My Father* at home,
and exterior view of the house, 1951.

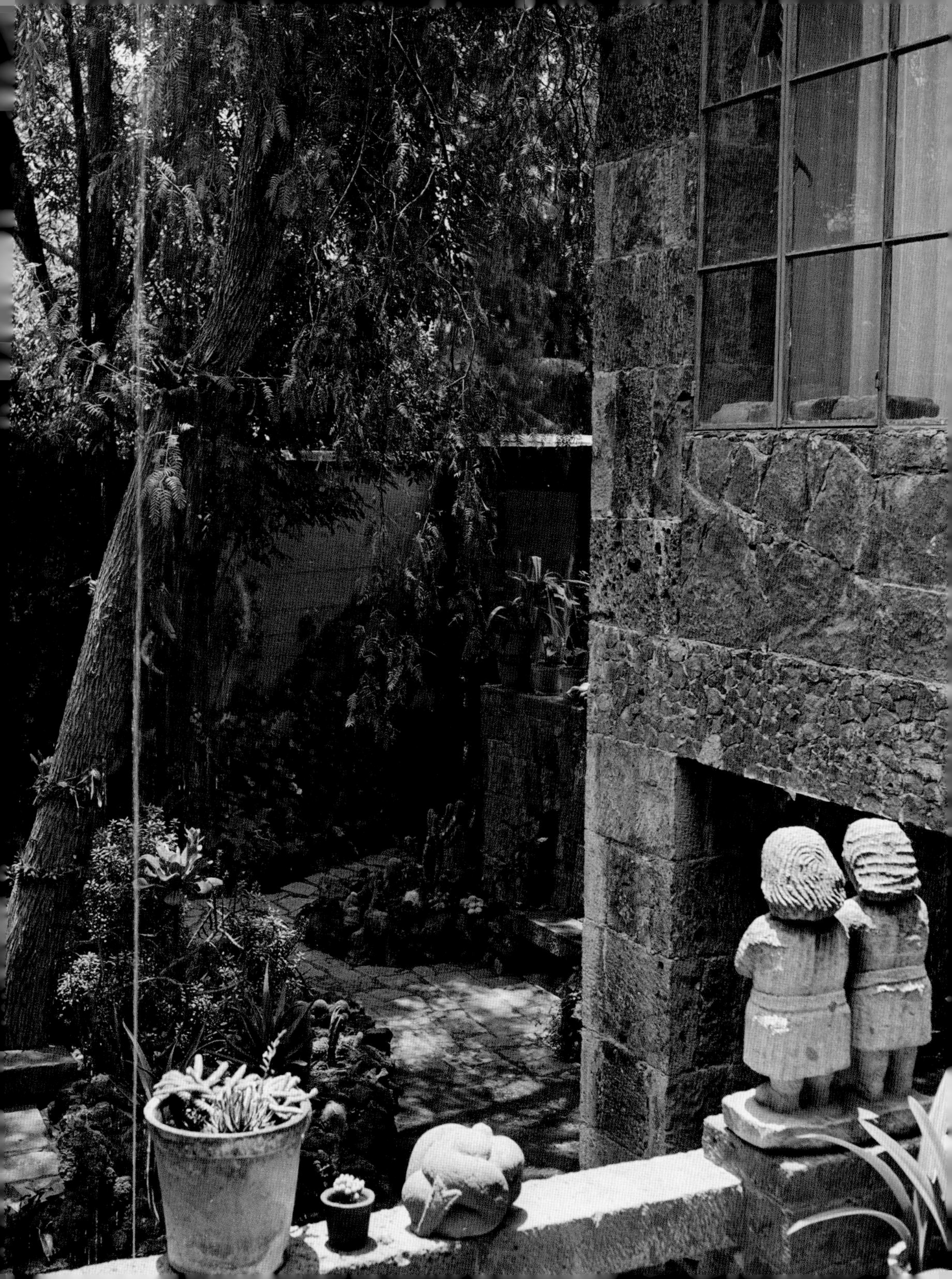

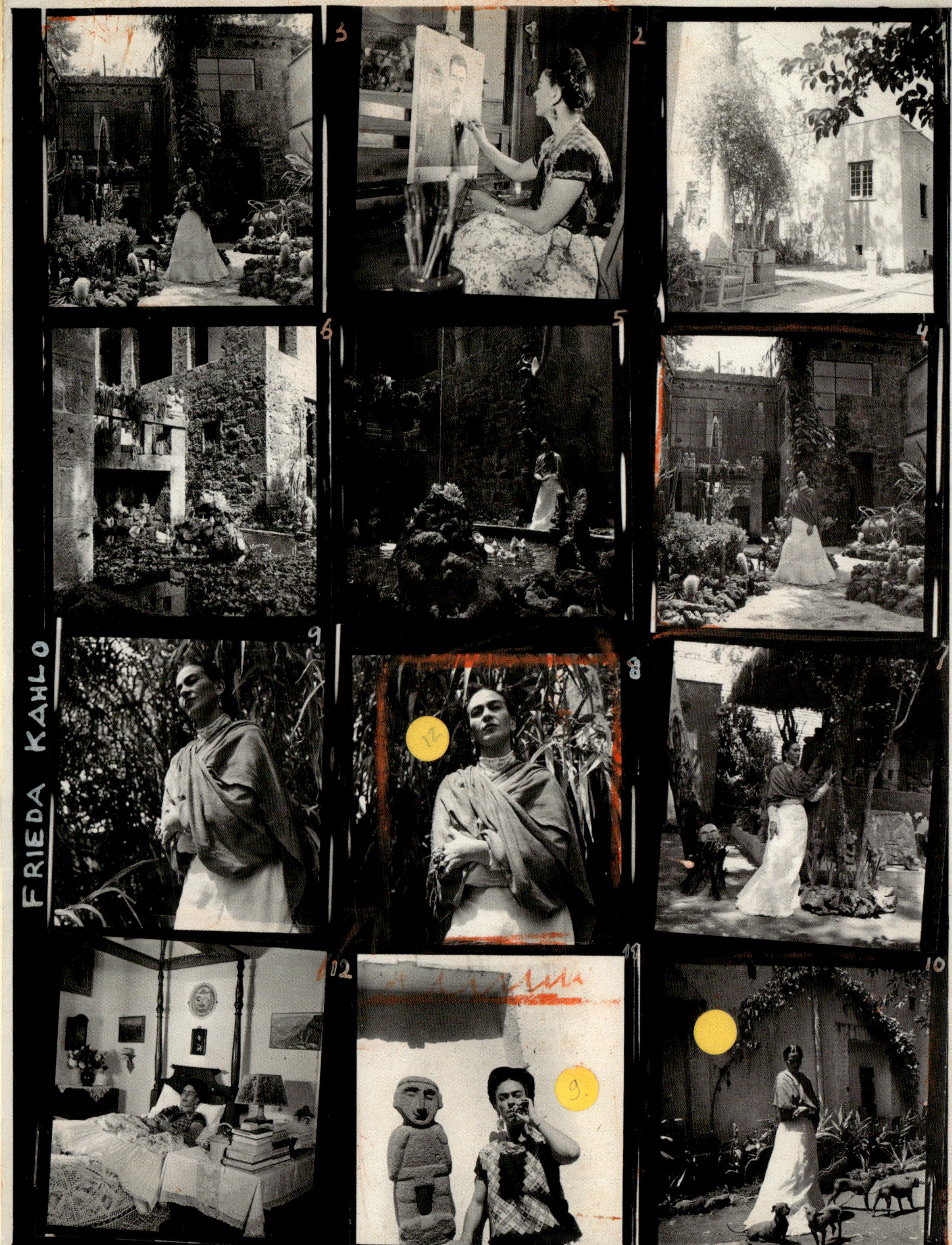
FRIEDA KAHLO

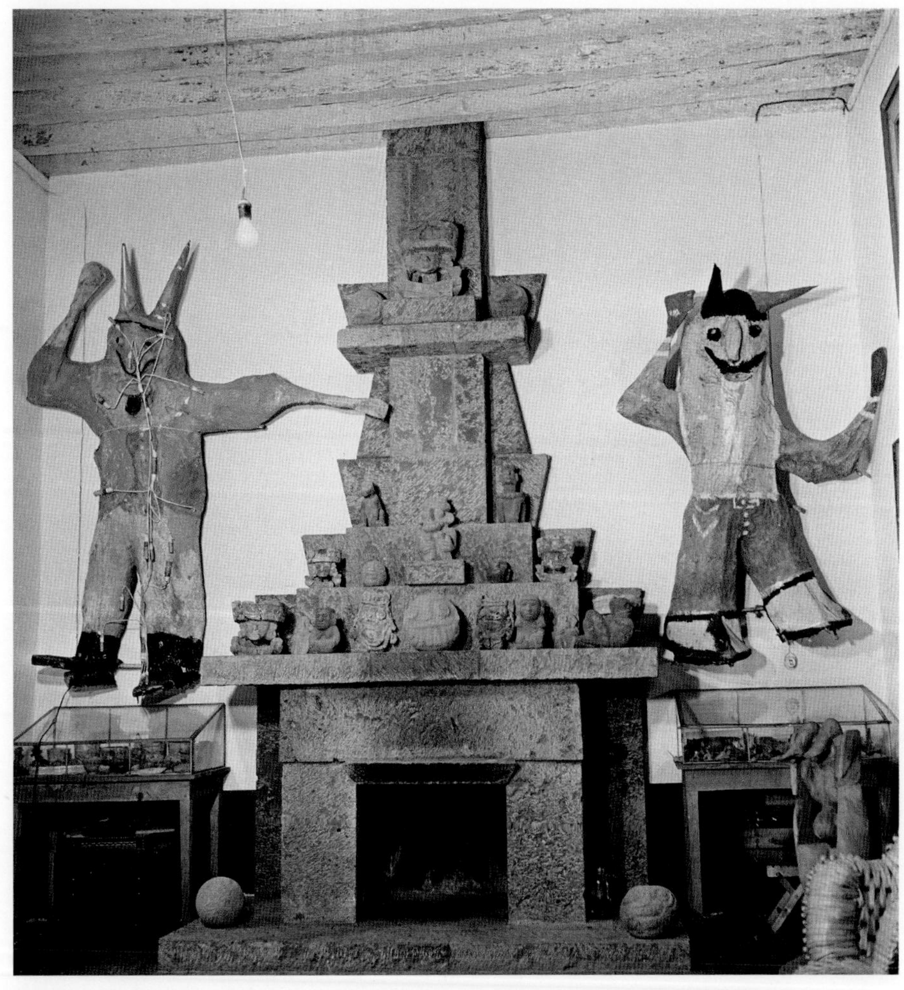

Contact print *Frida Kahlo*, 1951. "Frida Kahlo in Coyoacán, in her garden, a red silk serape on her shoulders, with her dogs, lying on her bed, working on her father's portrait." Interior view of the house, 1951. "A Mexican fireplace" (Gisèle Freund captions found on the back of press prints).

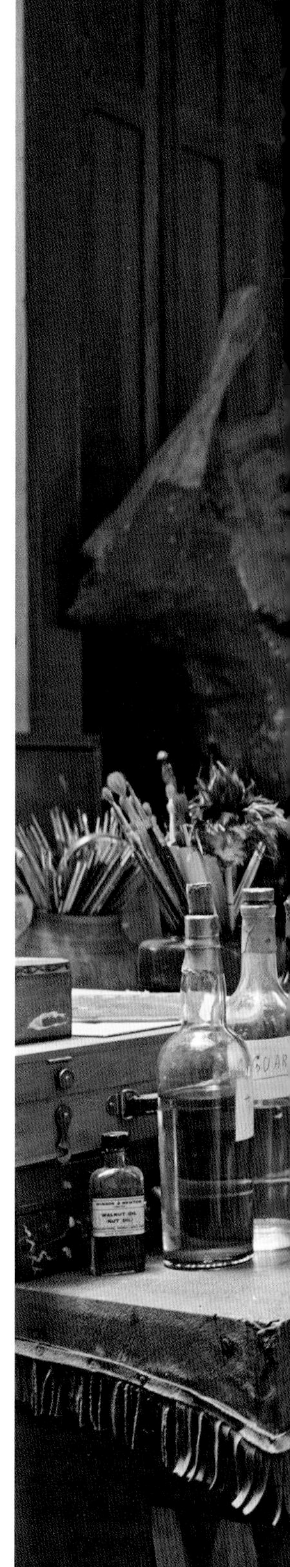

Frida Kahlo and Dr. Juan Farill photographed in her home, 1951.

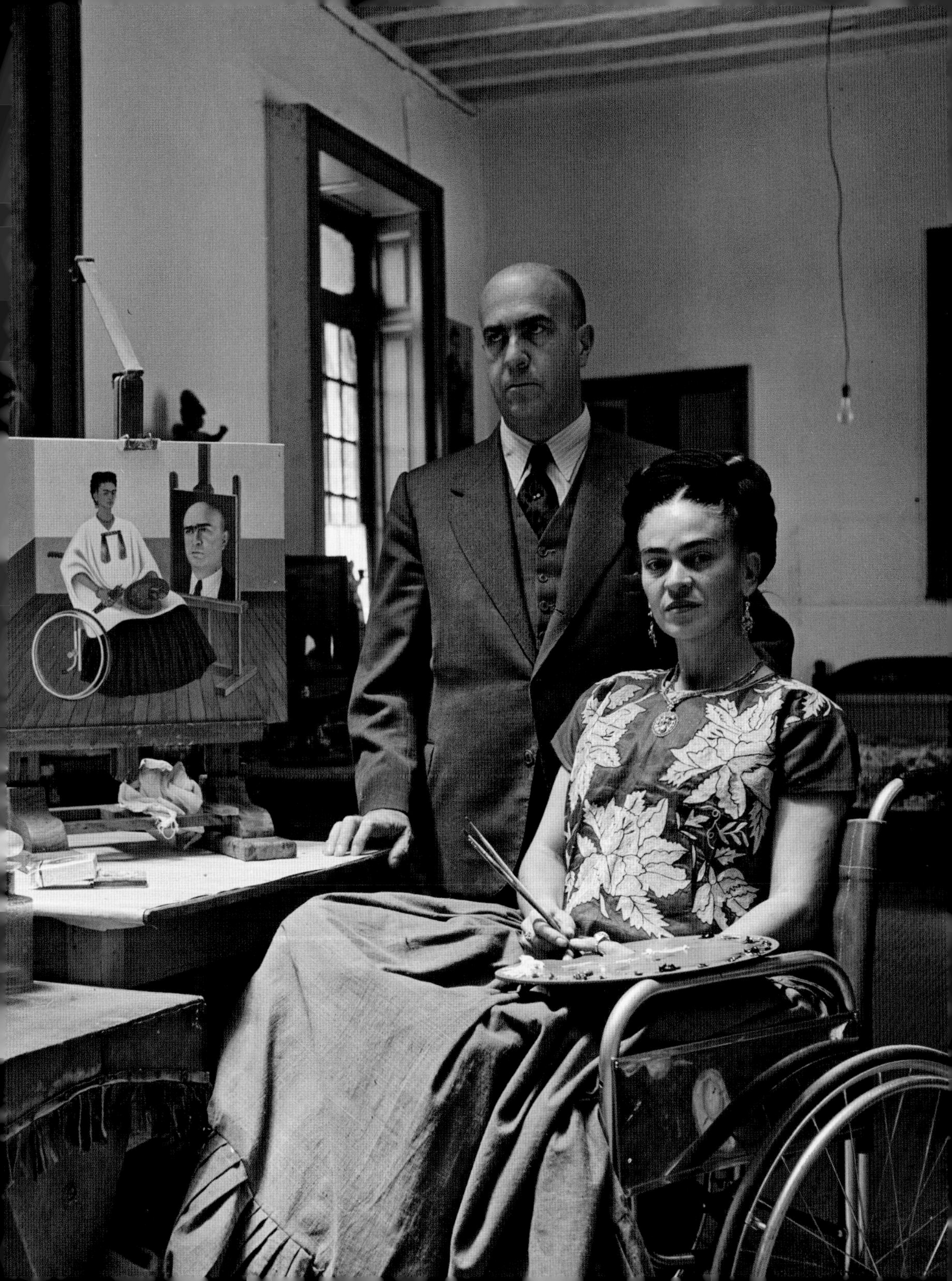

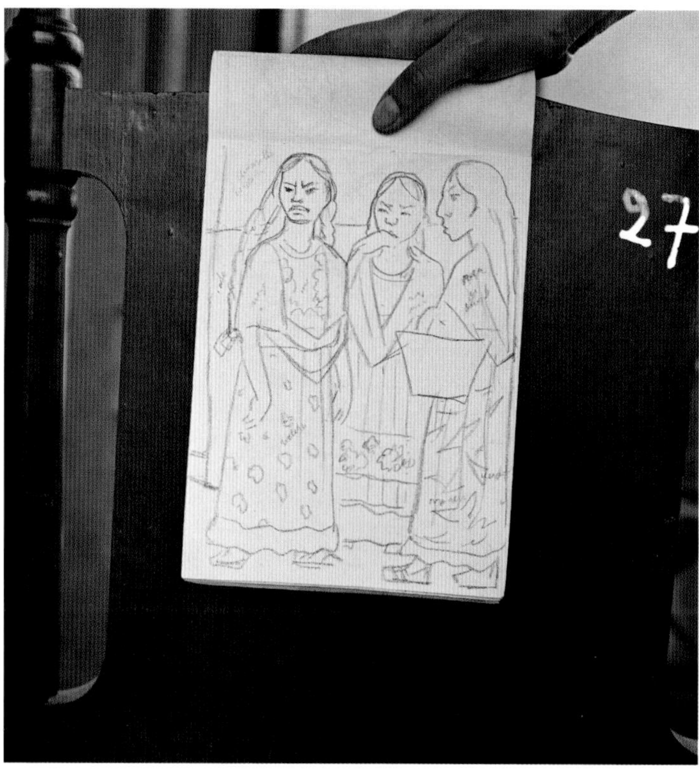

Diego Rivera at work in his studio inside the house, and, above, one of his sketches made during a trip to Tehuantepec, 1951. "Diego Rivera in his studio, writing his painter's memoirs. In the background [are] large effigies, Judases which the people burn on Easter Monday by stuffing them with *cuetes* [fireworks]. The effigies are made of painted newspaper and held in place by sticks" (Gisèle Freund caption for the photo story "Découverte d'une ville précortésienne près de Mexico City").

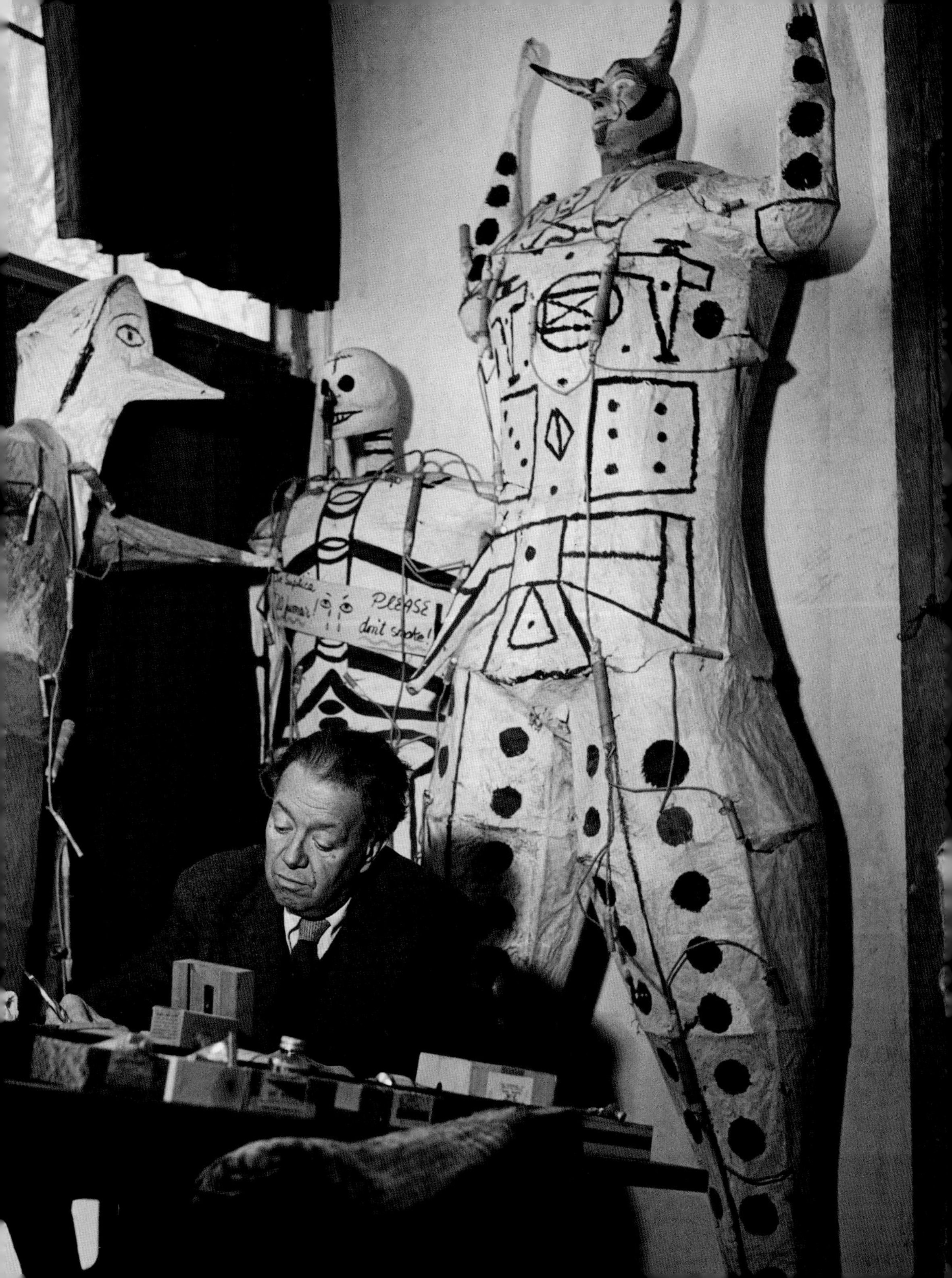
PLEASE
don't smoke!

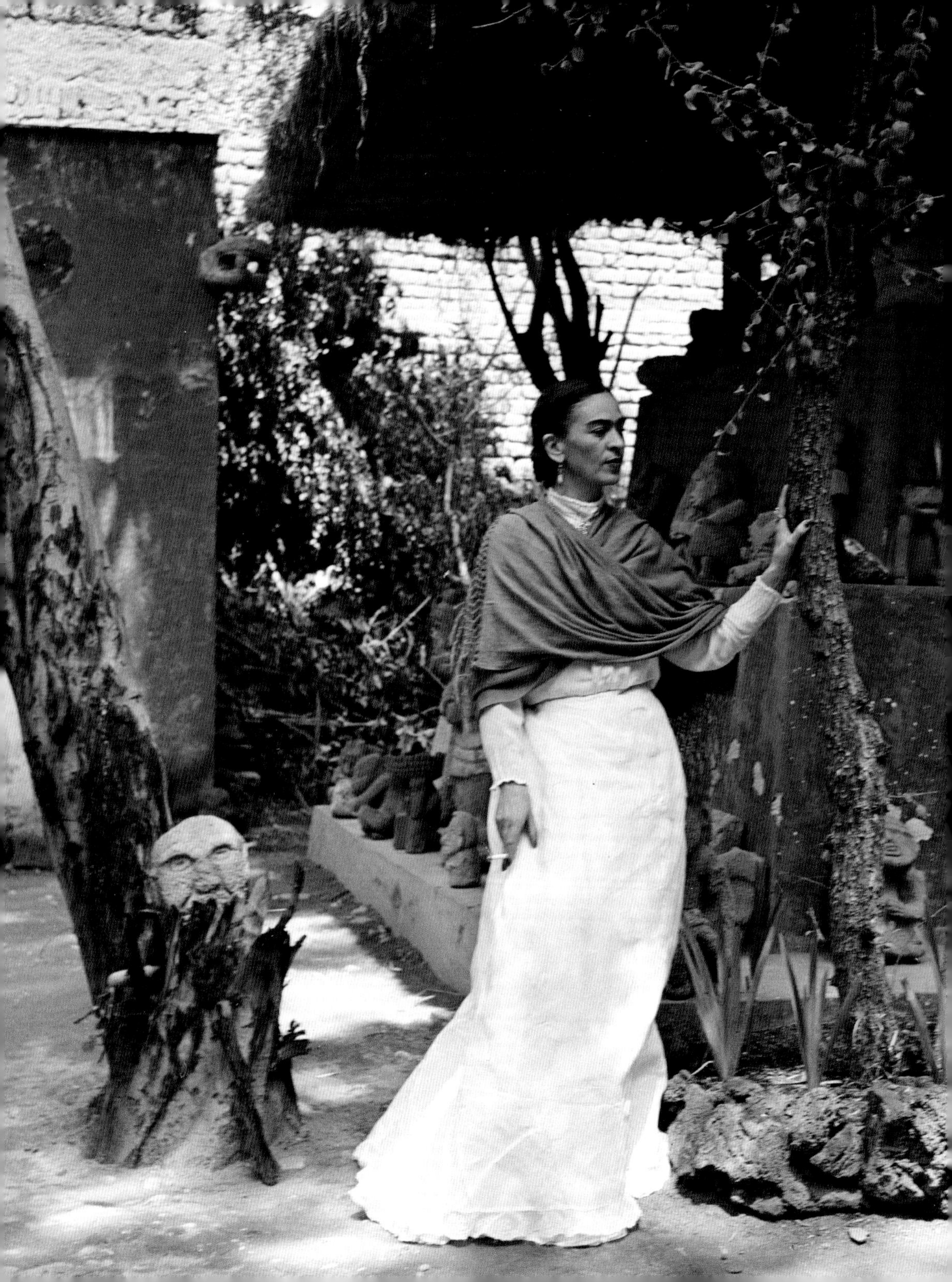

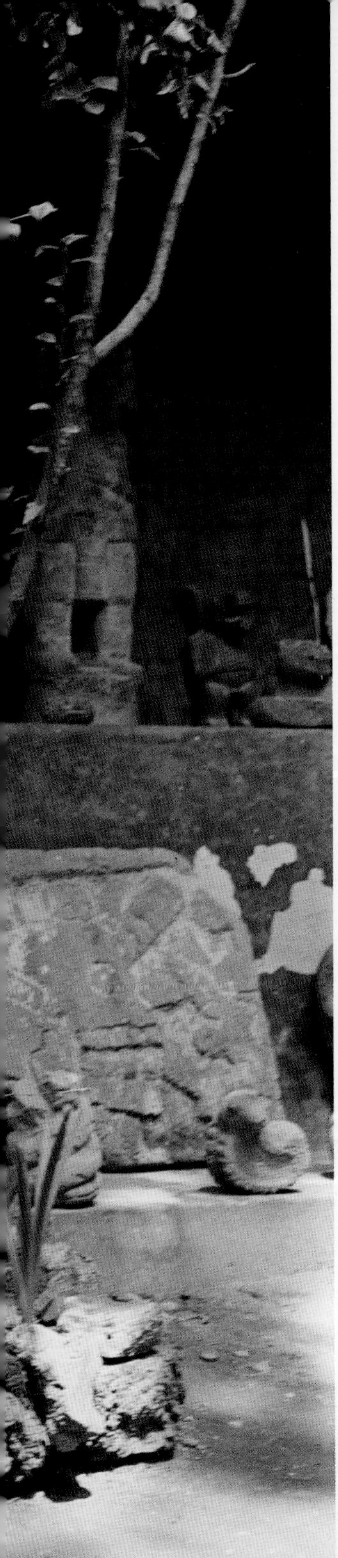

Frida Kahlo in her garden, 1951. “Frida’s painting was born of the terrible event of her life. At sixteen, she was hit by a car* and shattered her spinal column. Since then she has spent most of her life in her garden, full of trees and tropical flowers, where cactuses wrap around pre-Cortesian sculptures” (Giséle Freund, from the photo story “Femmes Mexicaines” [“Mexican Women”] published in *El Hogar,* Argentina, May 1950). *Editor’s Note: In actuality, the bus she had boarded was hit by a tram.

Frida Kahlo in front of the ornamental pool in her garden, 1951.

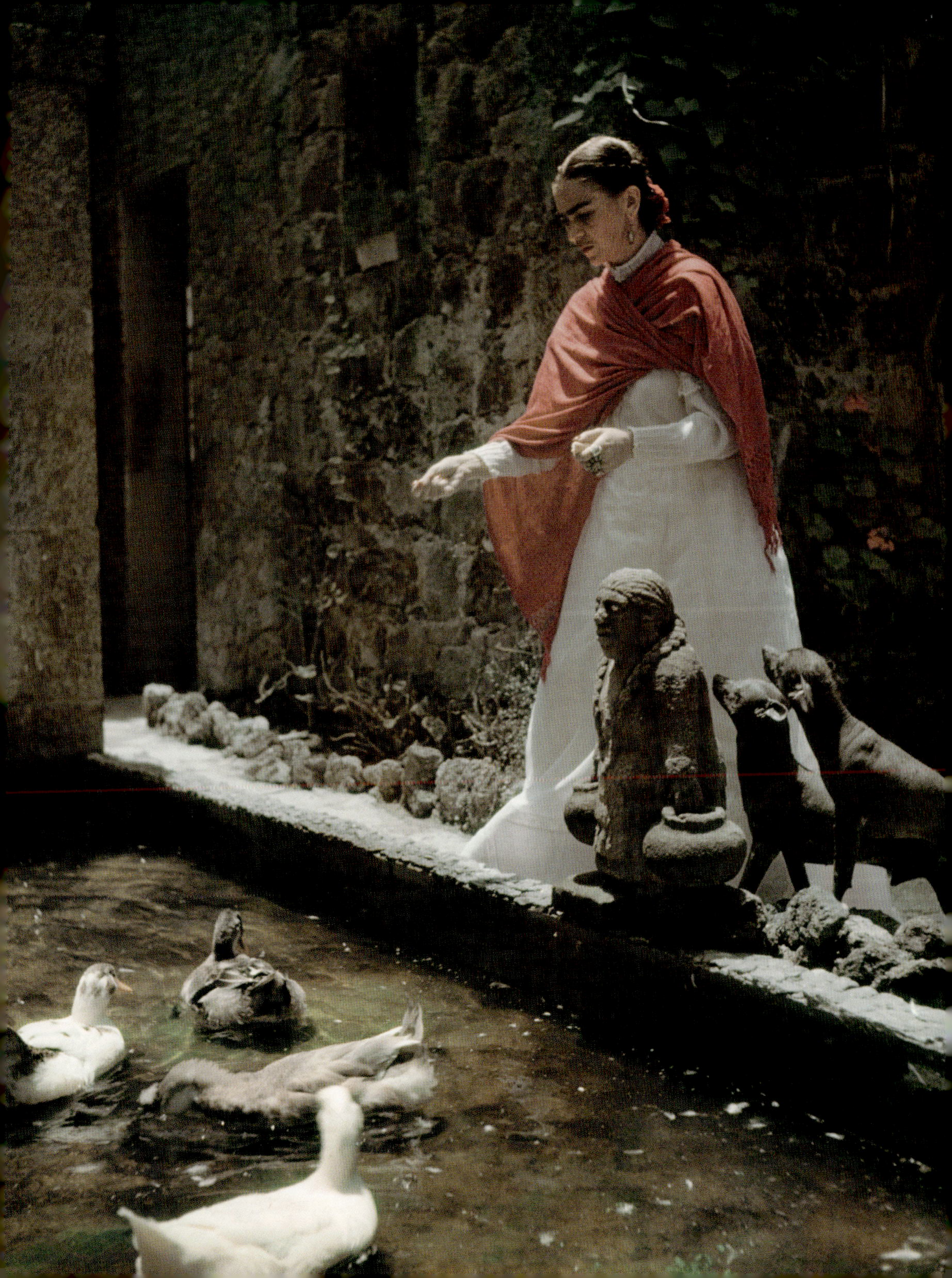

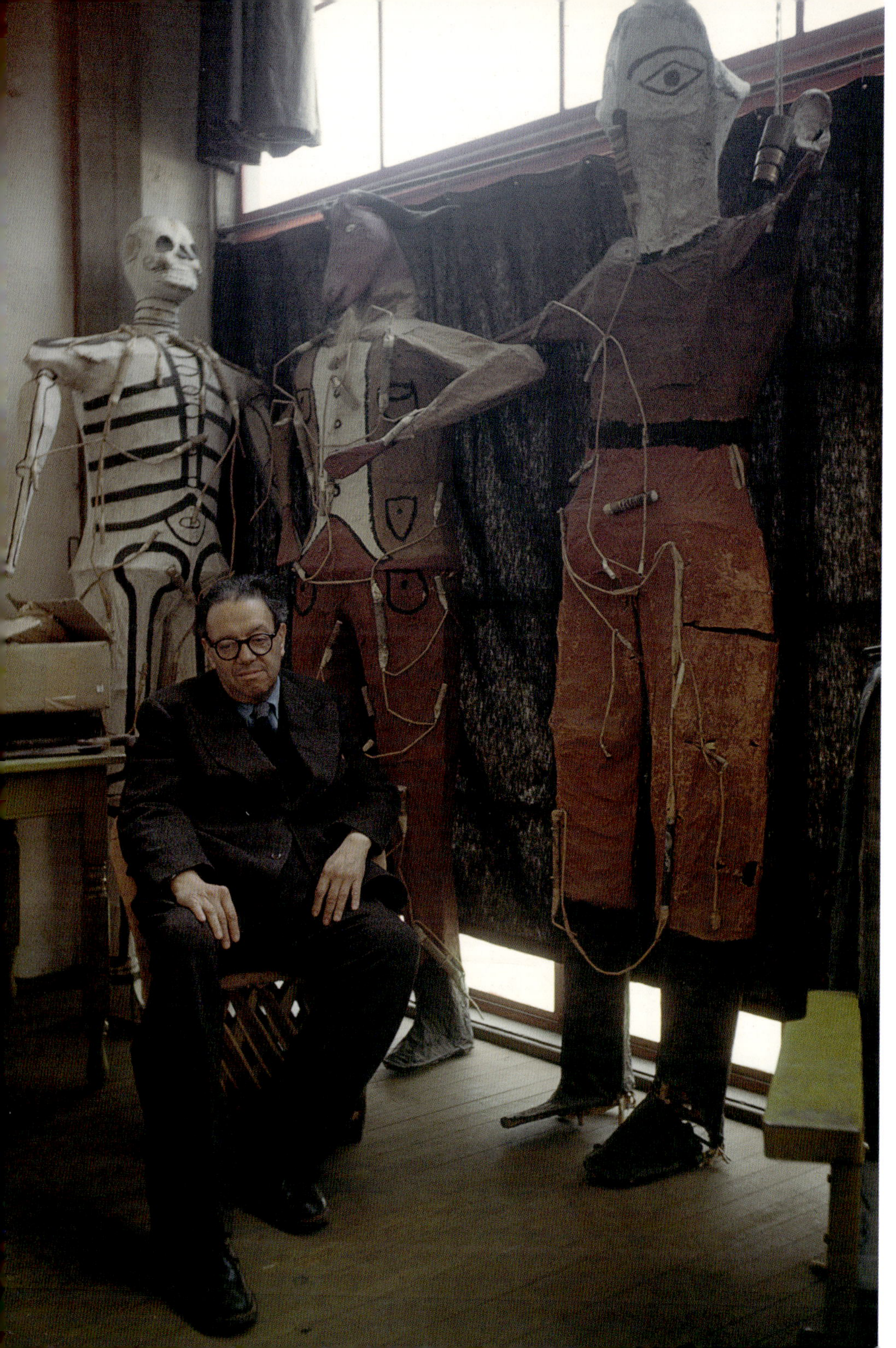

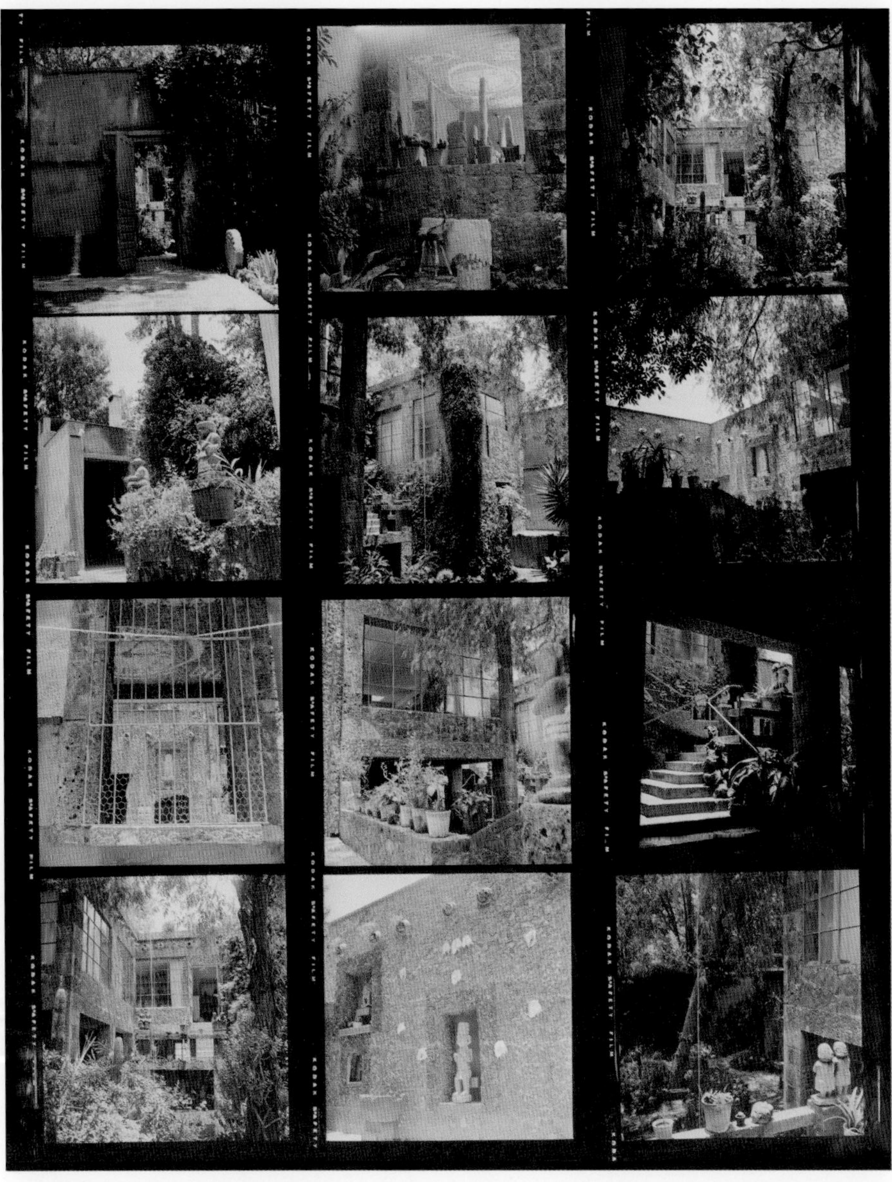

Diego Rivera in his studio, and contact print of photographs of Frida Kahlo's garden populated with pre-Cortesian sculptures, 1951. Following double-page spread: Frida Kahlo in her garden, 1951. (Editor's Note: Out of focus, but a rare period portrait in color.)

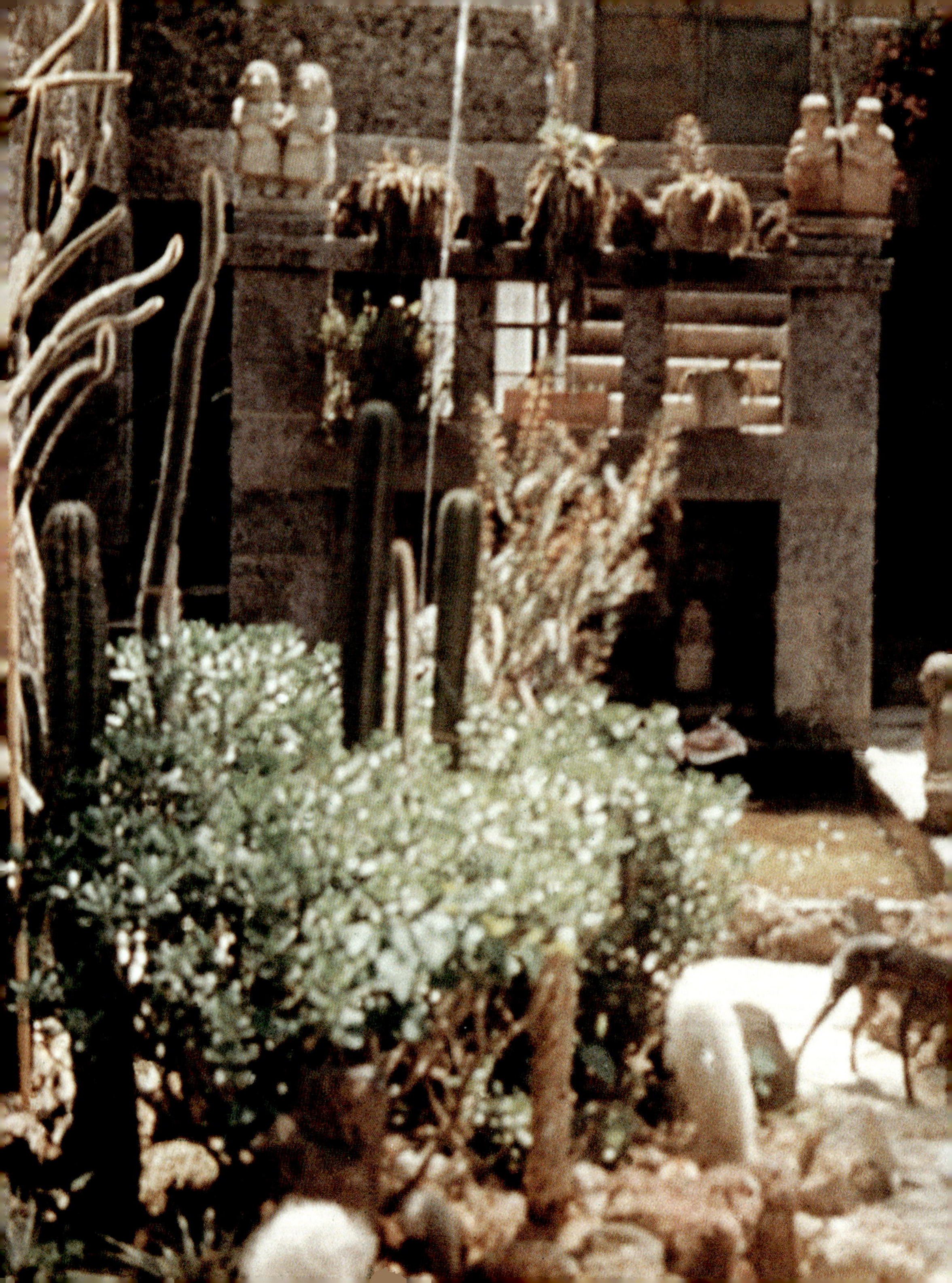

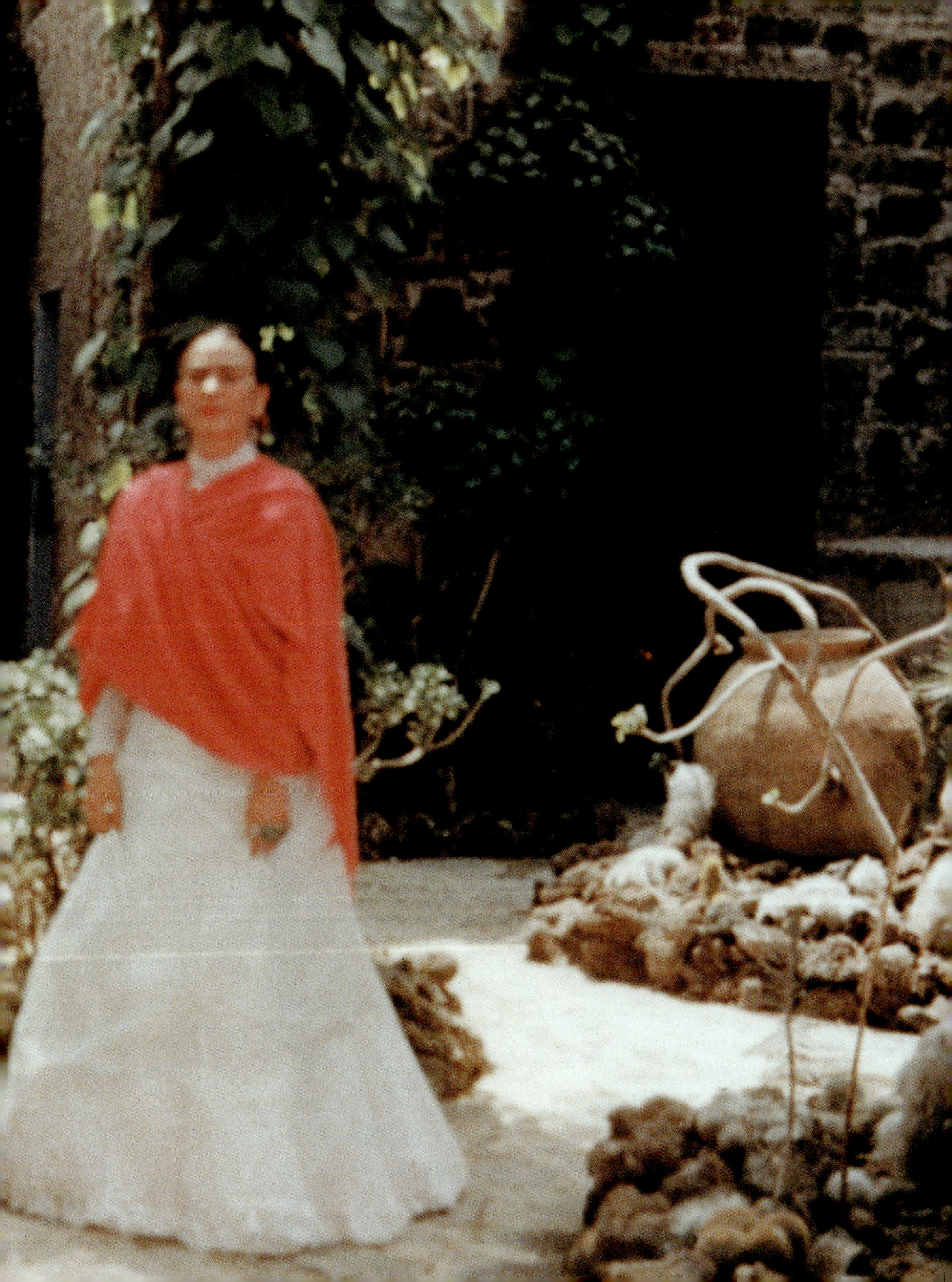

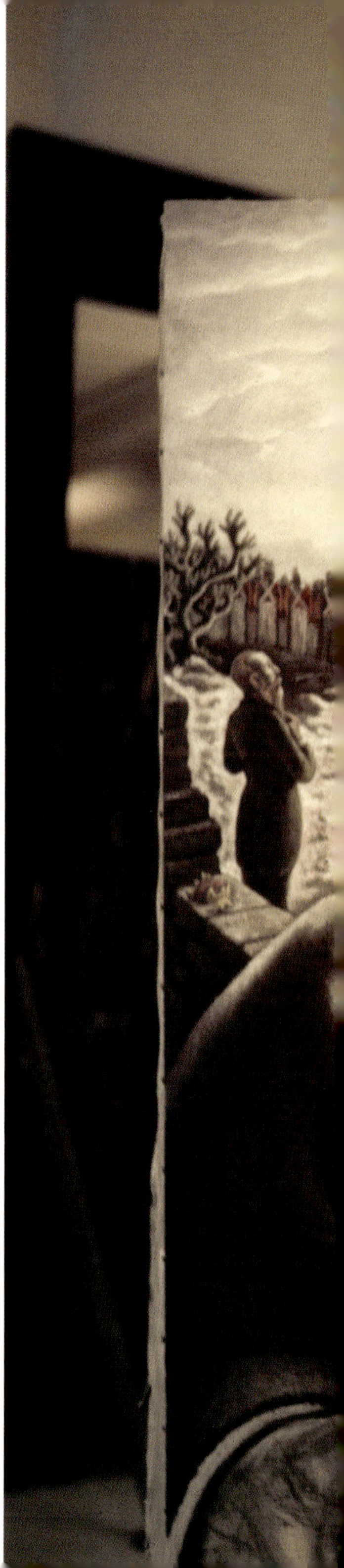

Diego Rivera in his studio, 1951. "The Mexican artist Diego Rivera painting a portrait of Benito Juárez, the great nineteenth-century Mexican statesman who wrote the Constitution. In the background, at left, Diego depicts the execution of Emperor Maximilian and, on the opposite side, farmers at work. This is his latest painting, recently completed for the Mexican government, created to be exhibited in the governmental palace. Diego is wearing the blue denim of a normal worker, a cheap model sold in American stores" (Gisèle Freund caption for the photo story "Mexican Painters at Work").

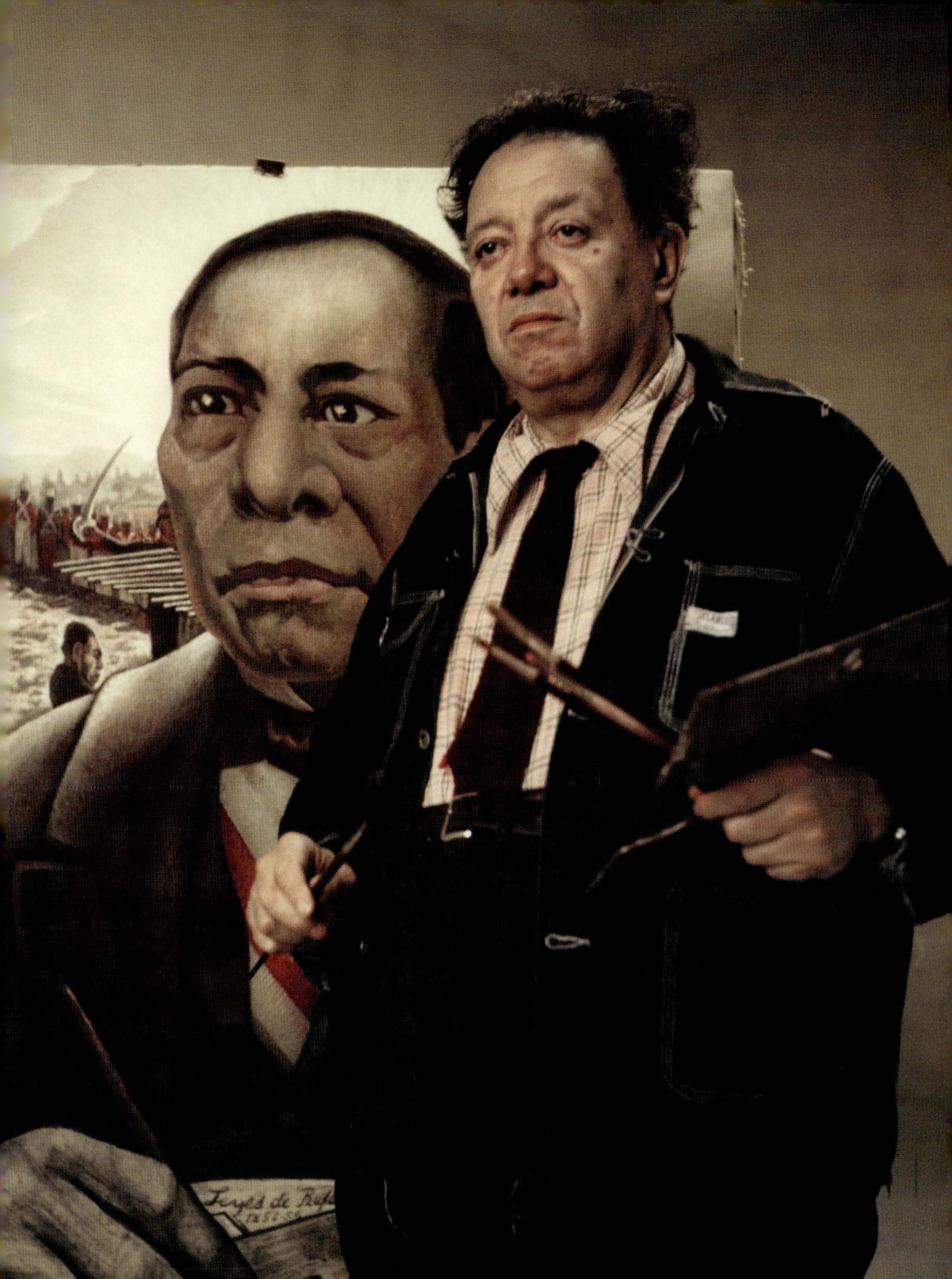

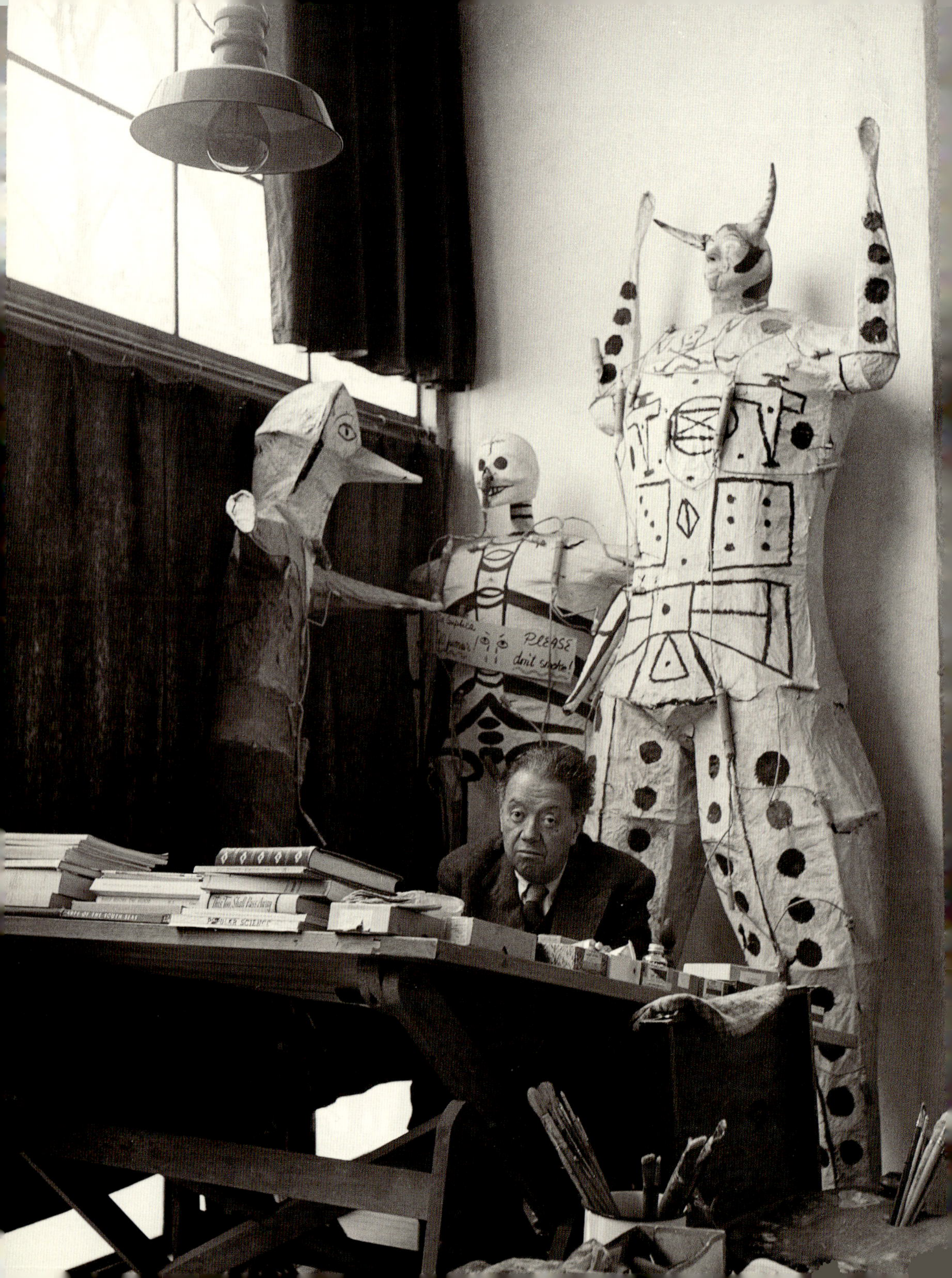
PLEASE
don't smoke!
This Too Shall Pass Away
POPULAR SCIENCE

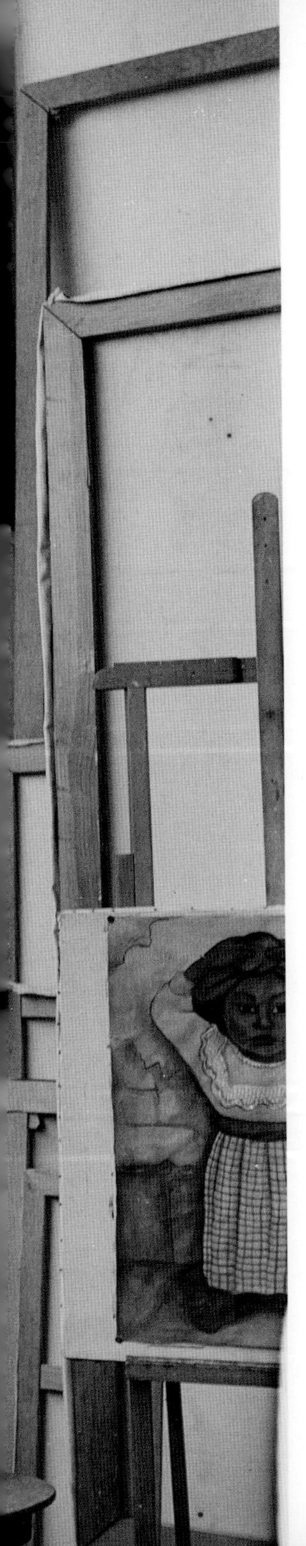

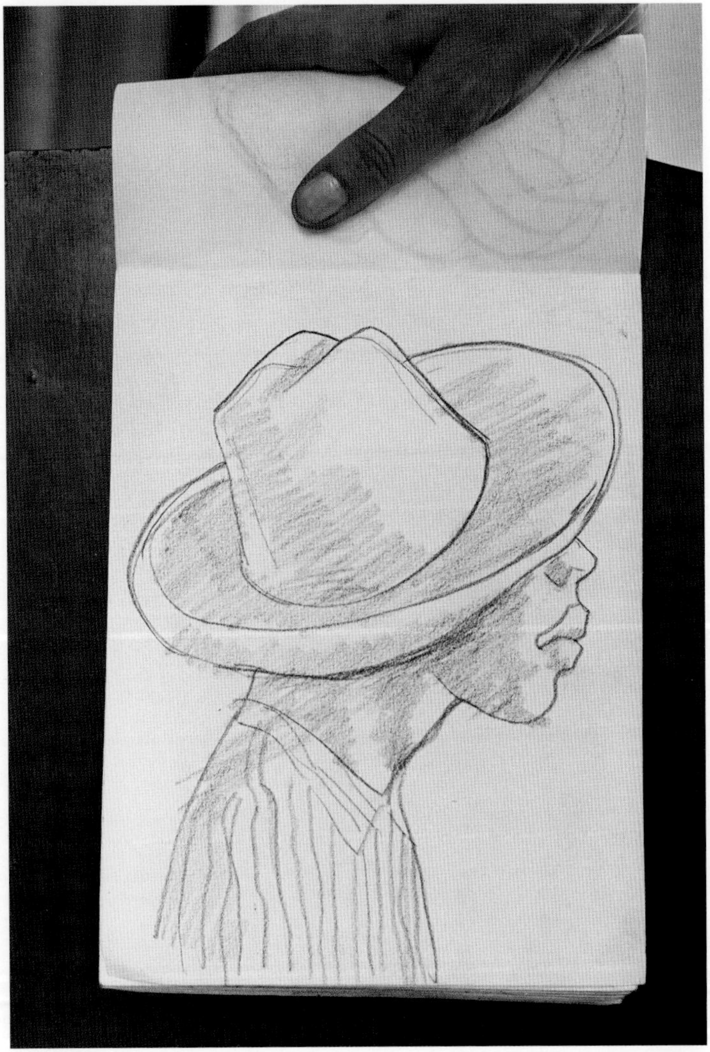

Diego Rivera in his studio, and one of his sketches, 1951.

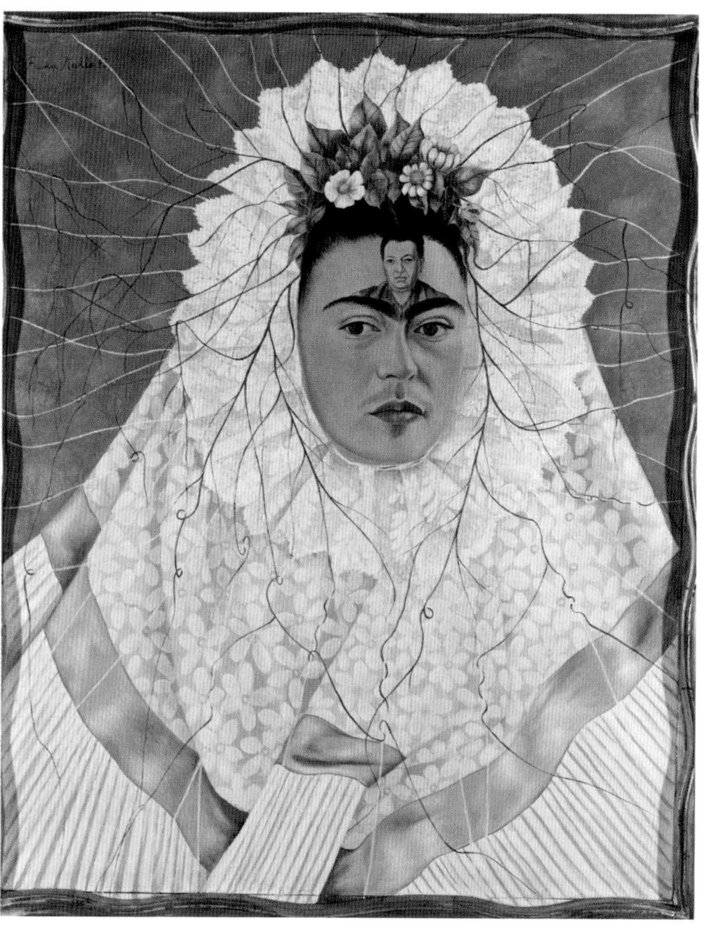

Self-Portrait as a Tehuana painted by Frida Kahlo, and Diego Rivera painting the portrait of Benito Juárez, photographed in the house, 1951.

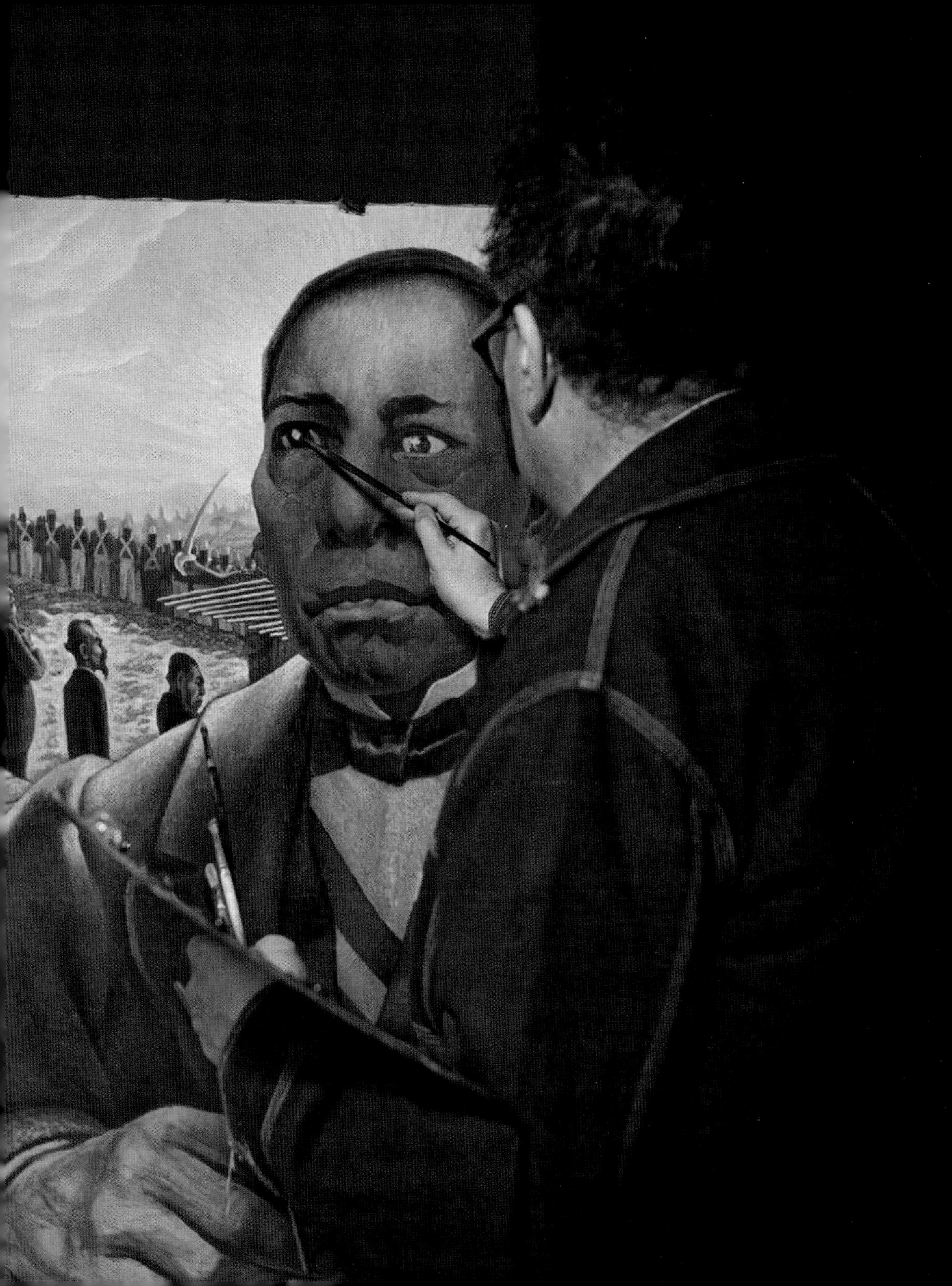

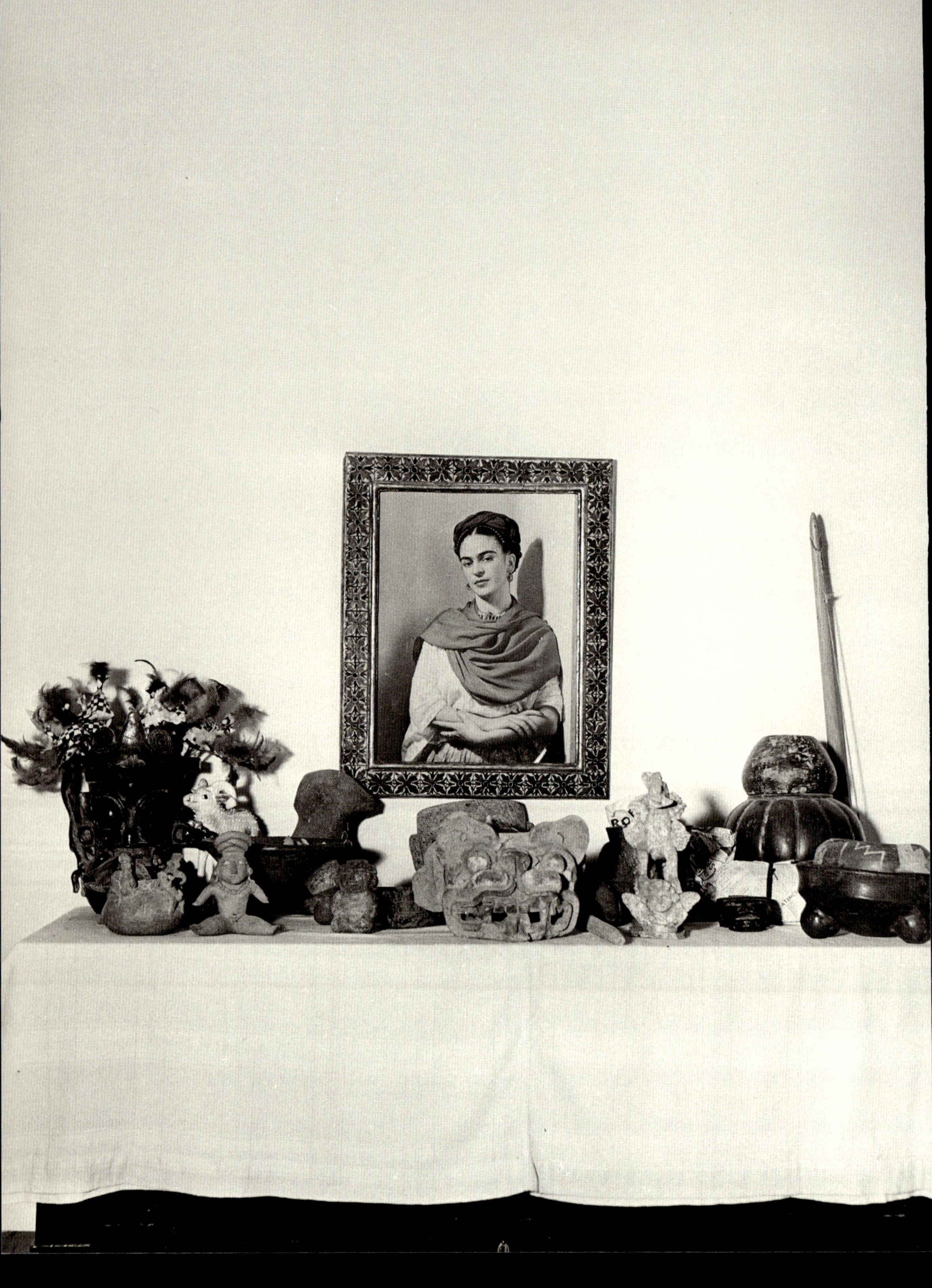

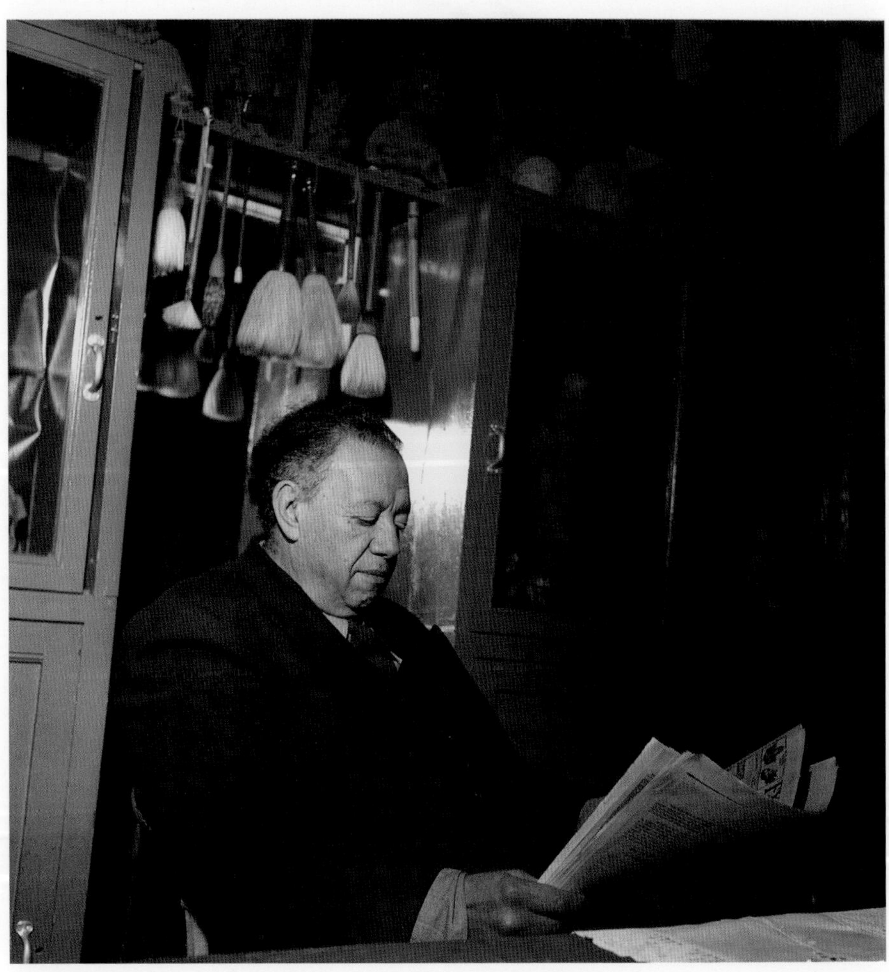

Interior view of the house, and Diego Rivera under the couple's collection of brushes, 1951.

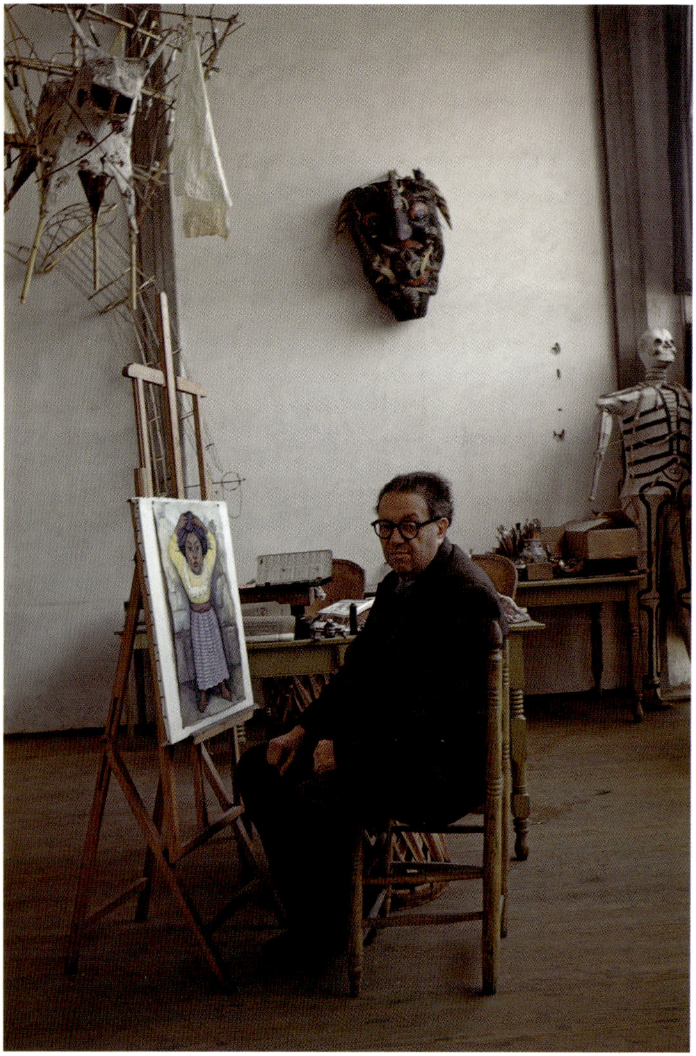

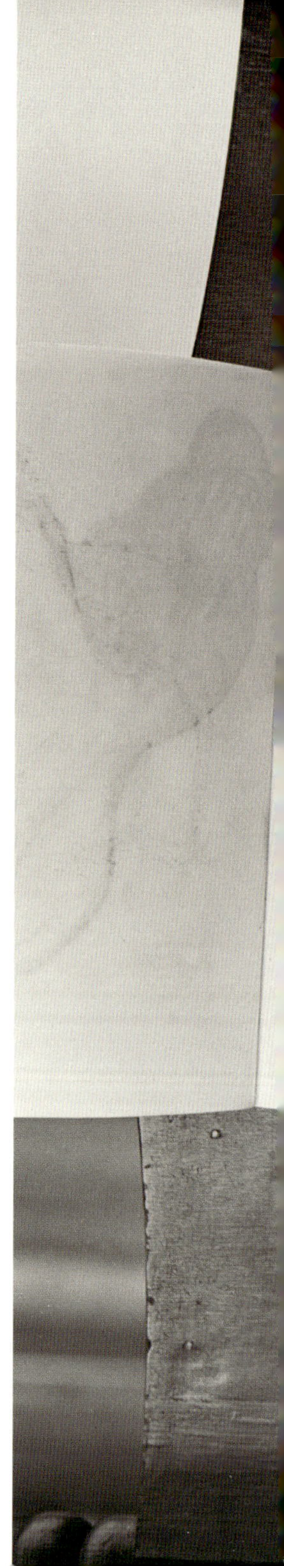

"Diego Rivera in his studio before one of his watercolors representing a little girl from Oaxaca" (Gisèle Freund caption found on the back of a press print, 1951), and sketch made by Diego Rivera during a trip to Tehuantepec, Mexico, 1951. "A page from Diego Rivera's sketchbook, Tehuanas bathing" (Gisèle Freund caption found on the back of a press print).

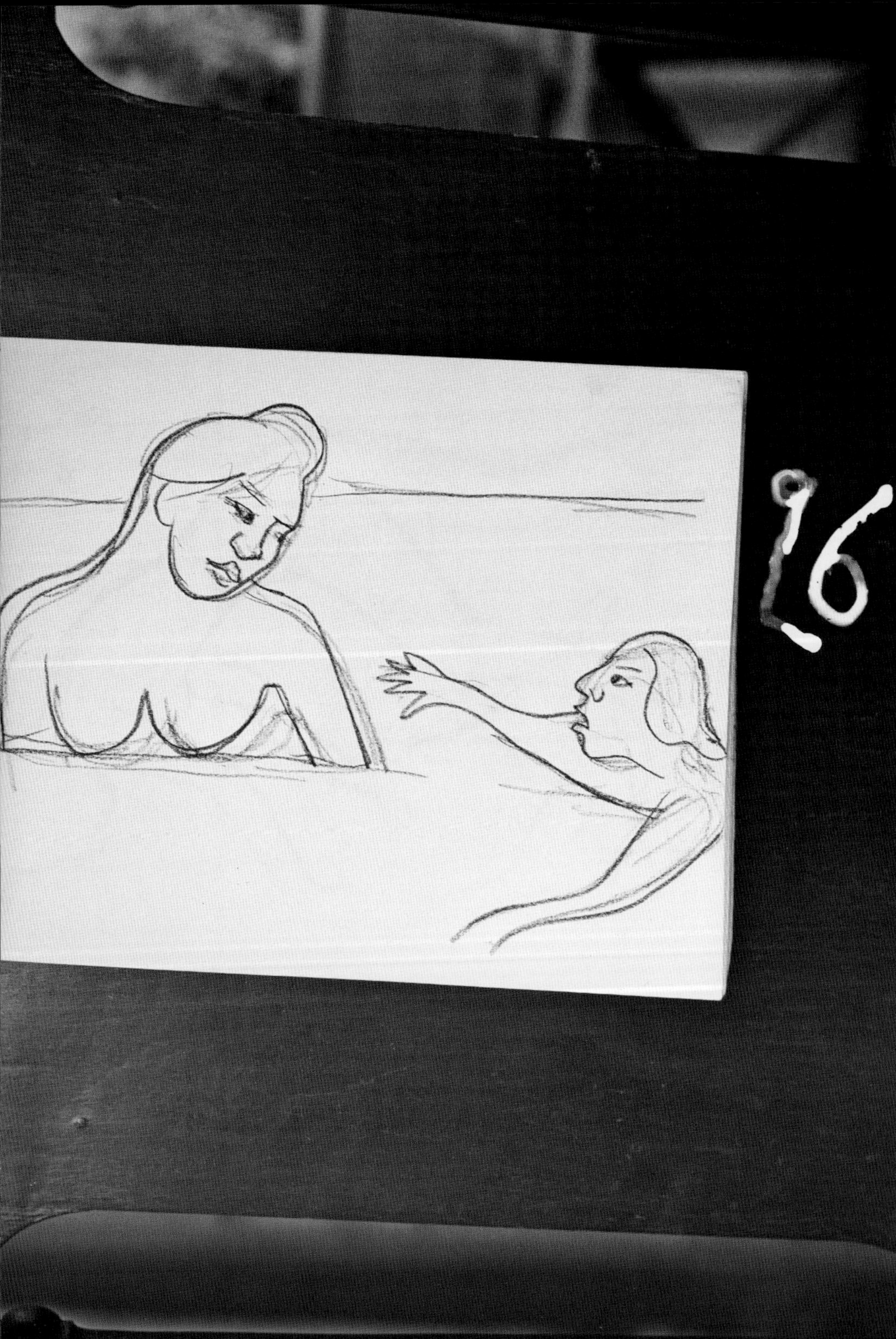
16

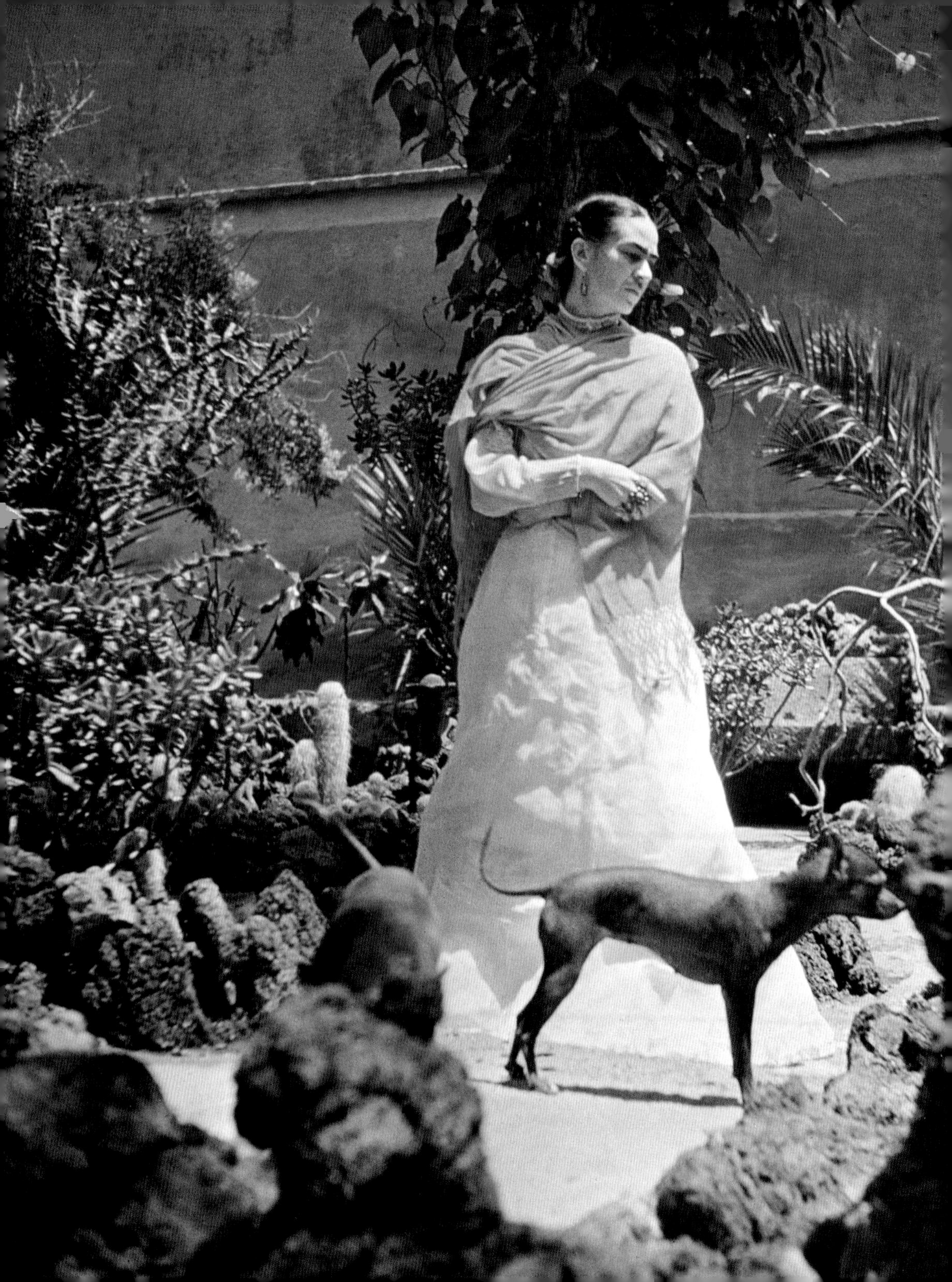

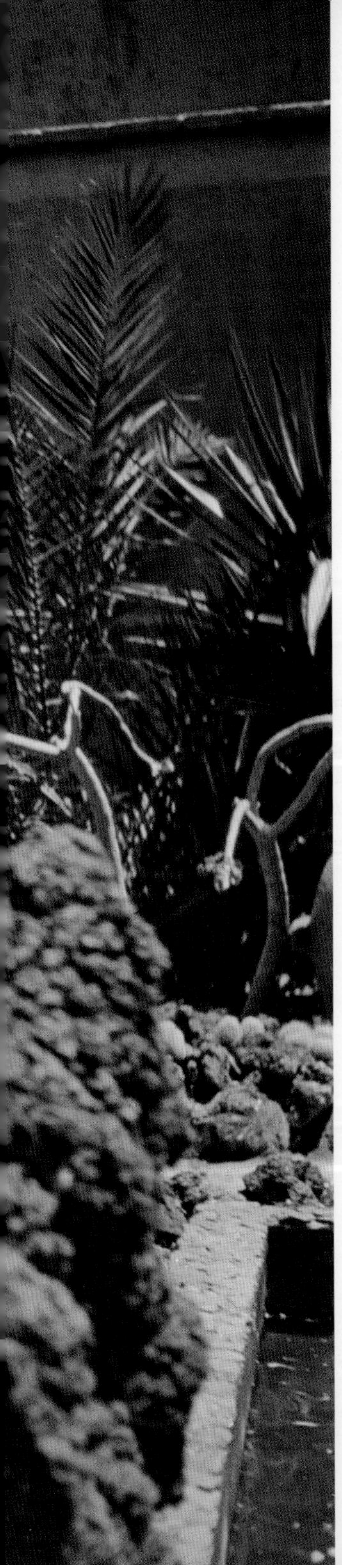

Frida Kahlo in her garden with her dogs, 1951.

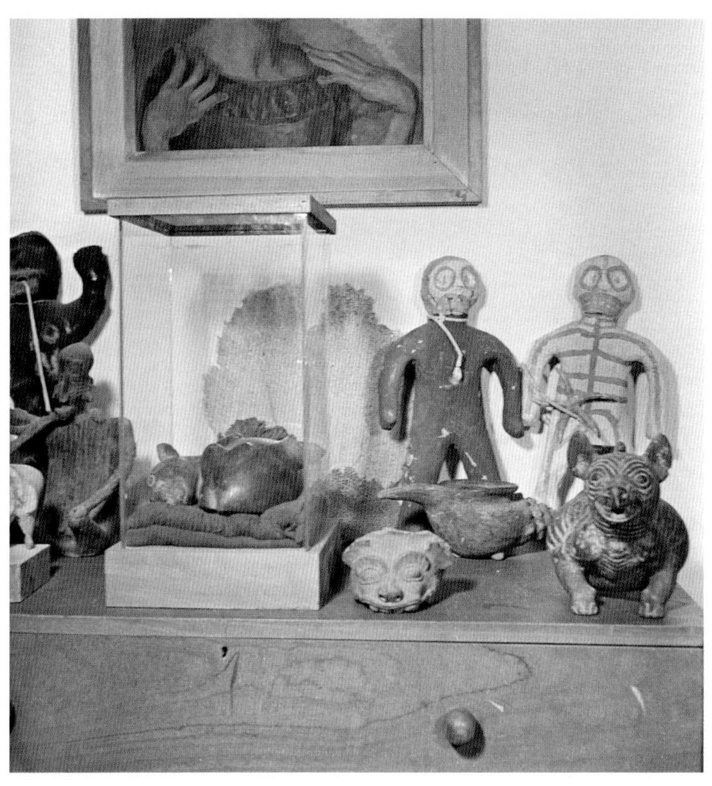

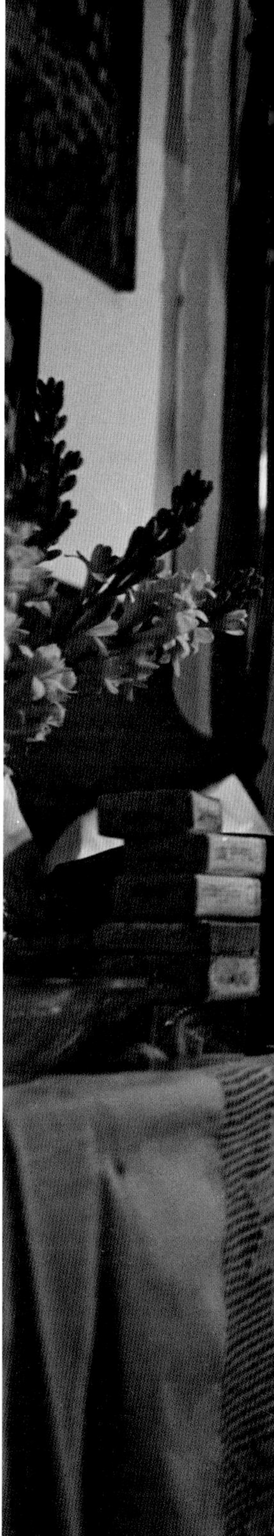

Figurines related to the Day of the Dead and pre-Columbian art collected by Diego Rivera, and Frida Kahlo, 1951.

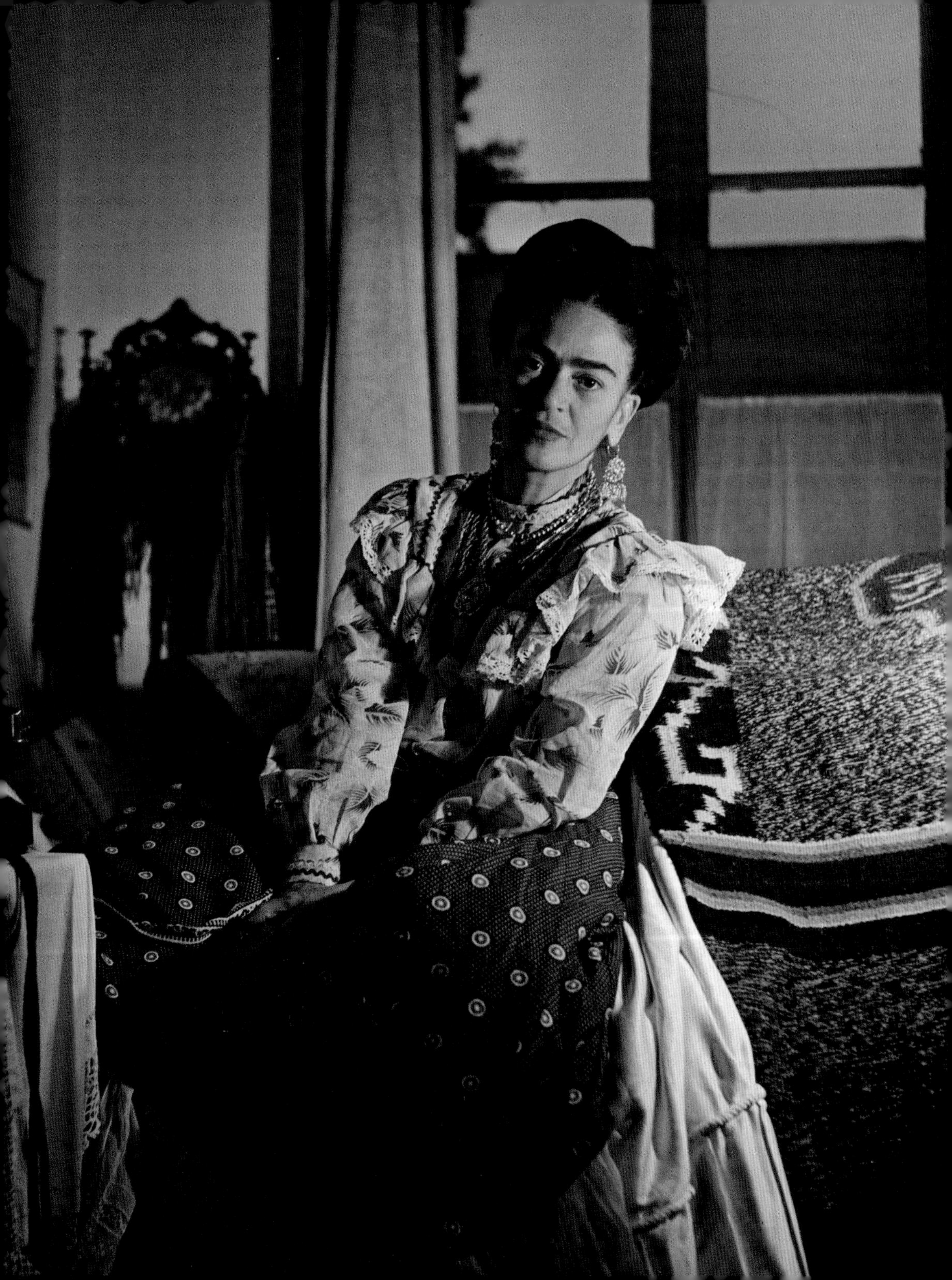

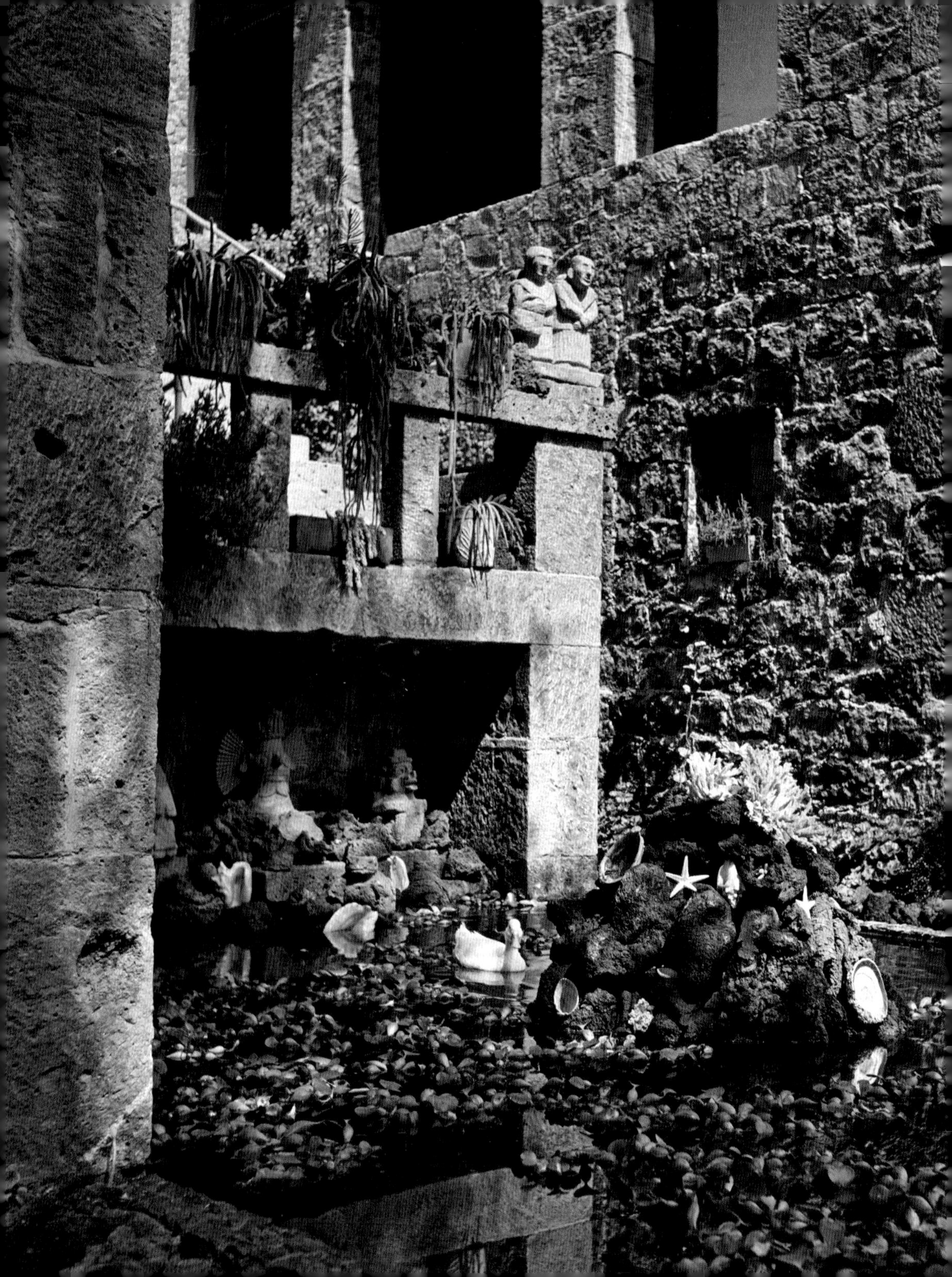

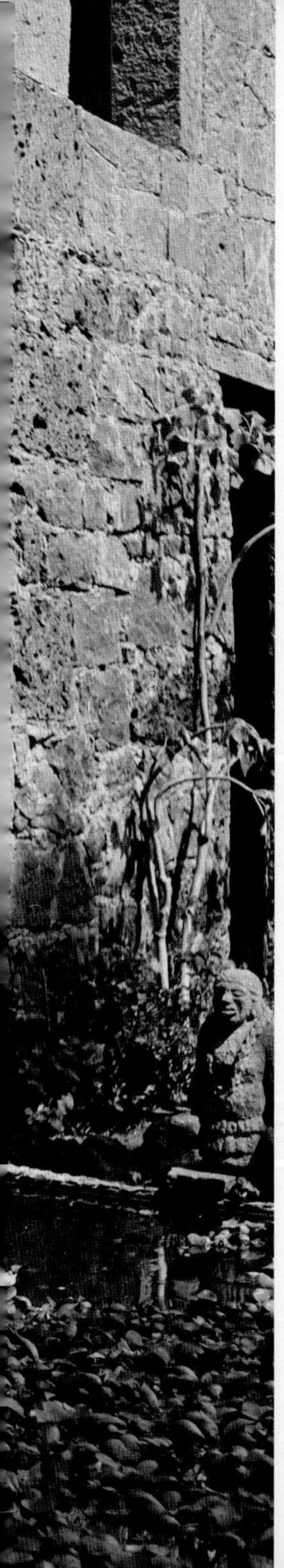

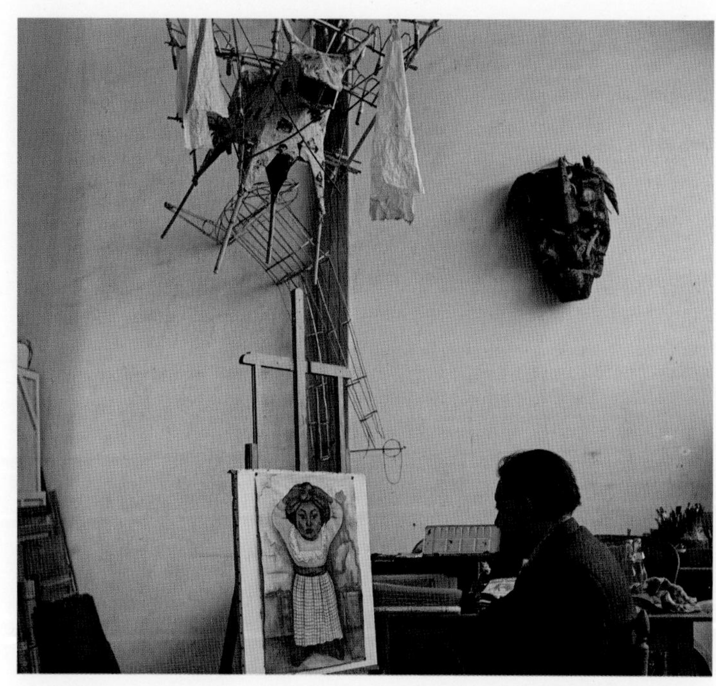

View of the ornamental pool in the garden, and Diego Rivera in his studio, 1951.

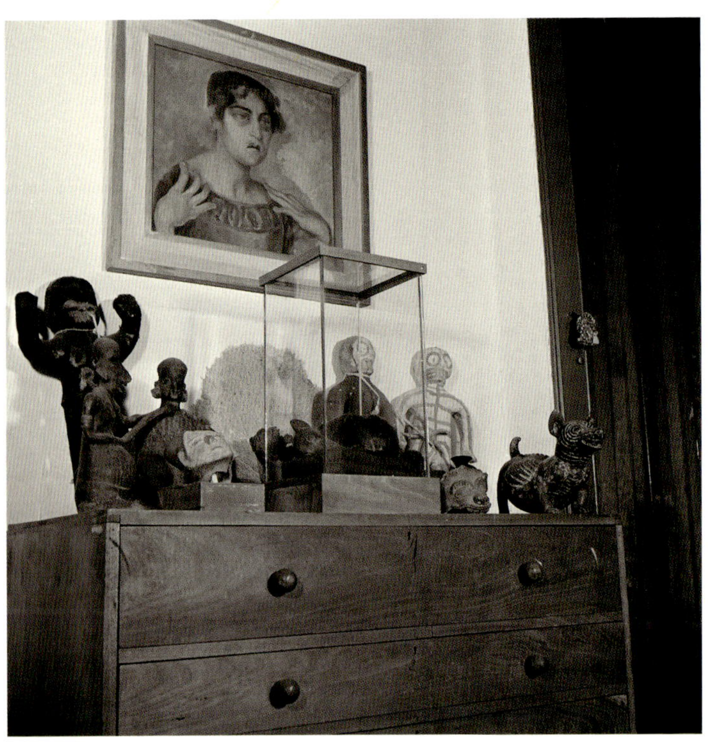

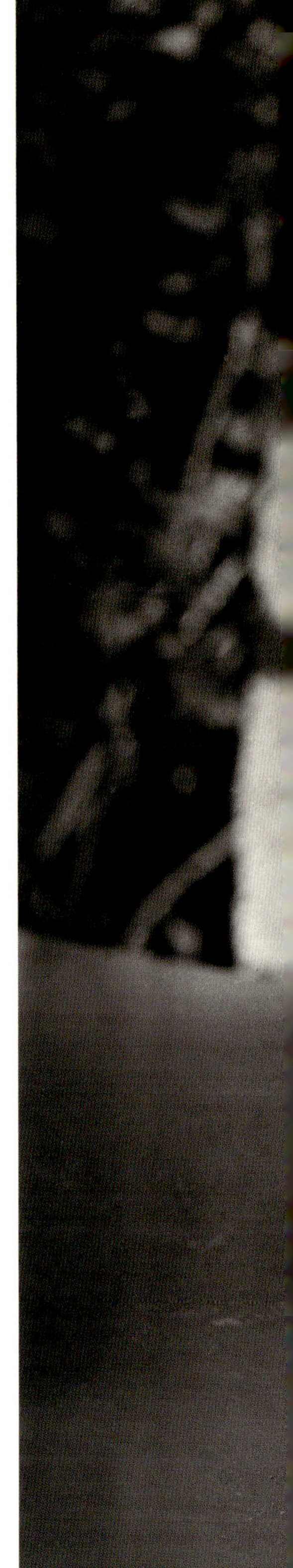

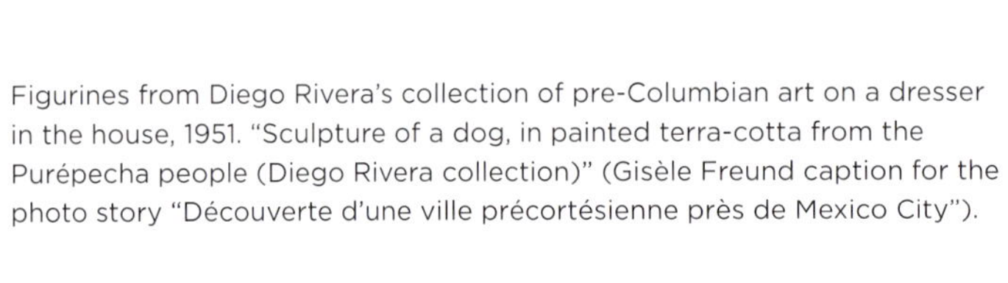

Figurines from Diego Rivera's collection of pre-Columbian art on a dresser in the house, 1951. "Sculpture of a dog, in painted terra-cotta from the Purépecha people (Diego Rivera collection)" (Gisèle Freund caption for the photo story "Découverte d'une ville précortésienne près de Mexico City").

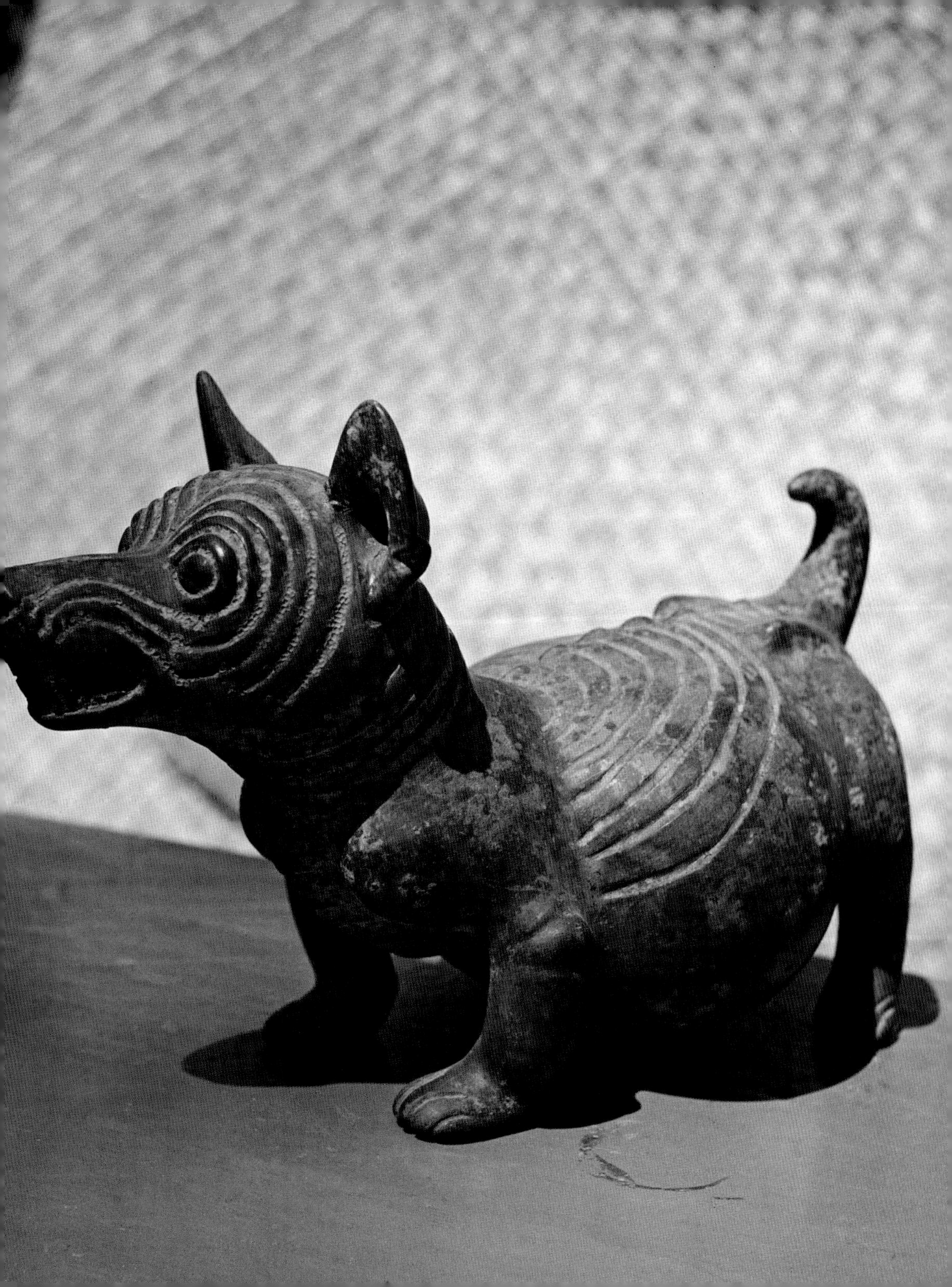

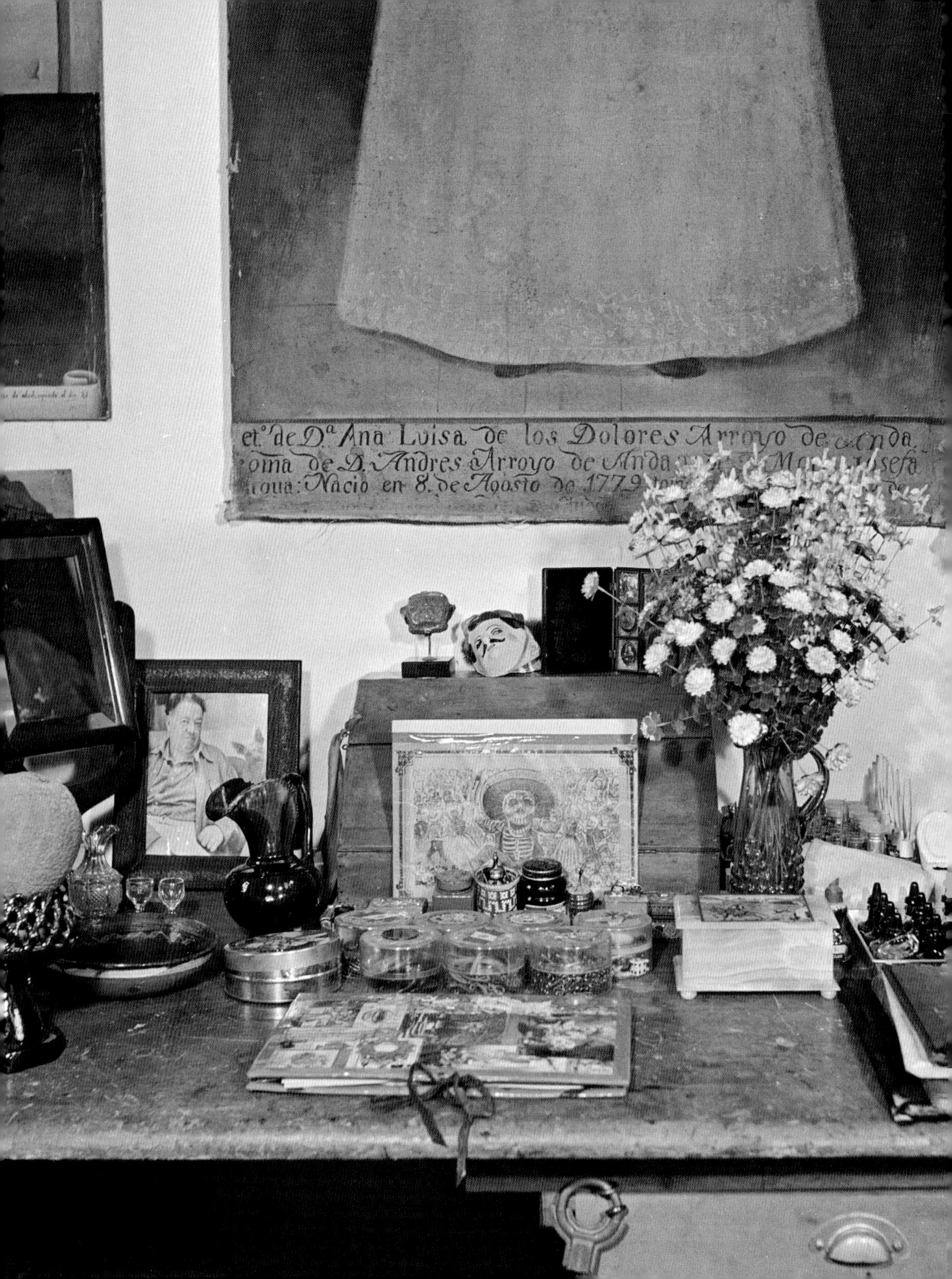
de Da Ana Luisa de los Dolores Arroyo de Anda.
de D. Andres Arroyo de Anda
Josefa
Nacio en 8. de Agosto de 1779

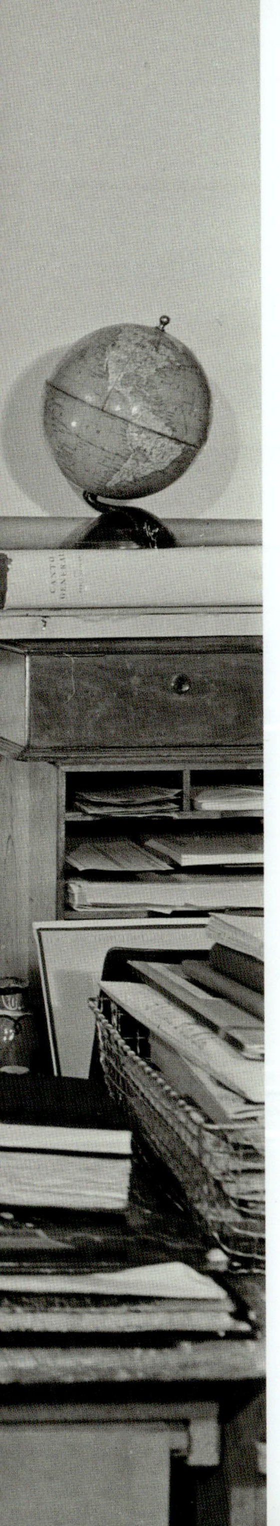

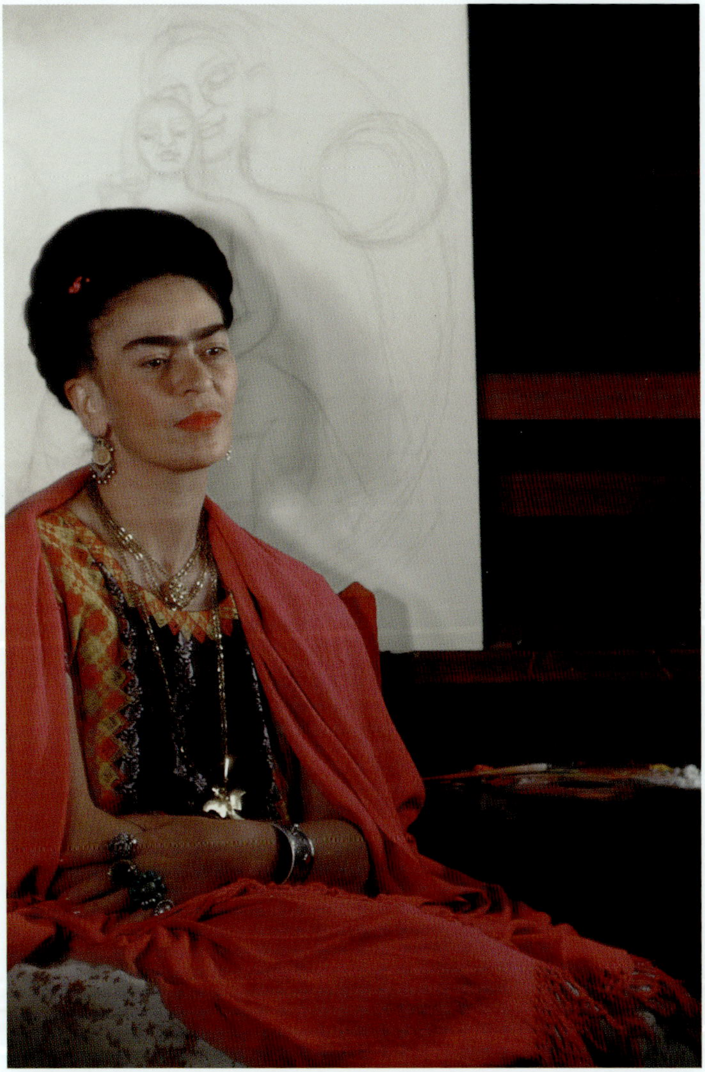

Detail of Frida Kahlo's desk, and Frida in front of the painting *The Love Embrace of the Universe, the Earth (Mexico), Myself, Diego, and Señor Xolotl*, 1951. "A heroic, nearly legendary figure, she sat in her wheelchair year after year painting terrifying canvases in the surrealist manner for which she became famous. She had a strange, moving beauty, which she had inherited from a Mexican mother and a German father; on top of that, she was very witty and had a lively intelligence" (Gisèle Freund, from the 1955 photo story "Diego Rivera construit sa tombe").

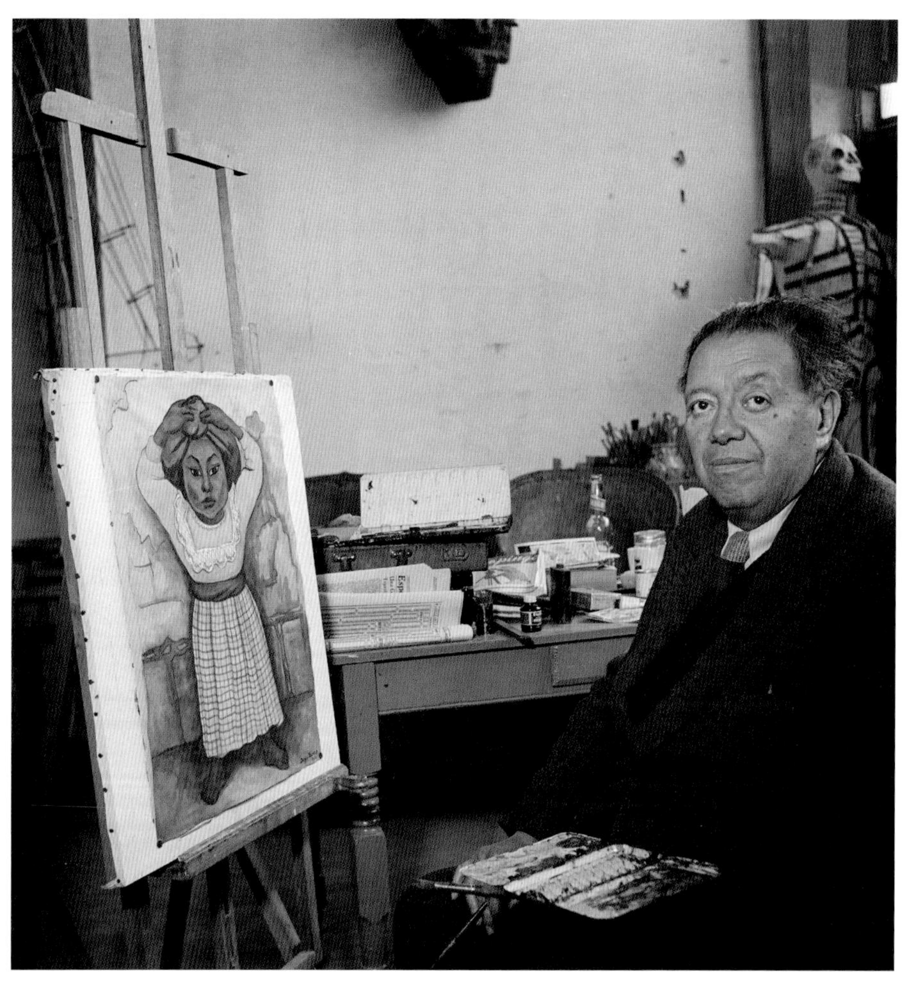

Diego Rivera in his studio, 1951,
and self-portrait painted by Diego Rivera and dated 1949 (press print).

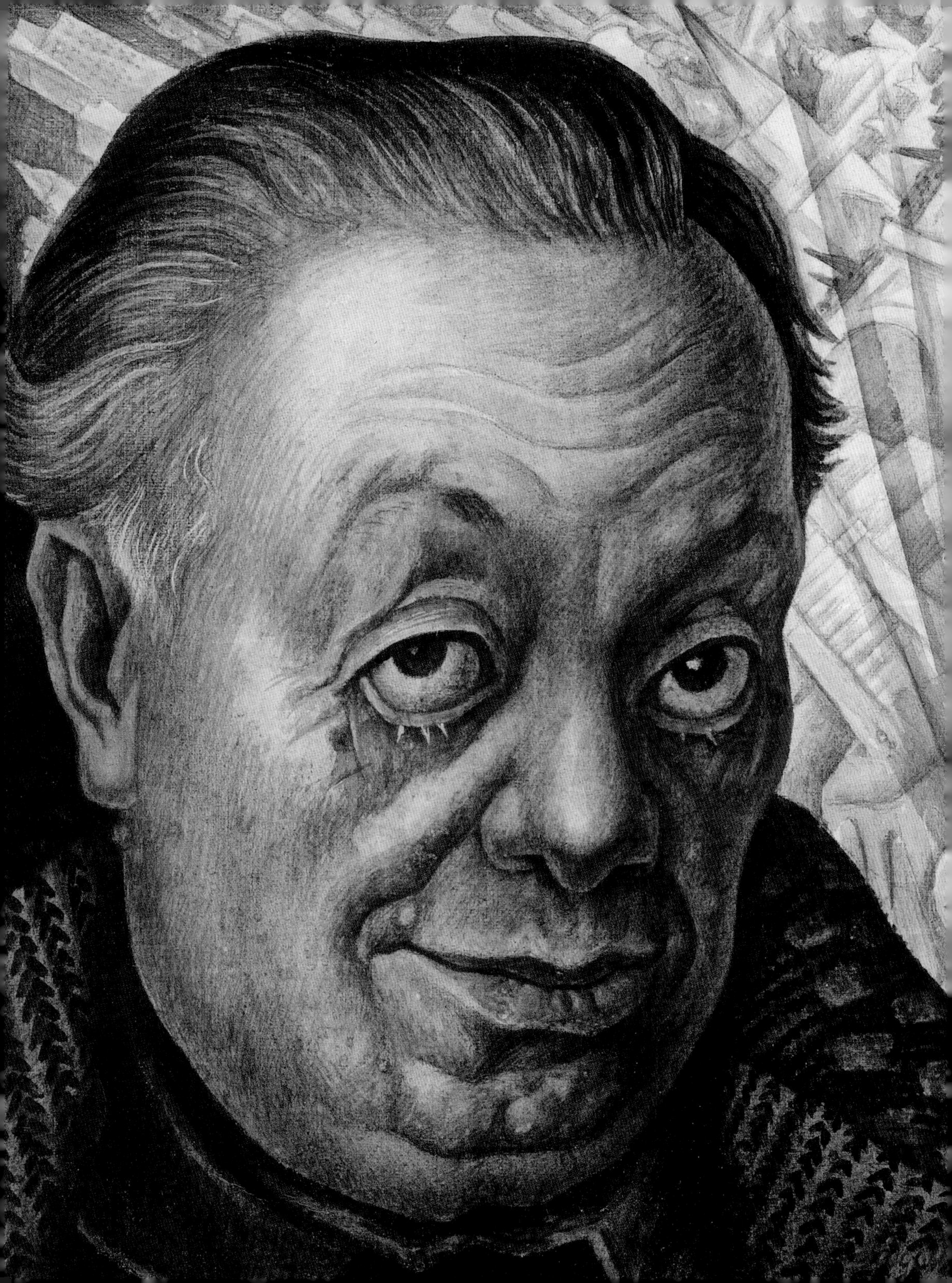

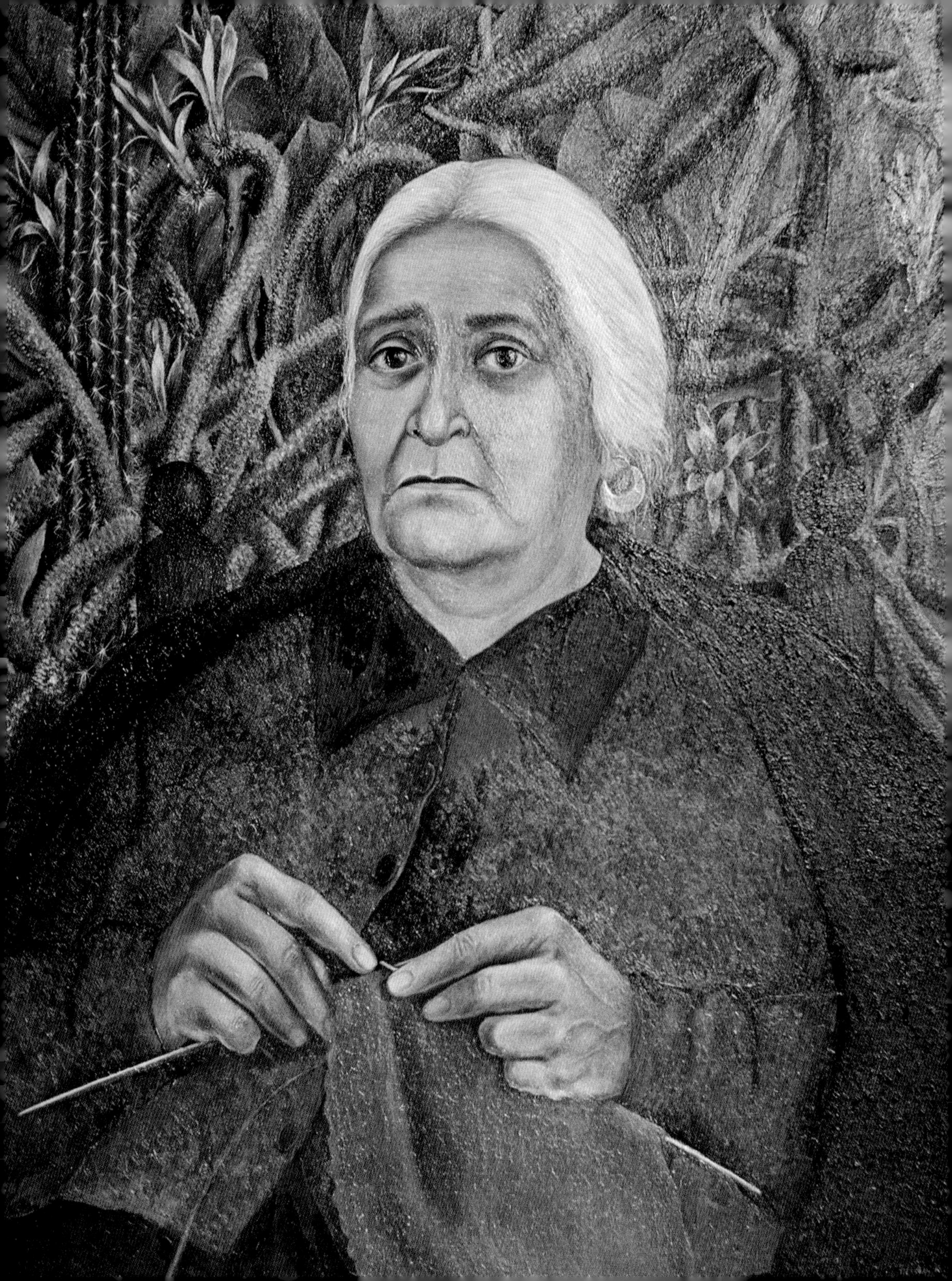

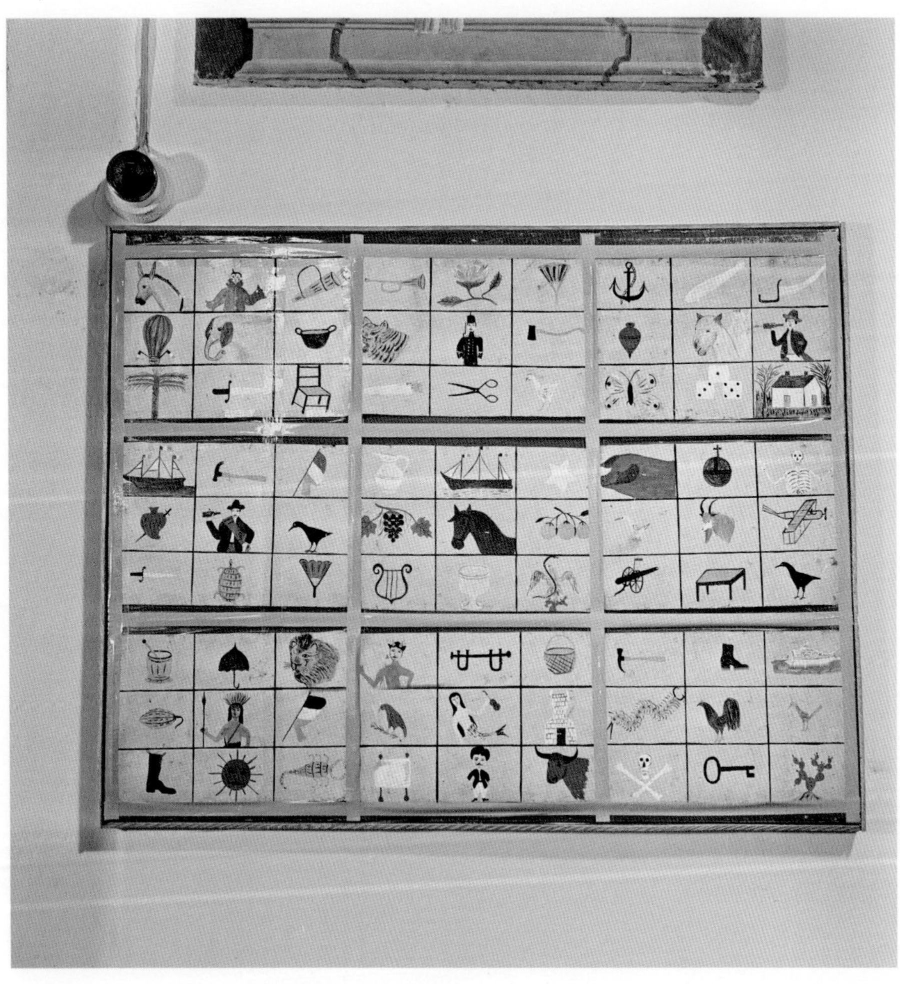

Portrait of Doña Rosita Morillo by Frida Kahlo, and view of an interior wall, 1951.

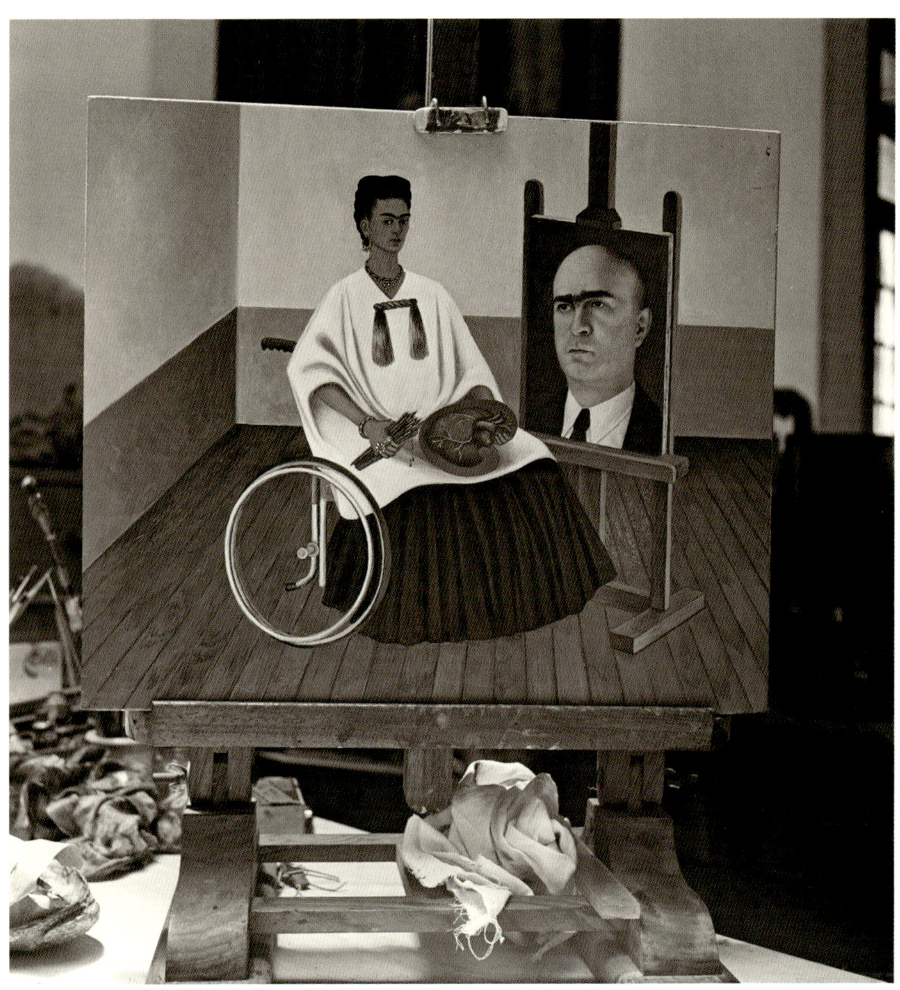

Self-Portrait with the Portrait of Doctor Farill by Frida Kahlo, 1951.

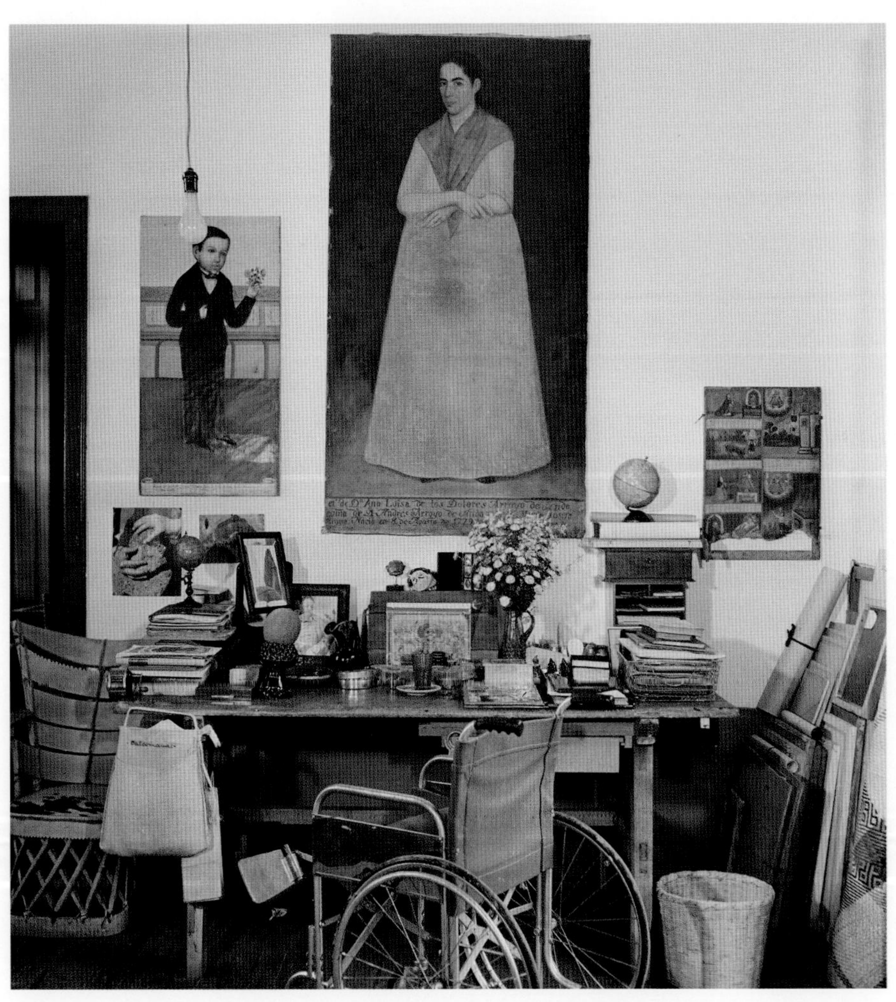

Frida Kahlo’s desk, 1951.

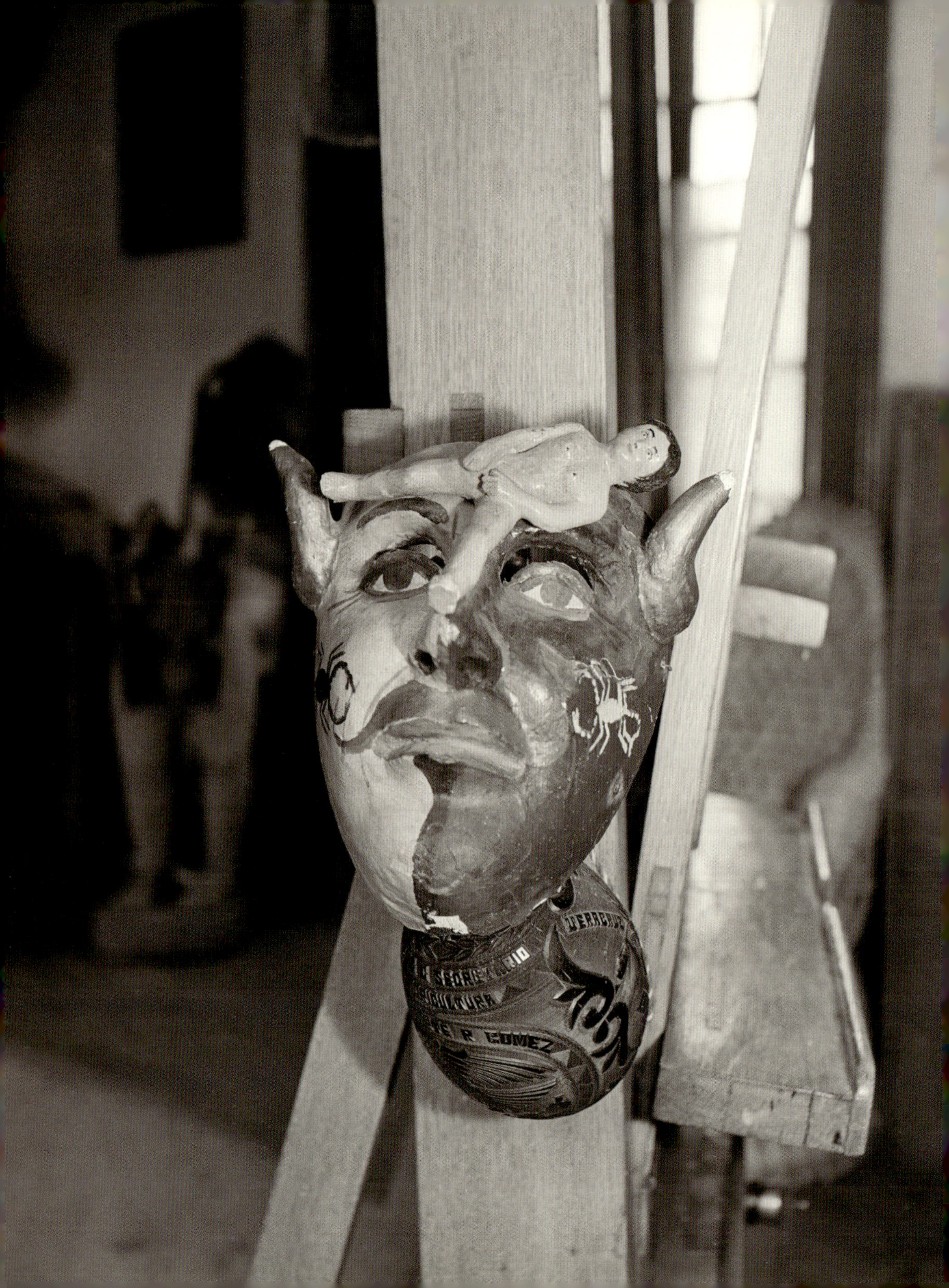

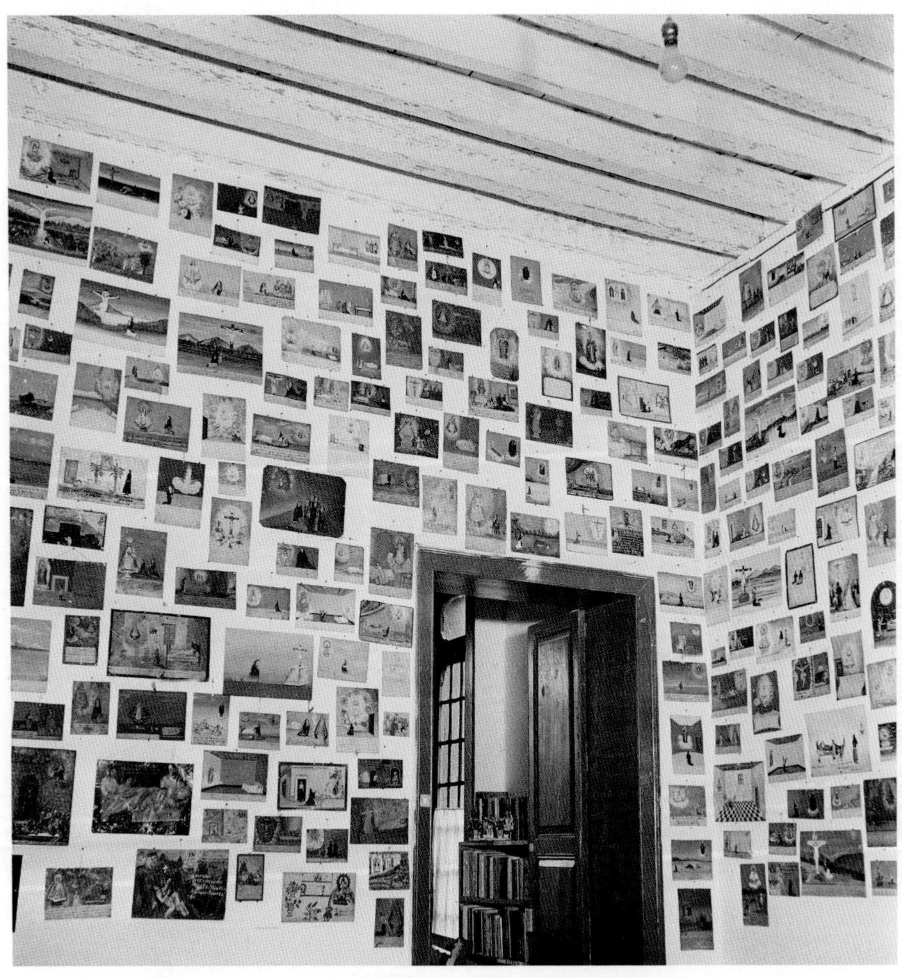

Mask, doll, and ex-votos in the house, 1951.

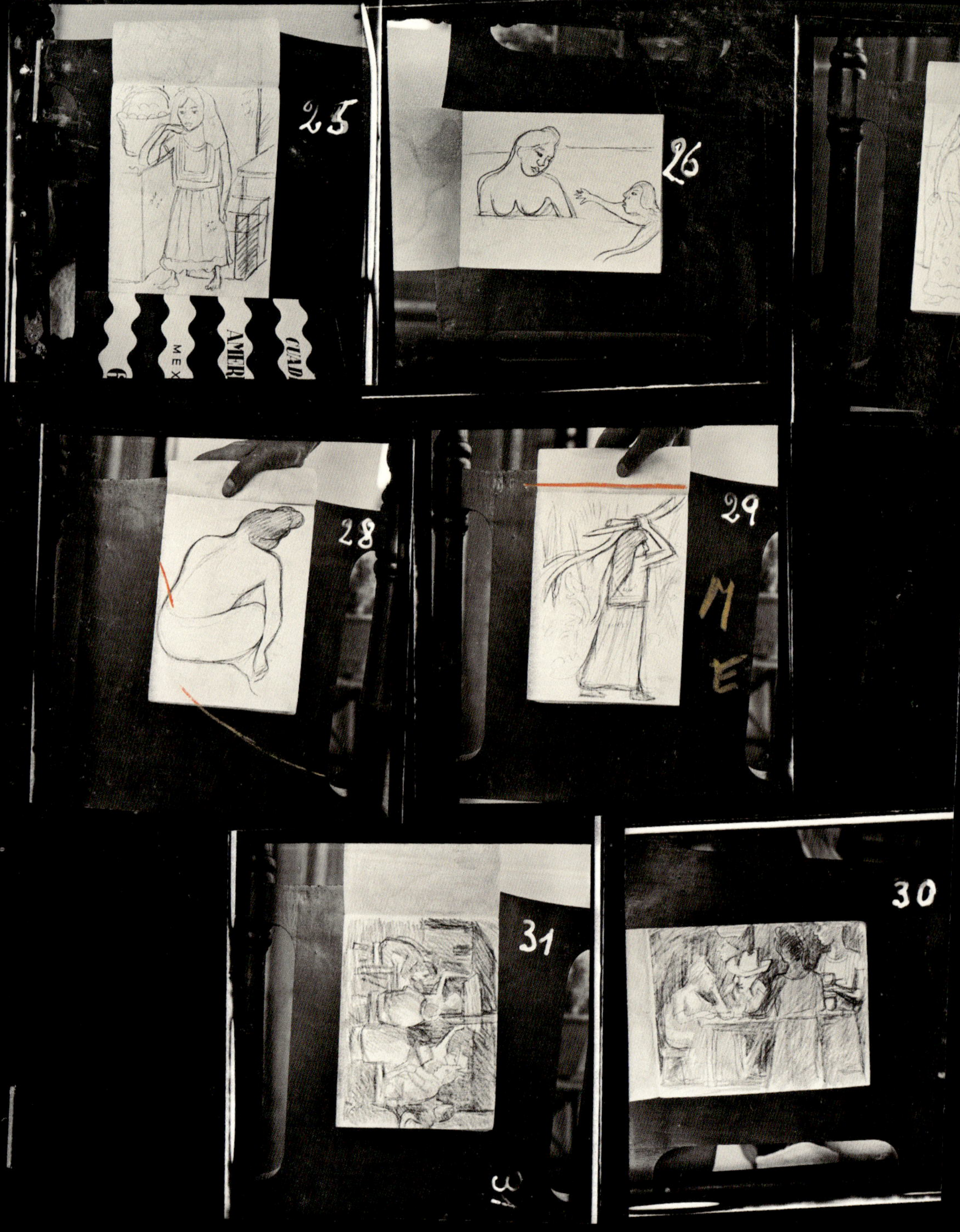
25
26
28
29
M
E
31
30

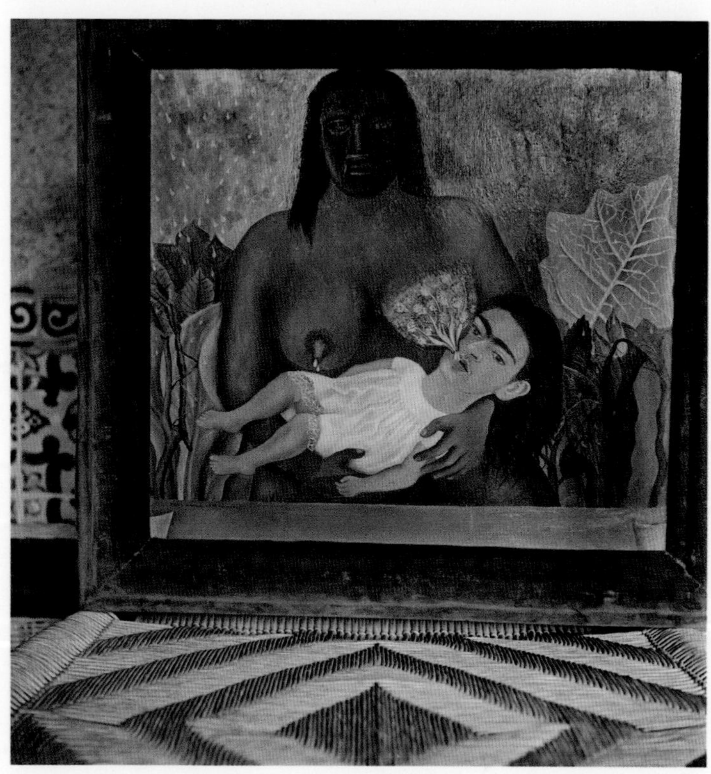

Contact print of photographs of Diego Rivera's sketchbook, made during a trip with Gisèle Freund to Tehuantepec, and *My Nurse and I* by Frida Kahlo, 1951.

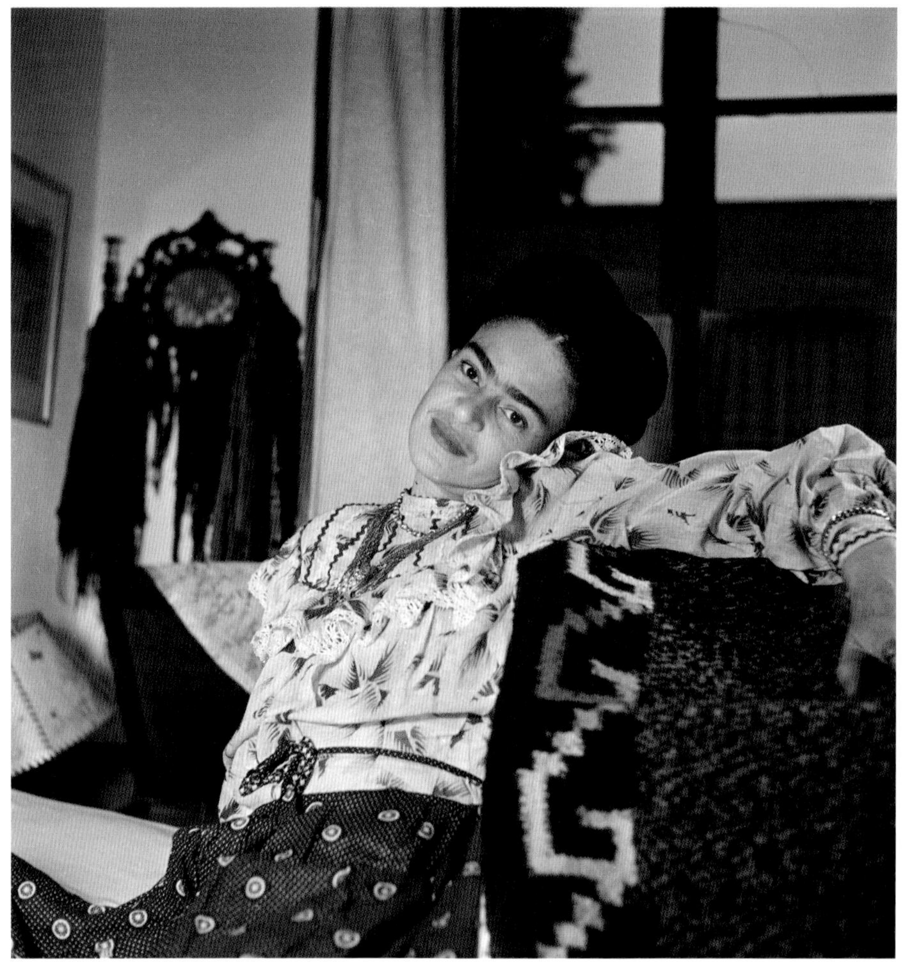

Frida Kahlo at forty-four years old,
and a view of a fireplace in the house, 1951.

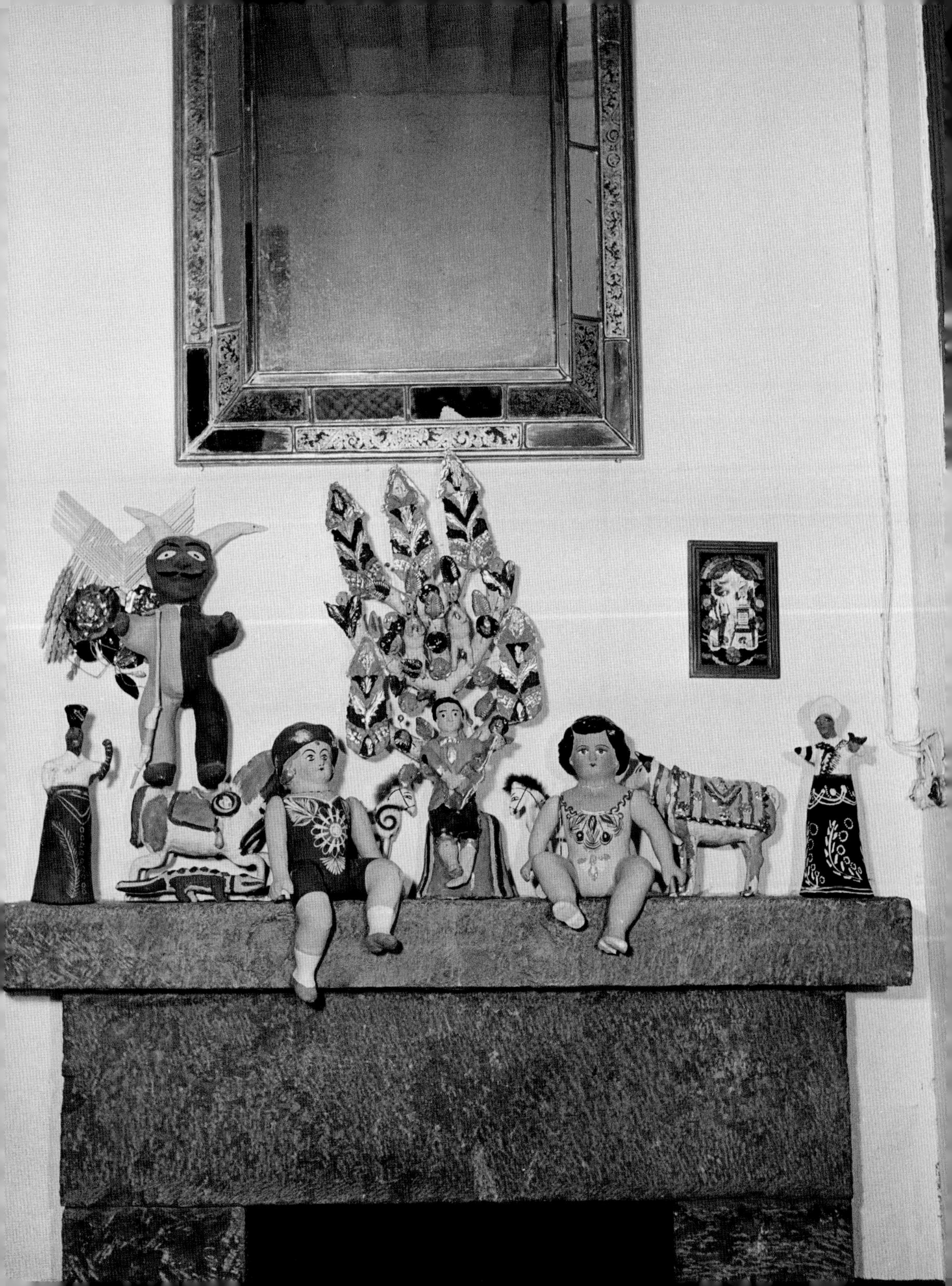

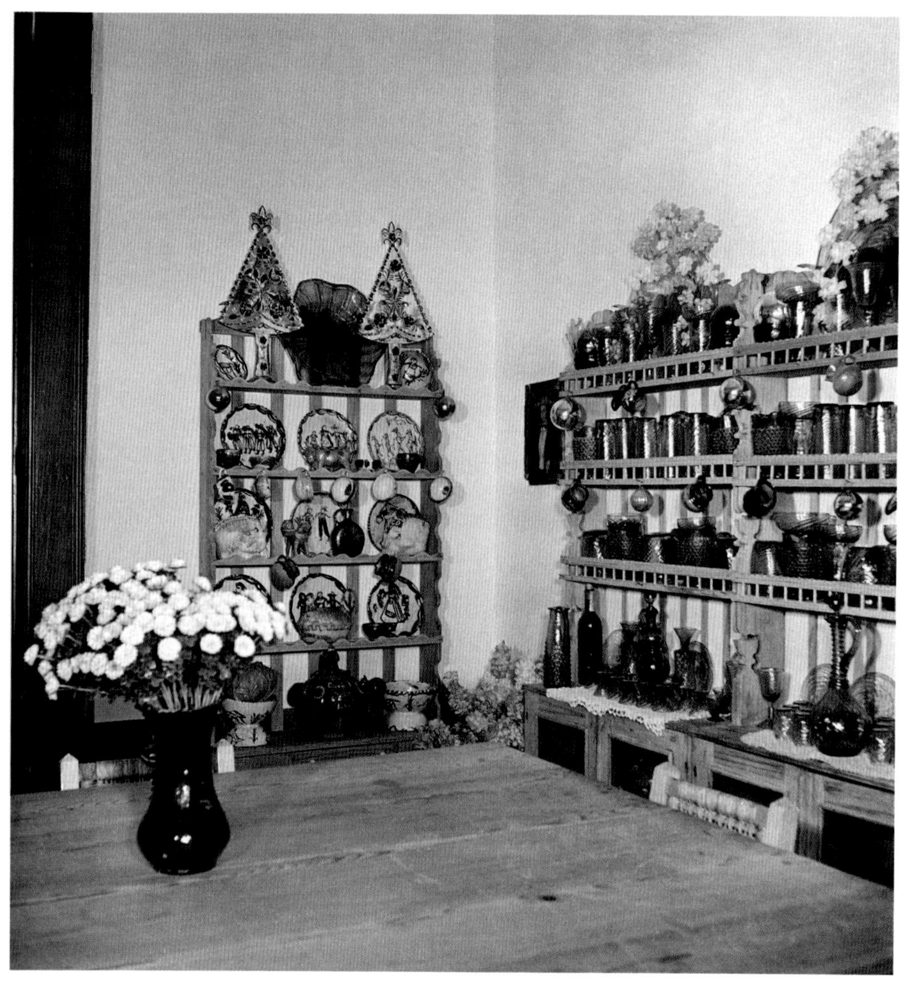

A collection of Mexican art, earthenware, and terra-cotta, and a contact print of photographs of La Casa Azul, 1951.

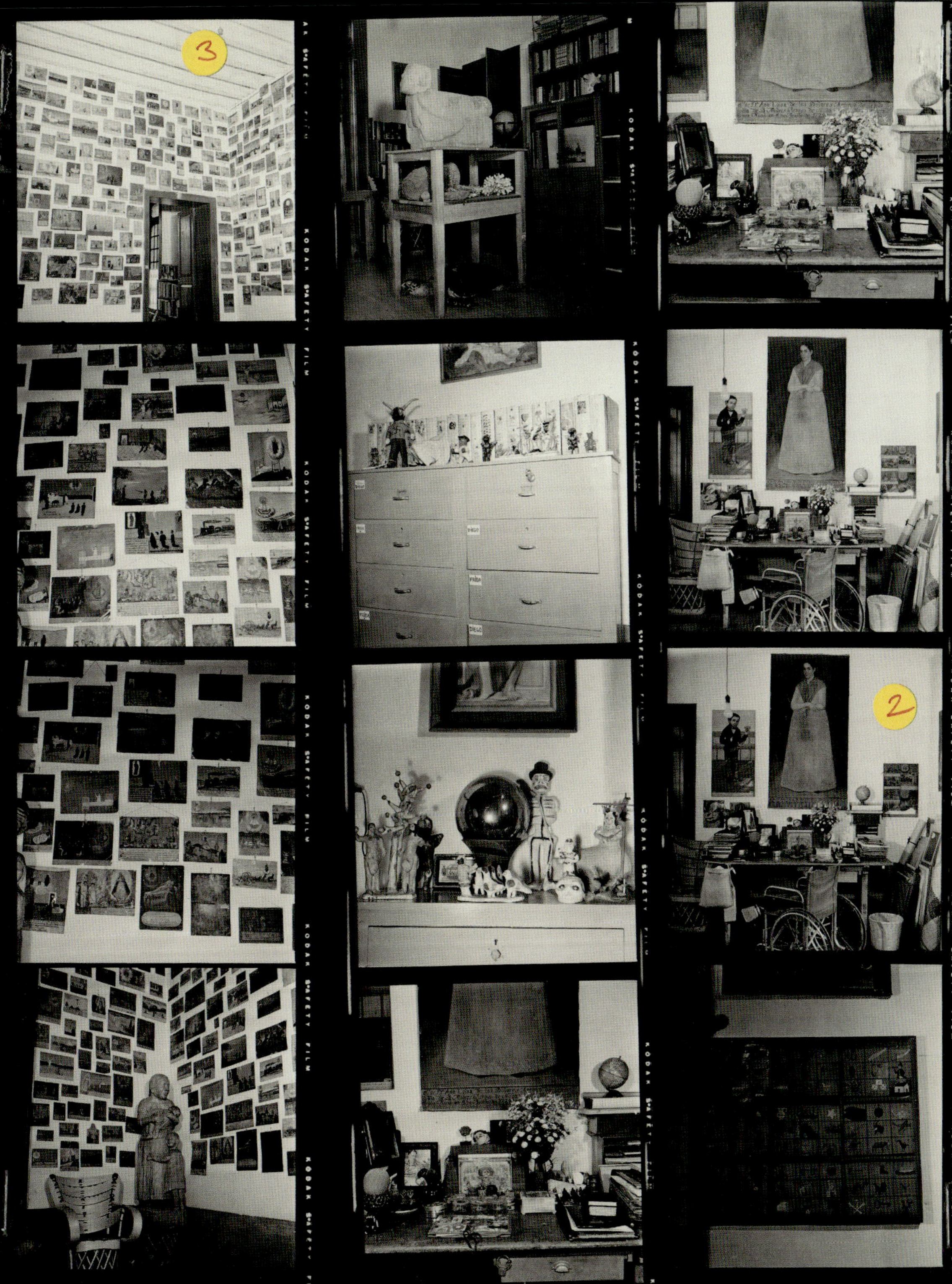

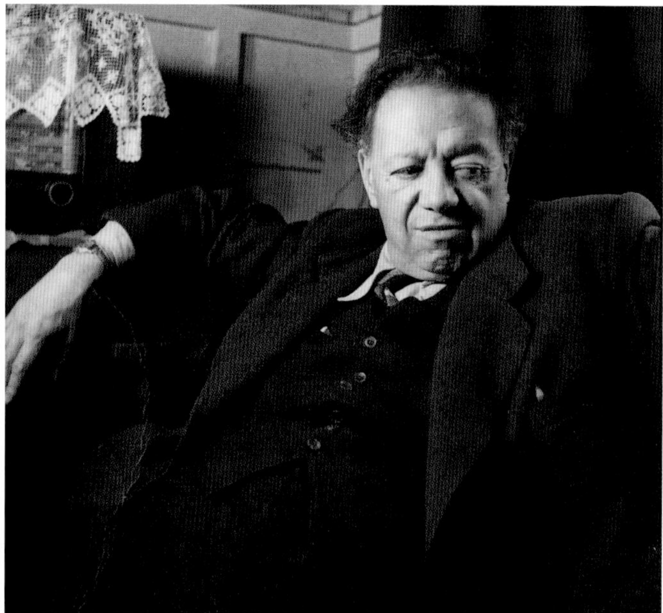

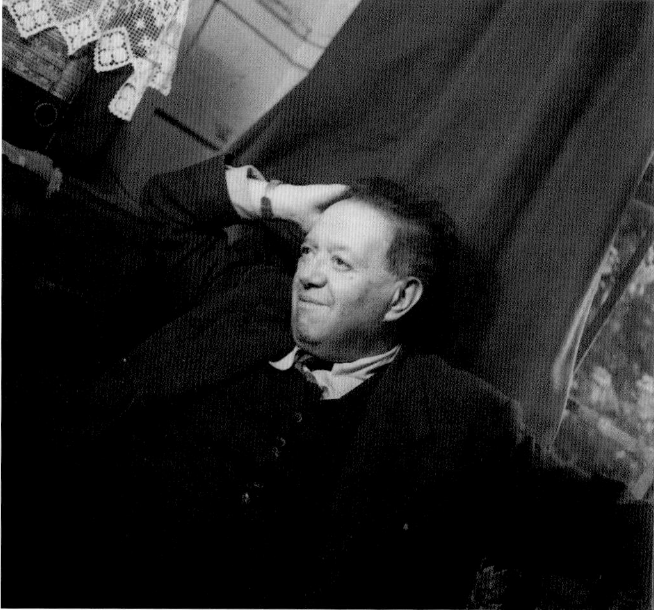

Diego Rivera photographed sitting with a child, c. 1955.

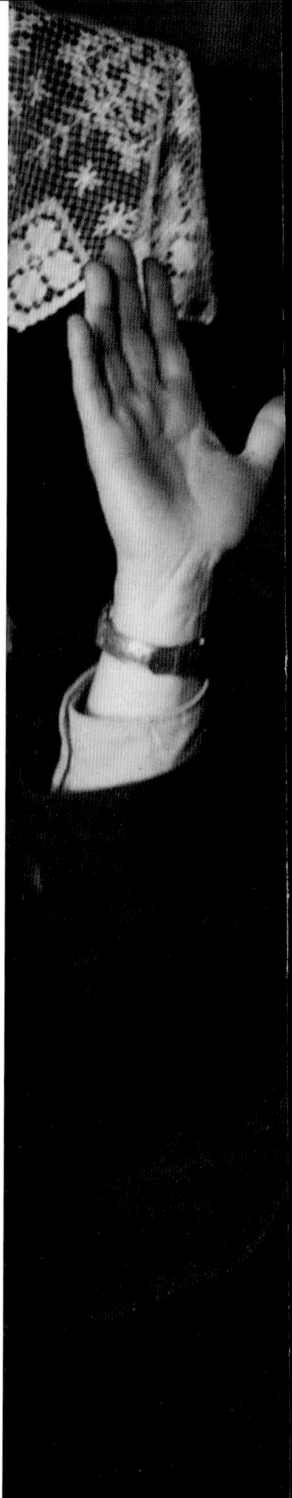

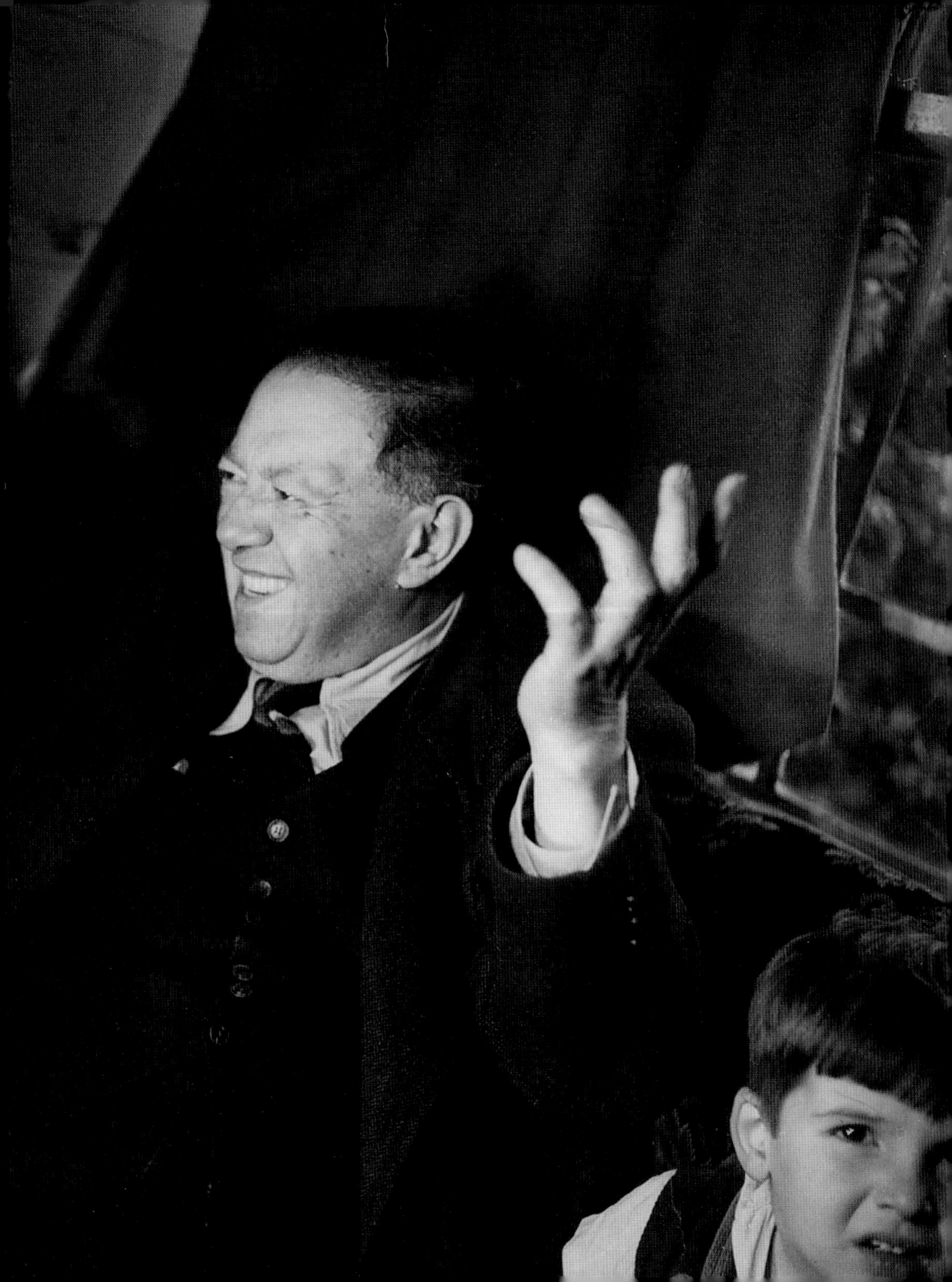

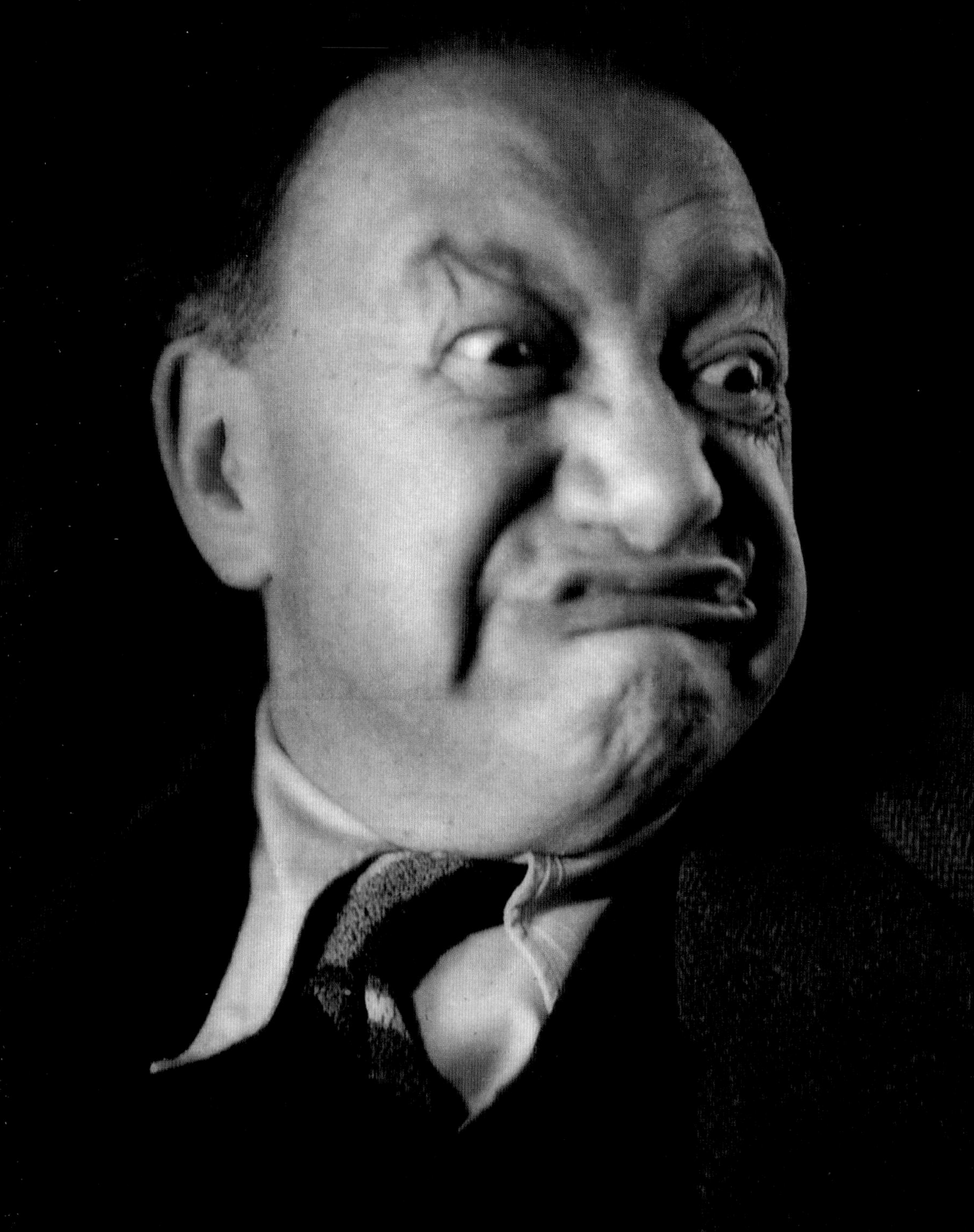

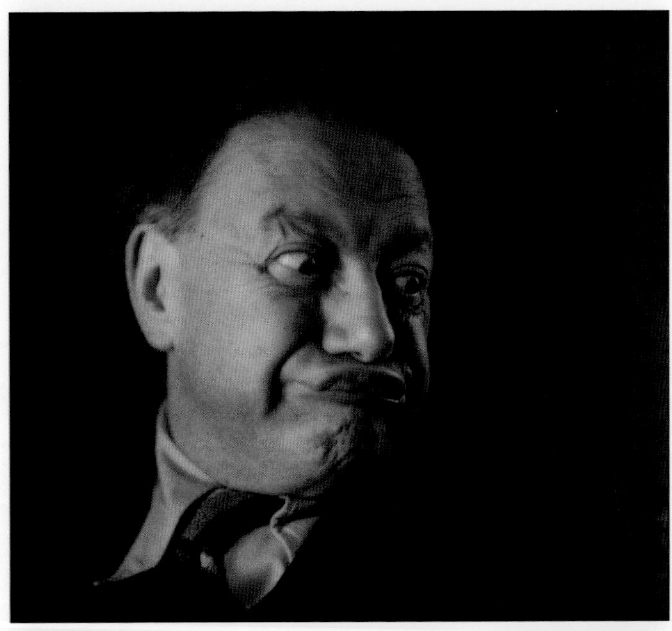

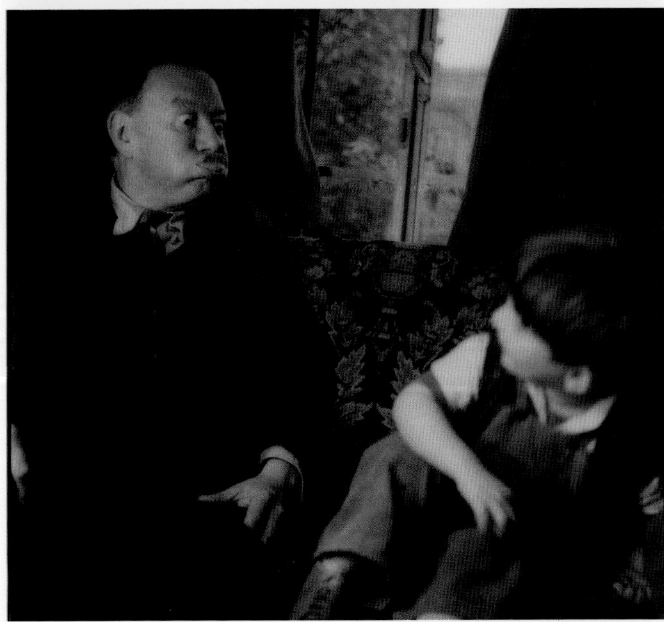

Diego Rivera making faces, c. 1955.

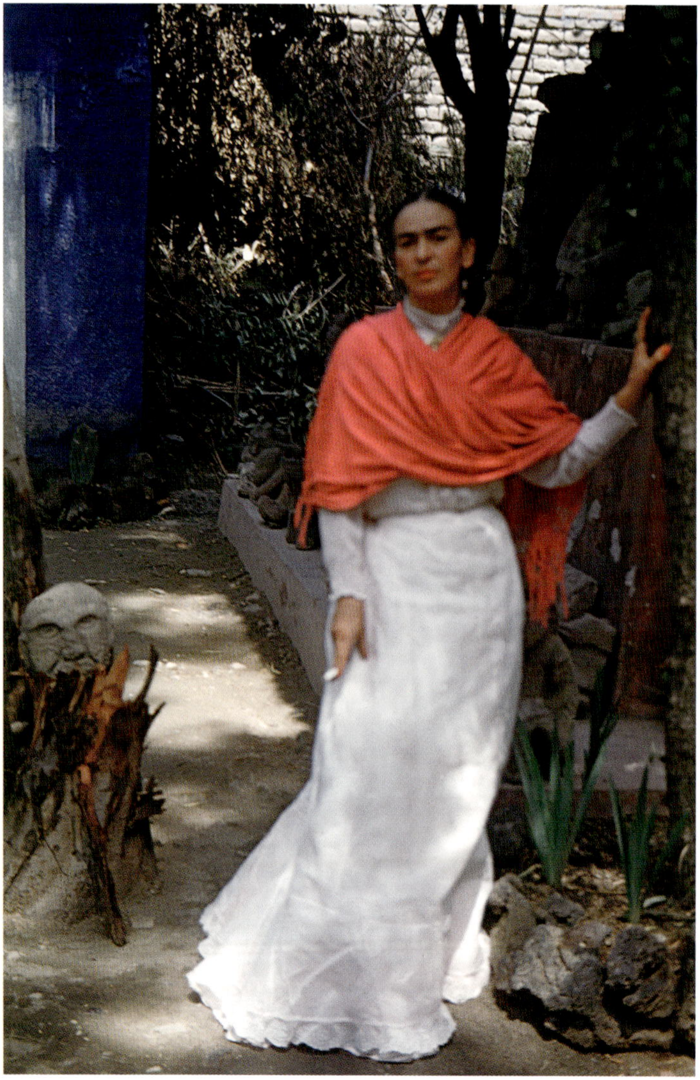

Frida Kahlo in her garden, and a Diego Rivera sketch, 1951. Following double-page spread: Diego Rivera in one of the house's storage spaces containing part of his antiquities collection, 1951.

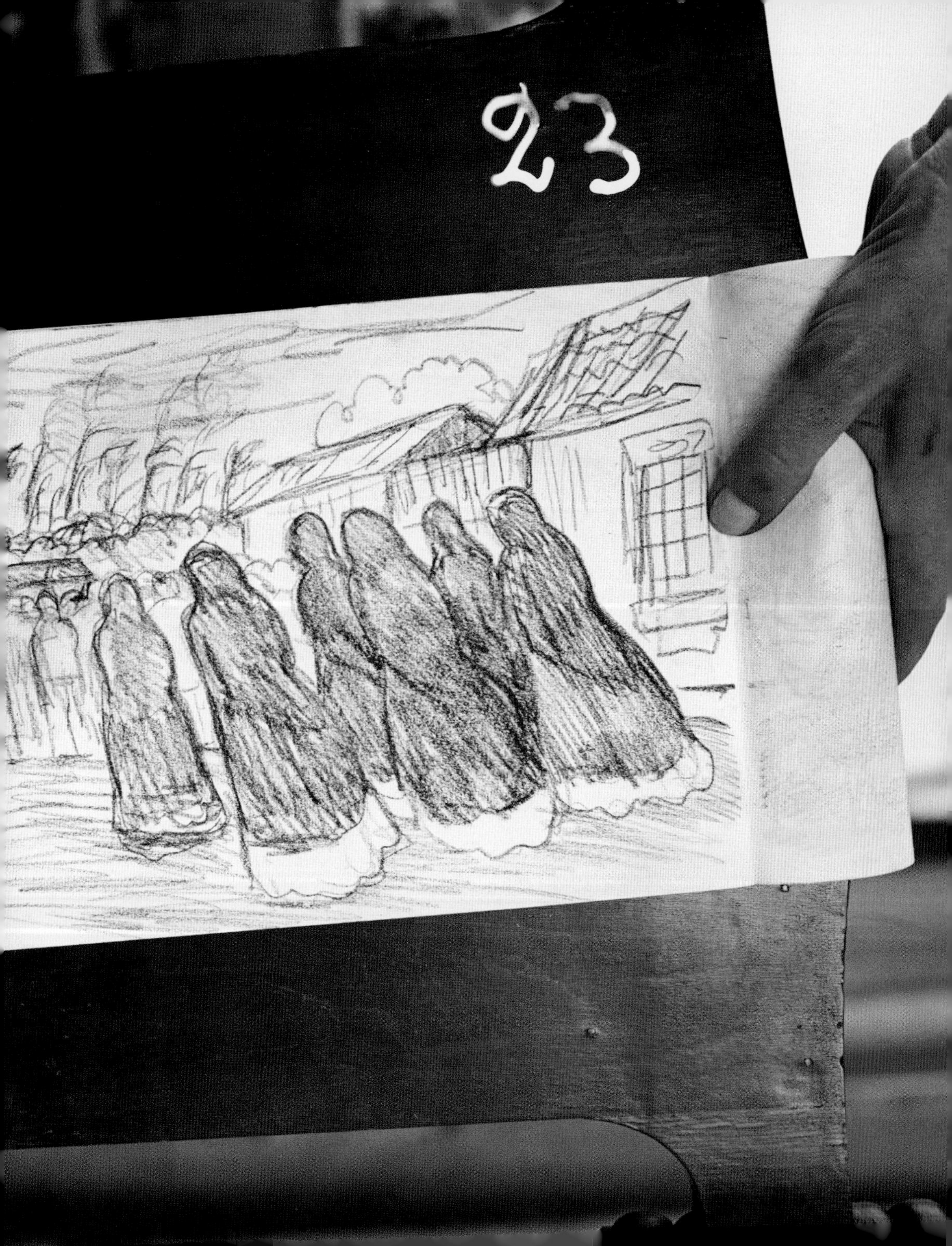
23

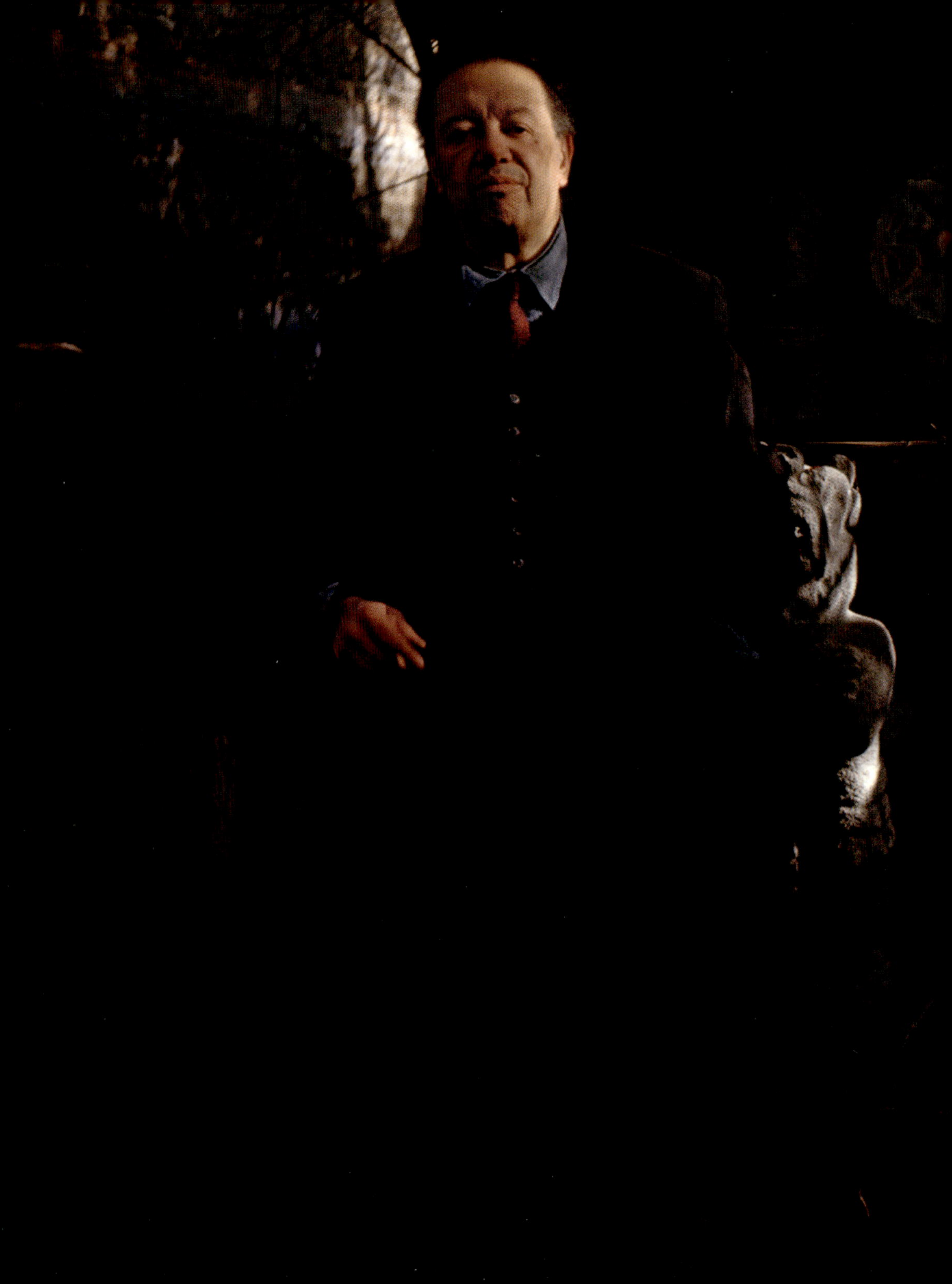

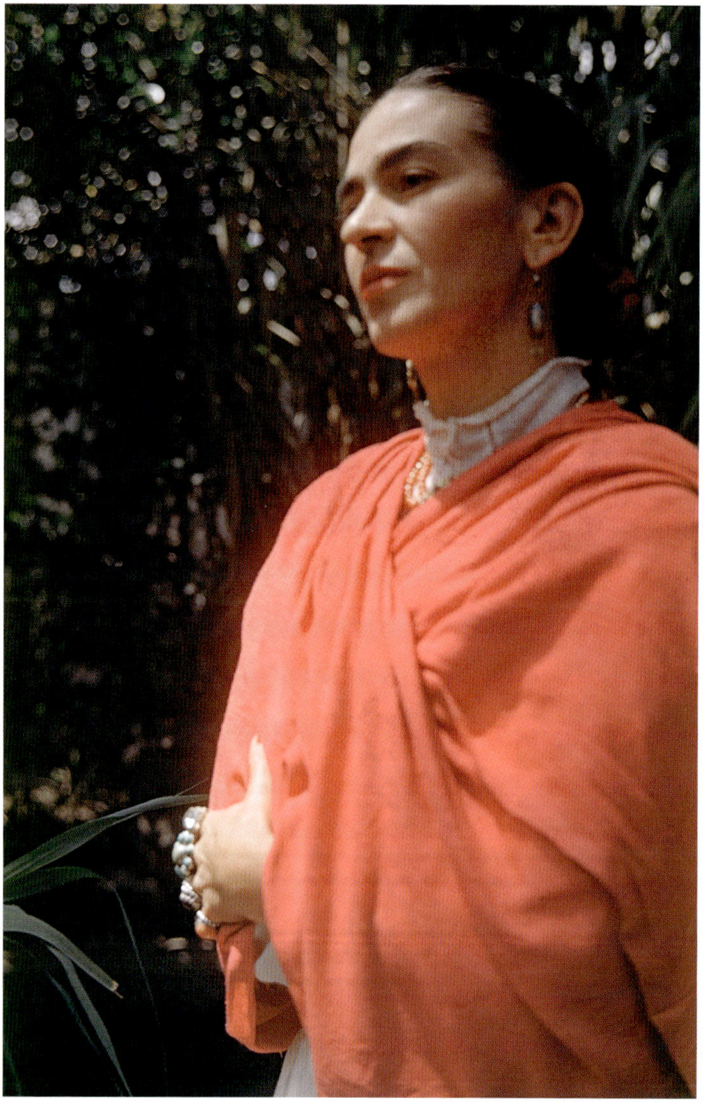

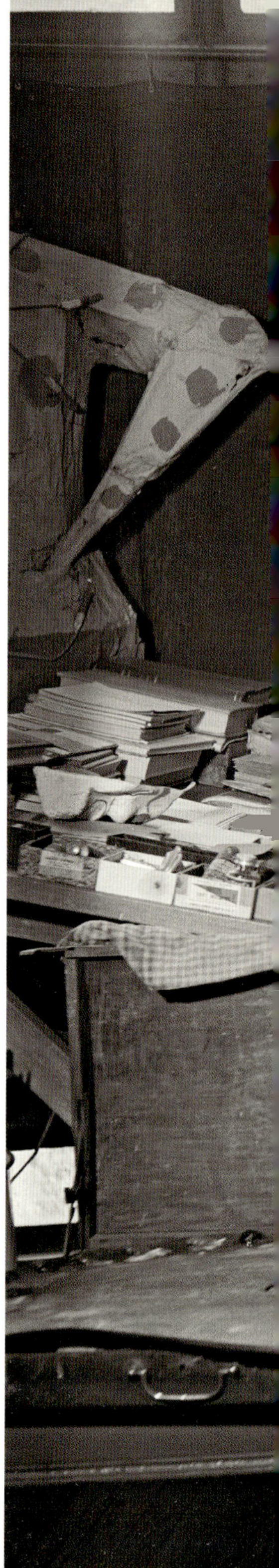

Frida Kahlo in the garden, and Diego Rivera in his studio, 1951. Following double-page spread: Frida Kahlo in her studio painting *Portrait of My Father*, 1951.

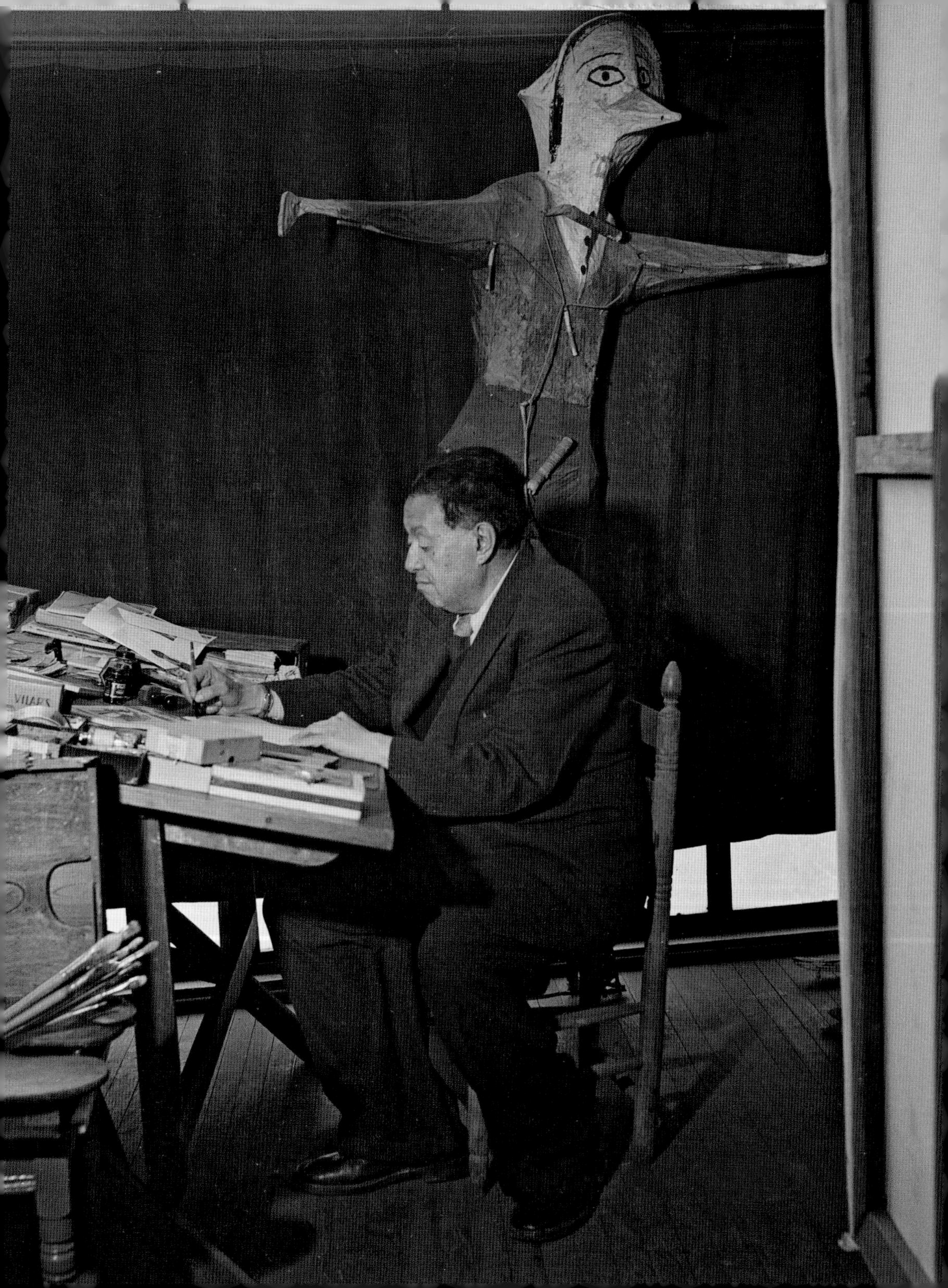

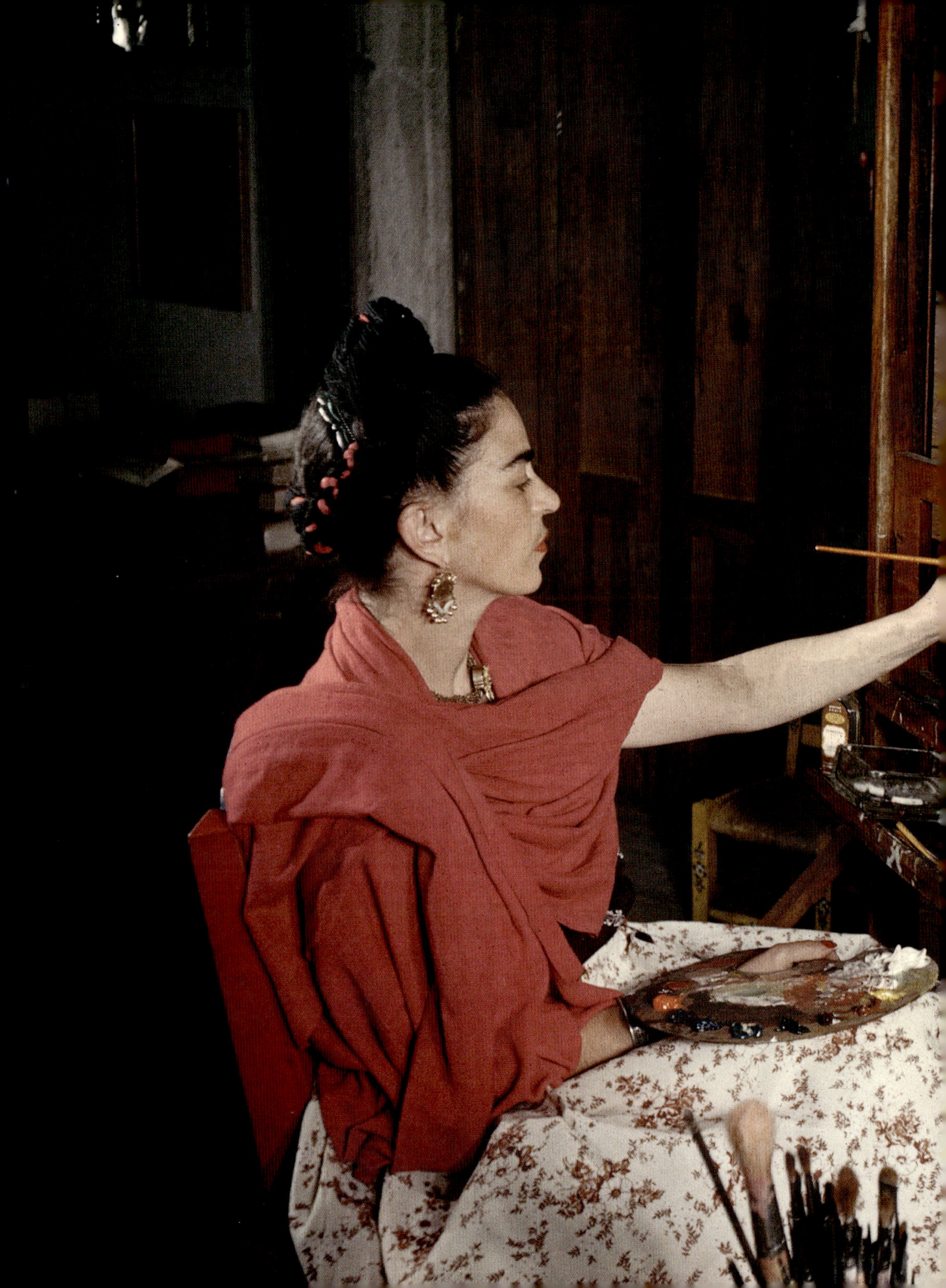

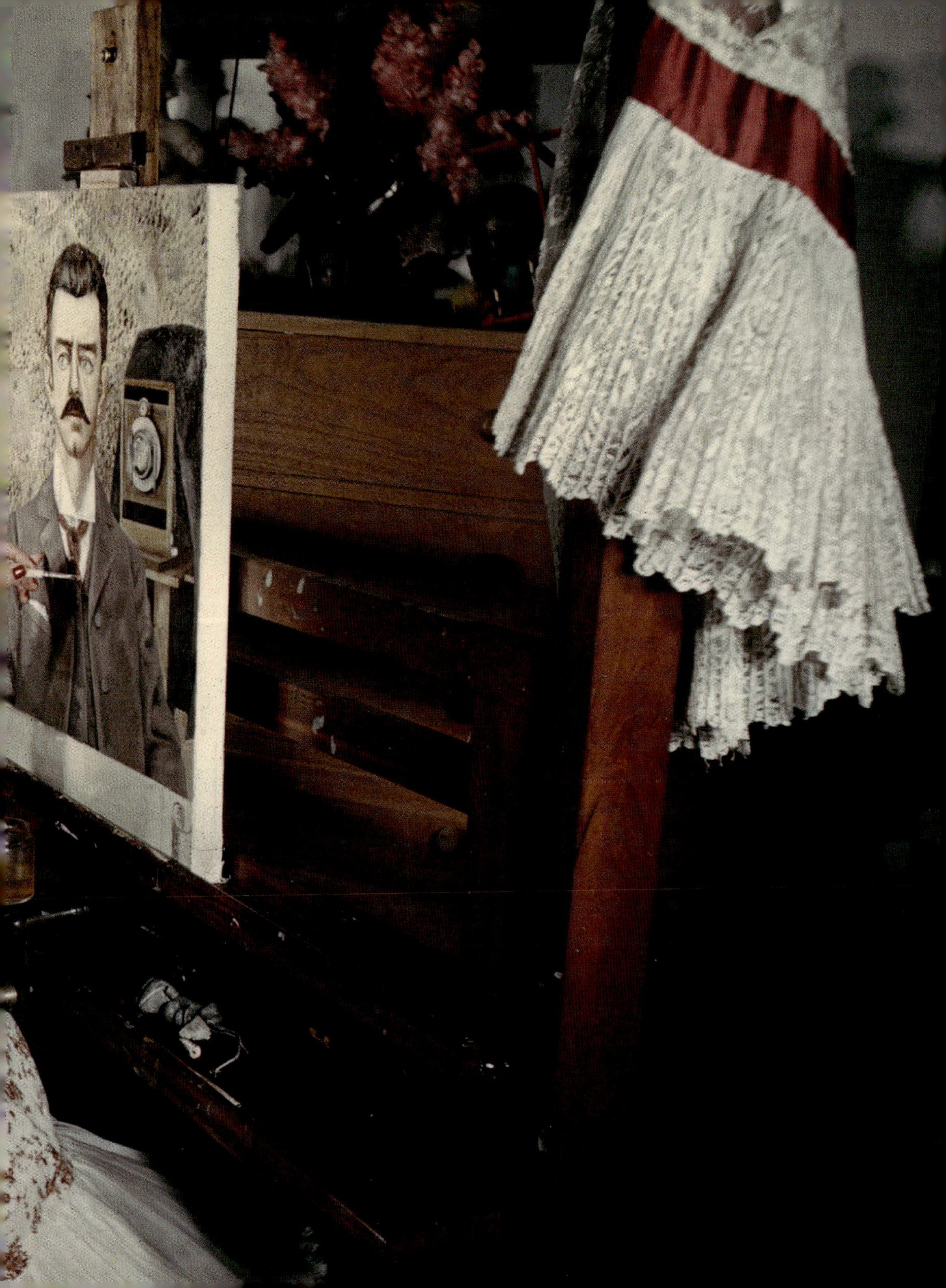

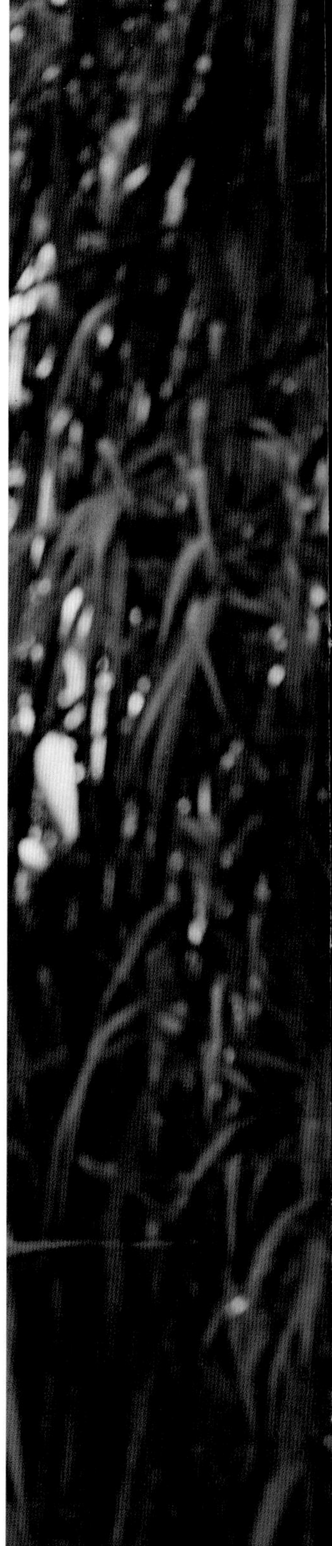

Frida Kahlo in her garden, 1951.

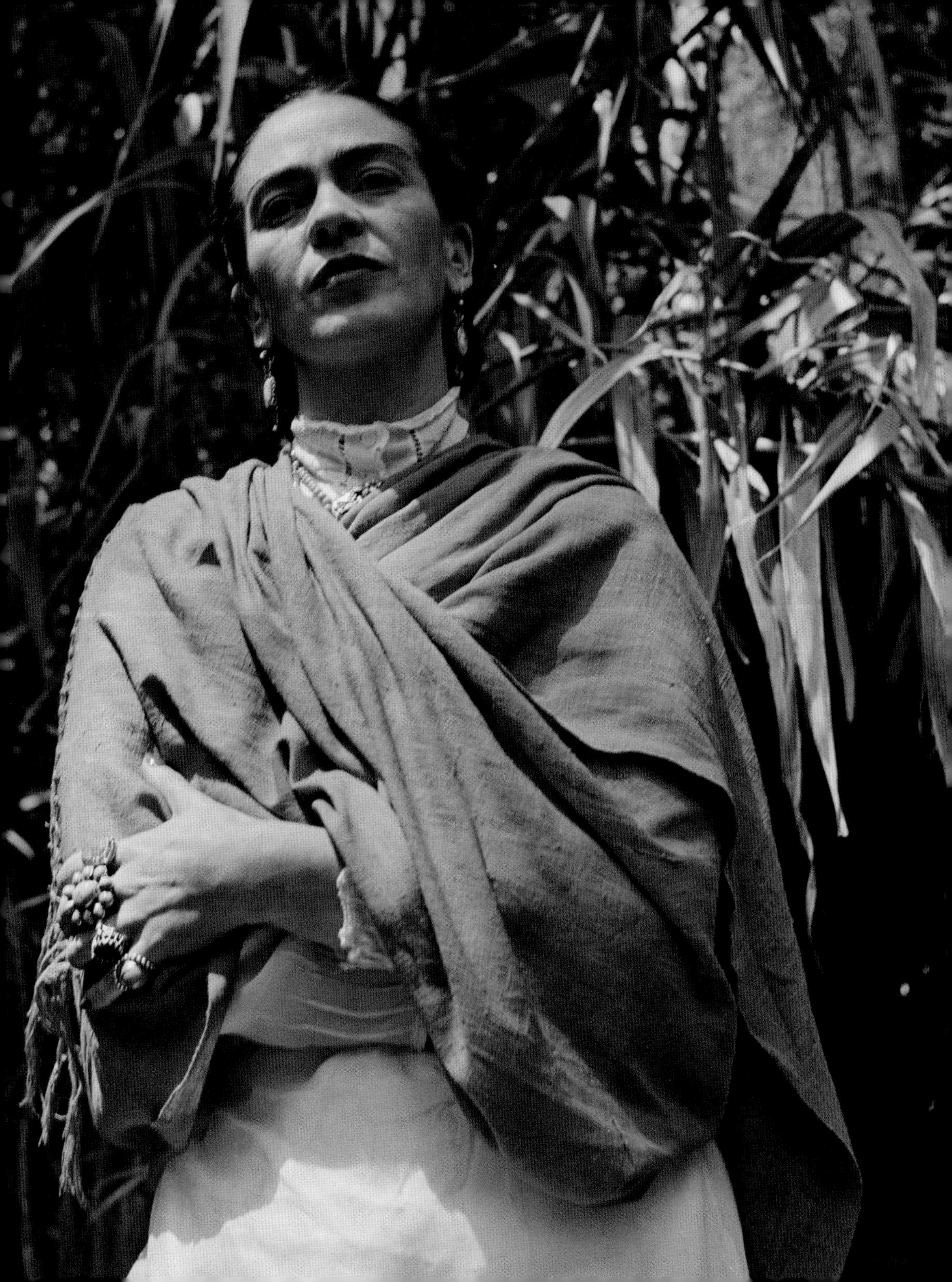

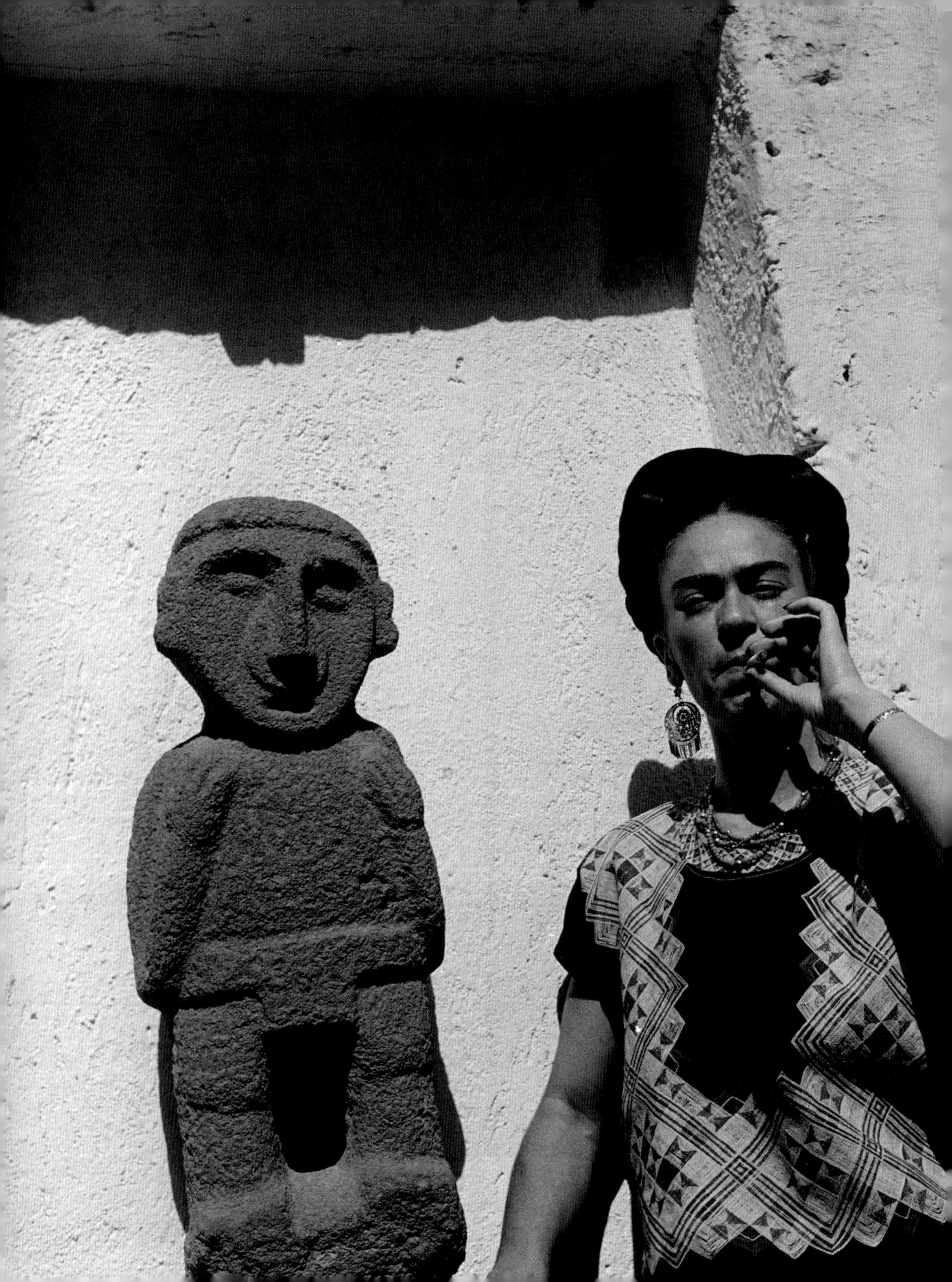

Frida Kahlo in her garden, 1951.

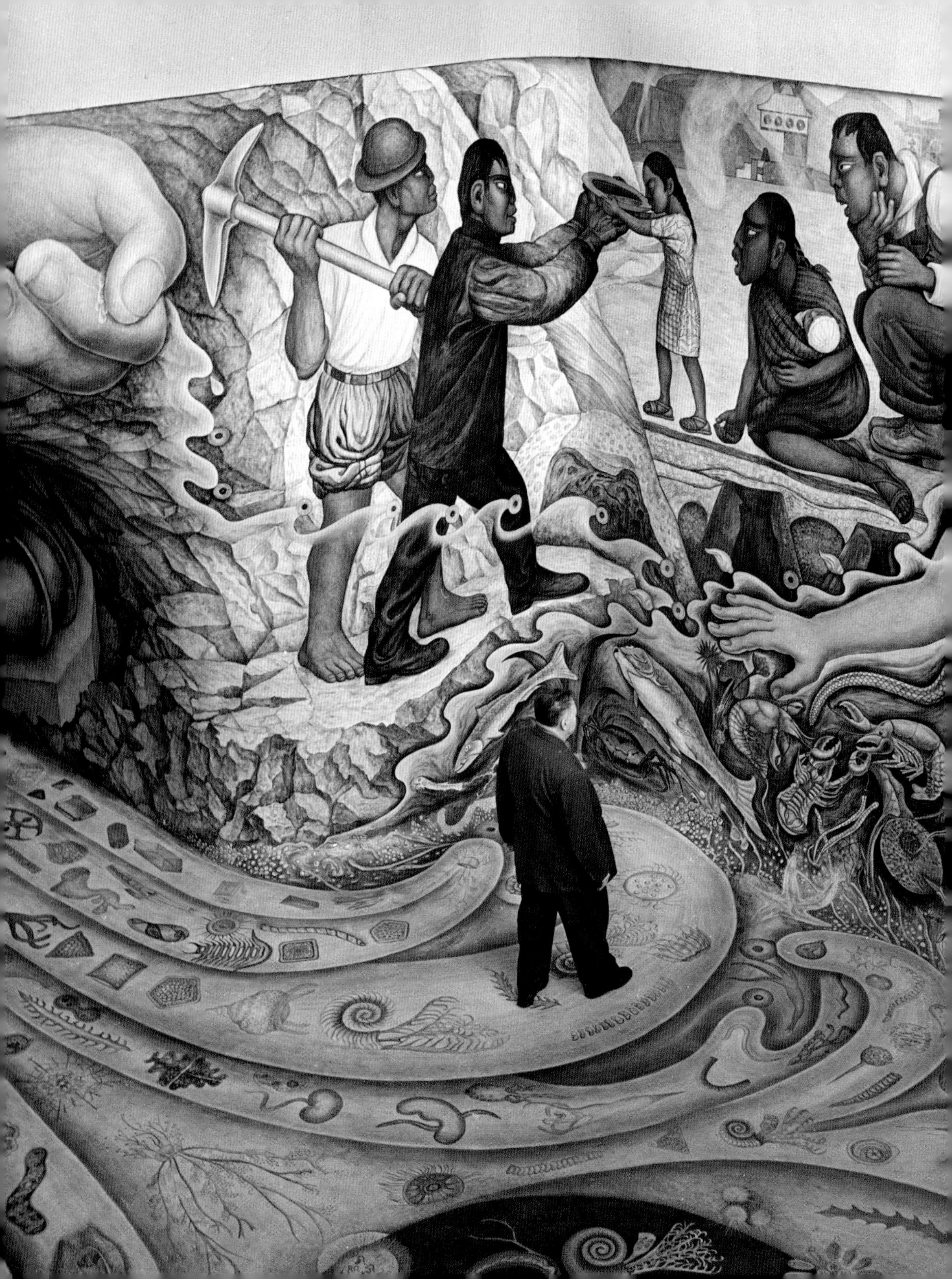

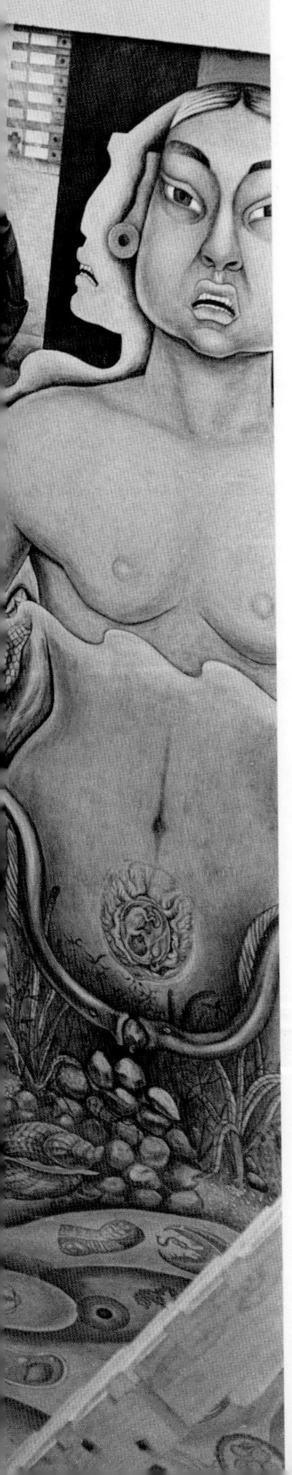

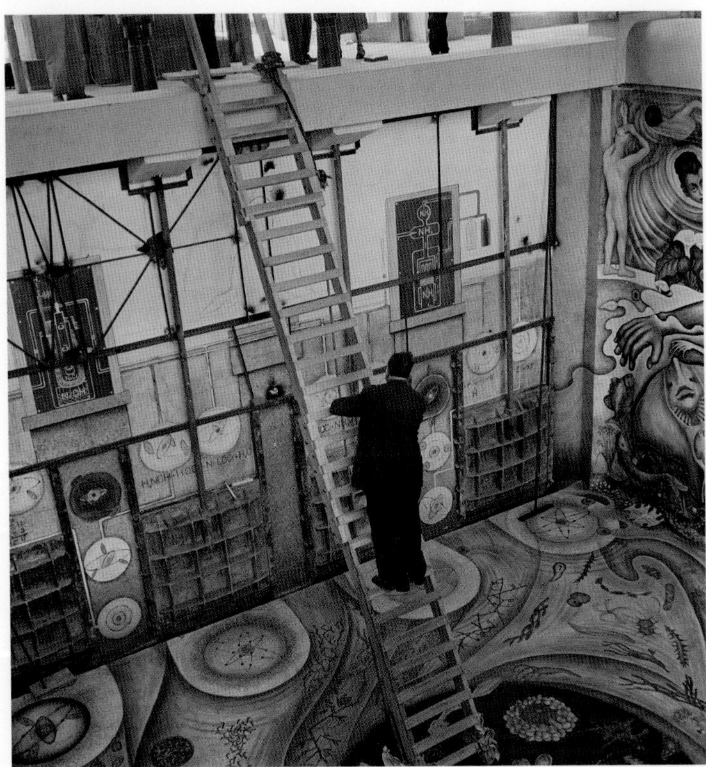

Diego Rivera in front of and at work on his fresco *Water, Origin of Life,* Mexico City, 1951. "One of the most curious works that Rivera has recently finished is an underwater painting. The reservoir was built in the middle of Chapultepec Park in Mexico City; the waters of the Lerma River flow through a tunnel approximately twelve miles long, passing under the mountains that separate the valleys of Mexico and Toluca, and is then channeled into the city to quench its inhabitants' thirst. The mural paintings illustrate the history of mankind" (Gisèle Freund caption found on the back of a press print).

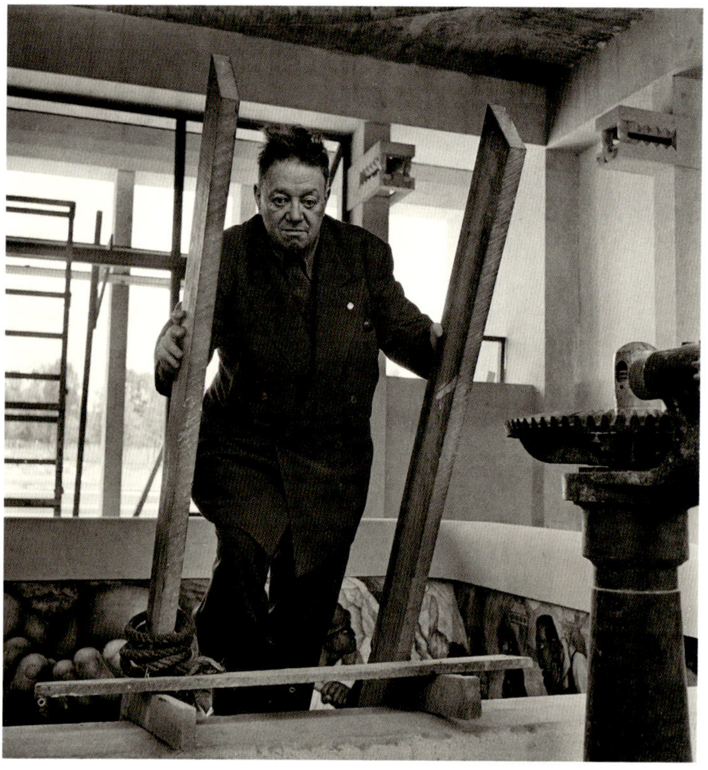

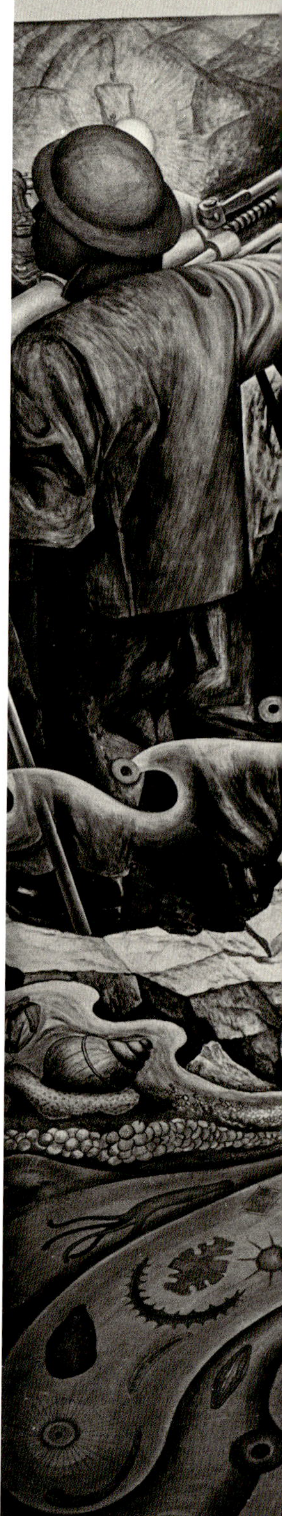

Diego Rivera at work on his fresco *Water, Origin of Life,* Mexico City, 1951.
Following double-page spread: Diego Rivera fresco in the Palace of Cortés, Cuernavaca, Mexico, 1951.

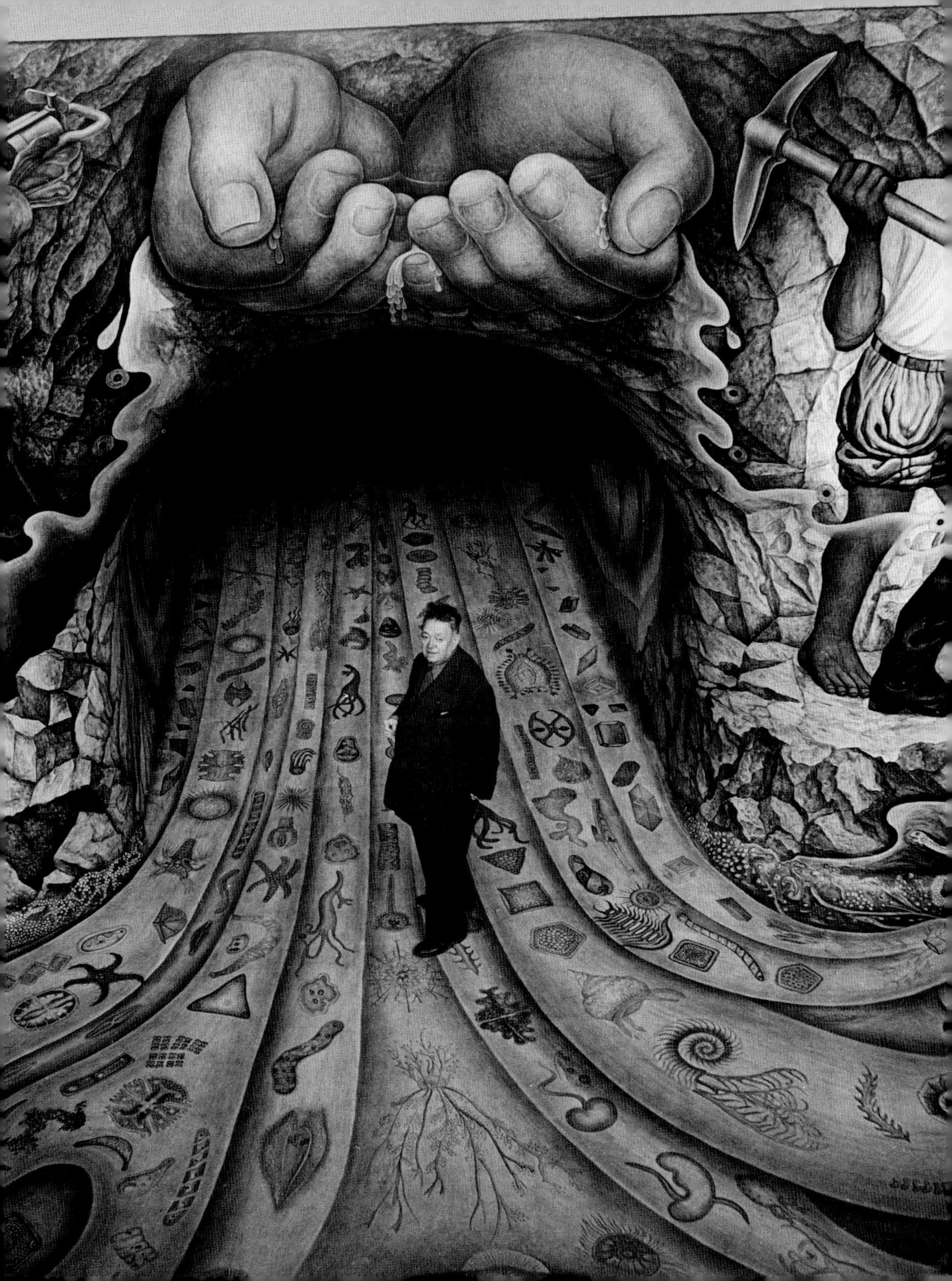

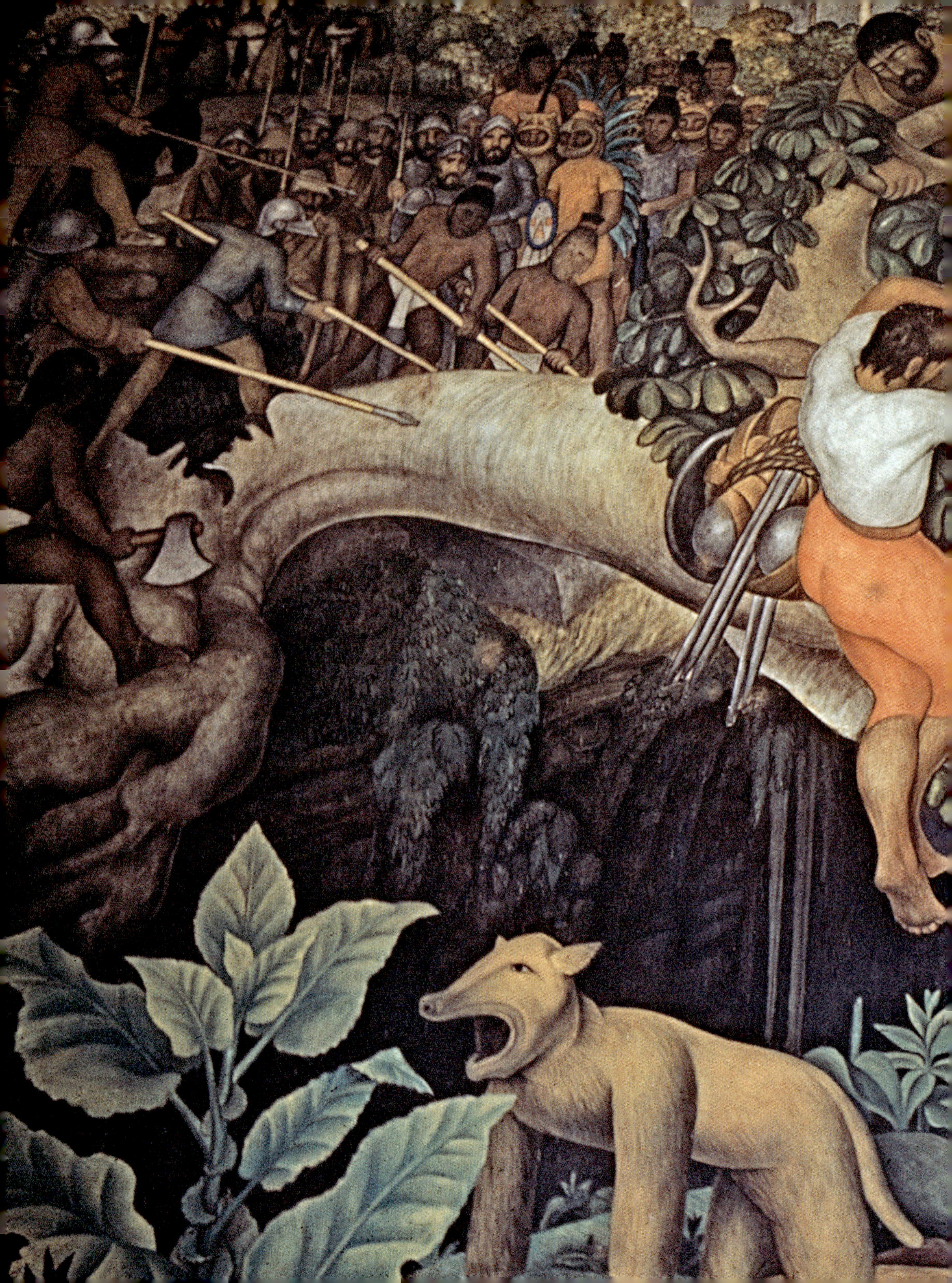

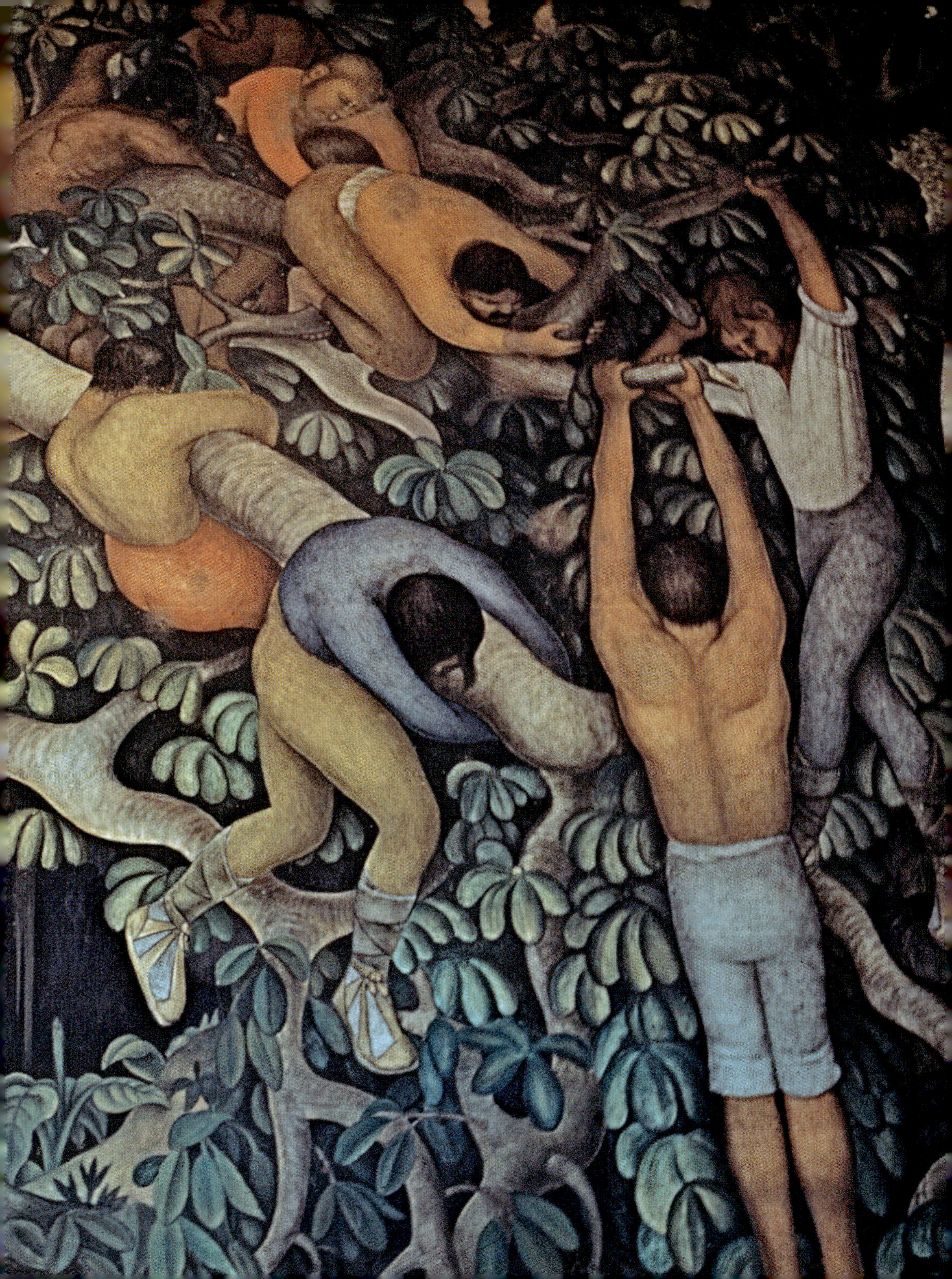

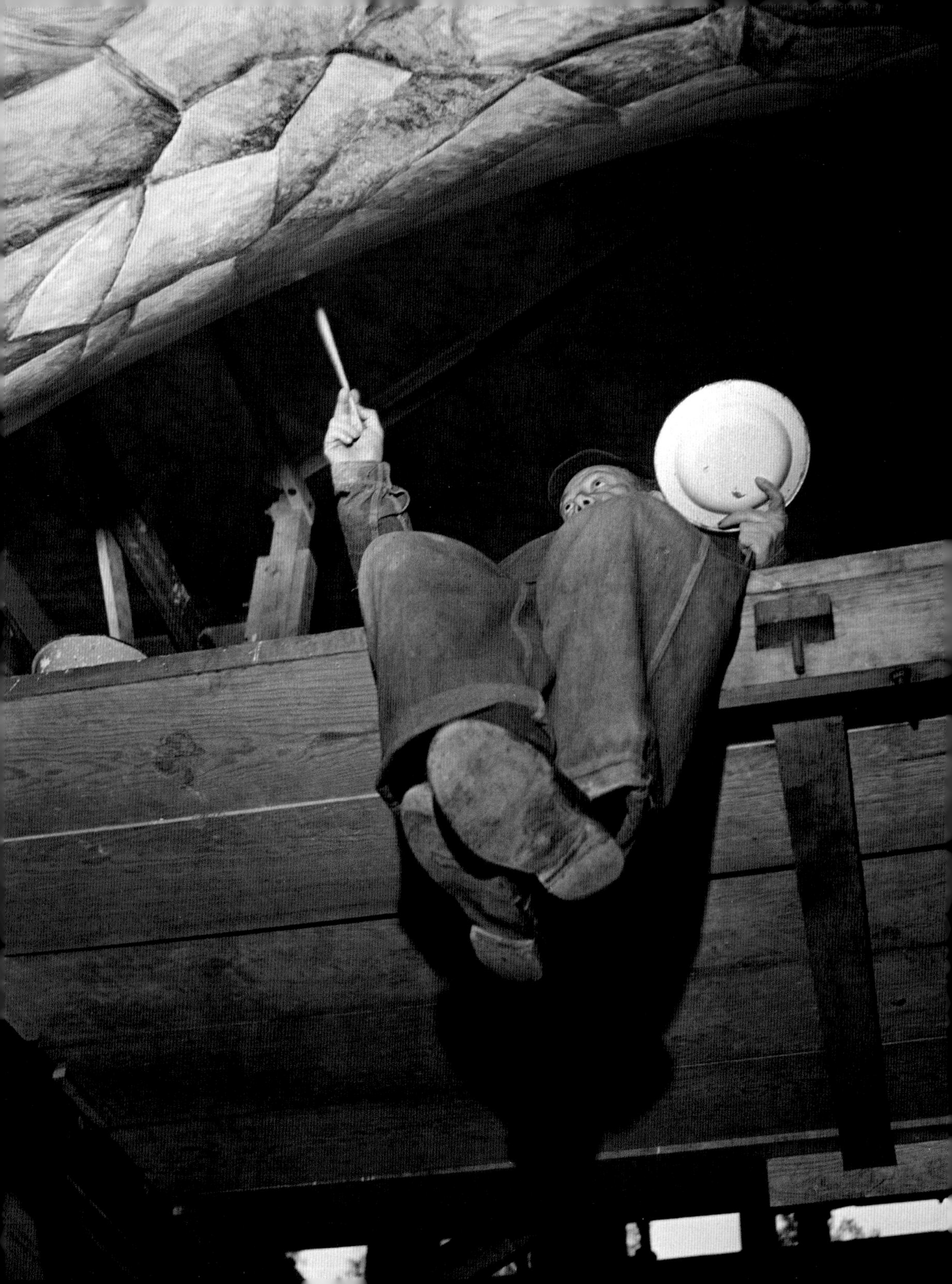

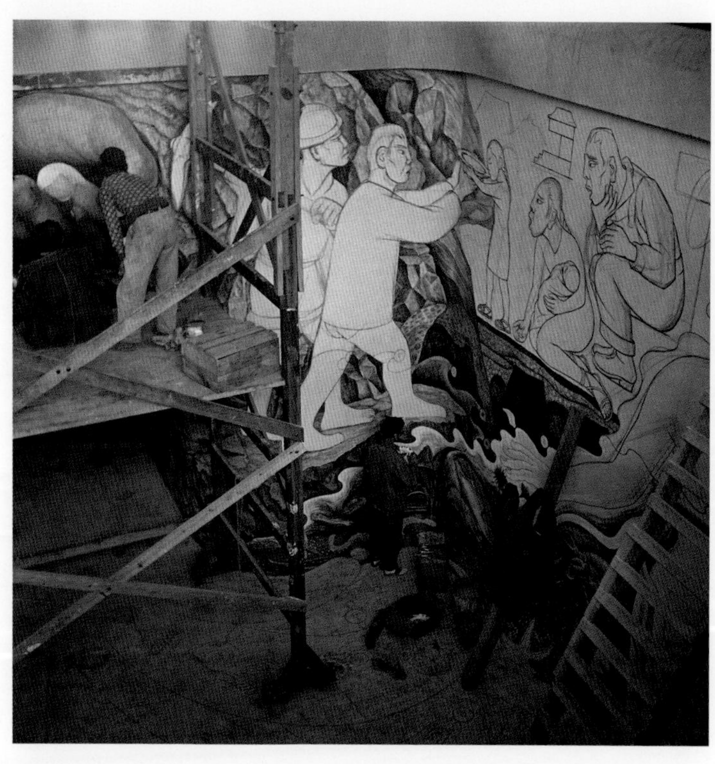

Diego Rivera at work on his fresco *Water, Origin of Life,* 1951.

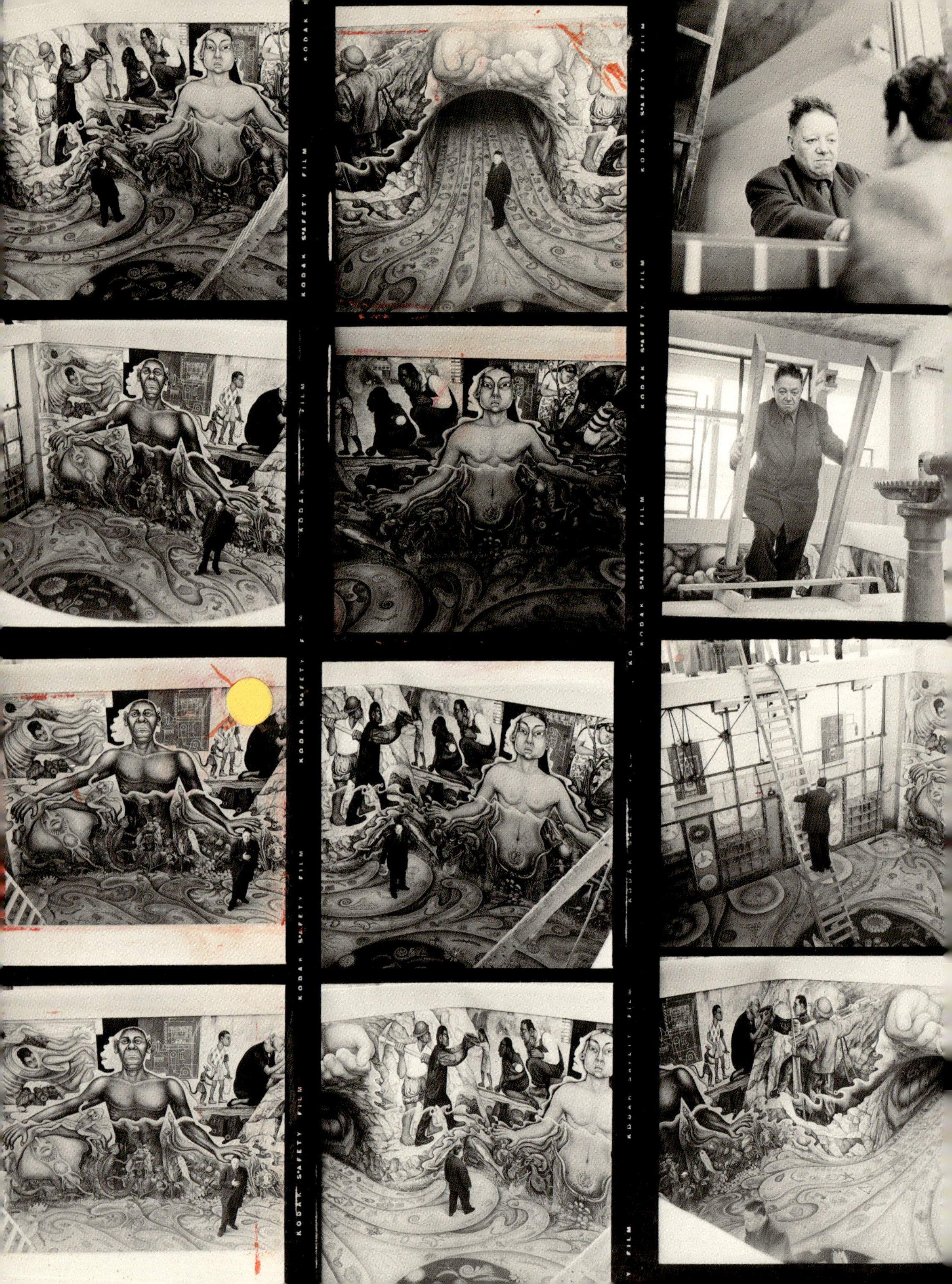
KODAK SAFETY FILM

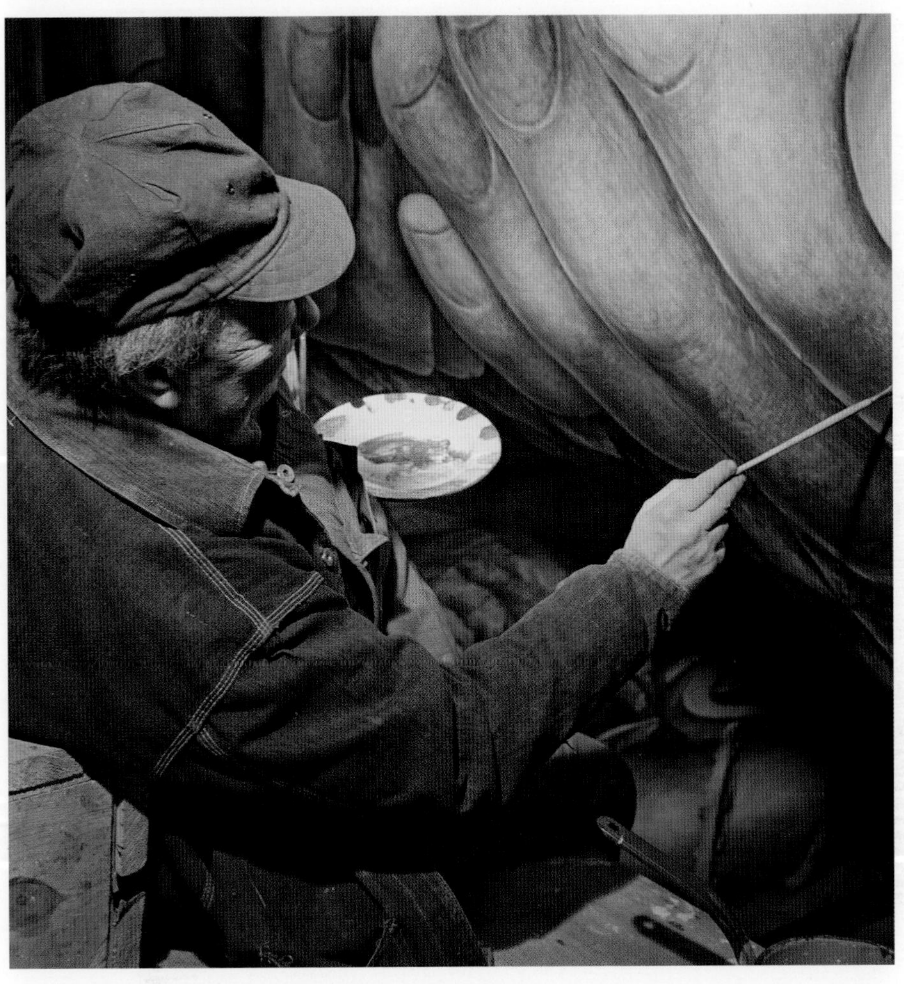

Contact print of photographs of Diego Rivera and his fresco *Water, Origin of Life* (a view in color is on the following double-page spread), and Rivera at work on it, 1951.

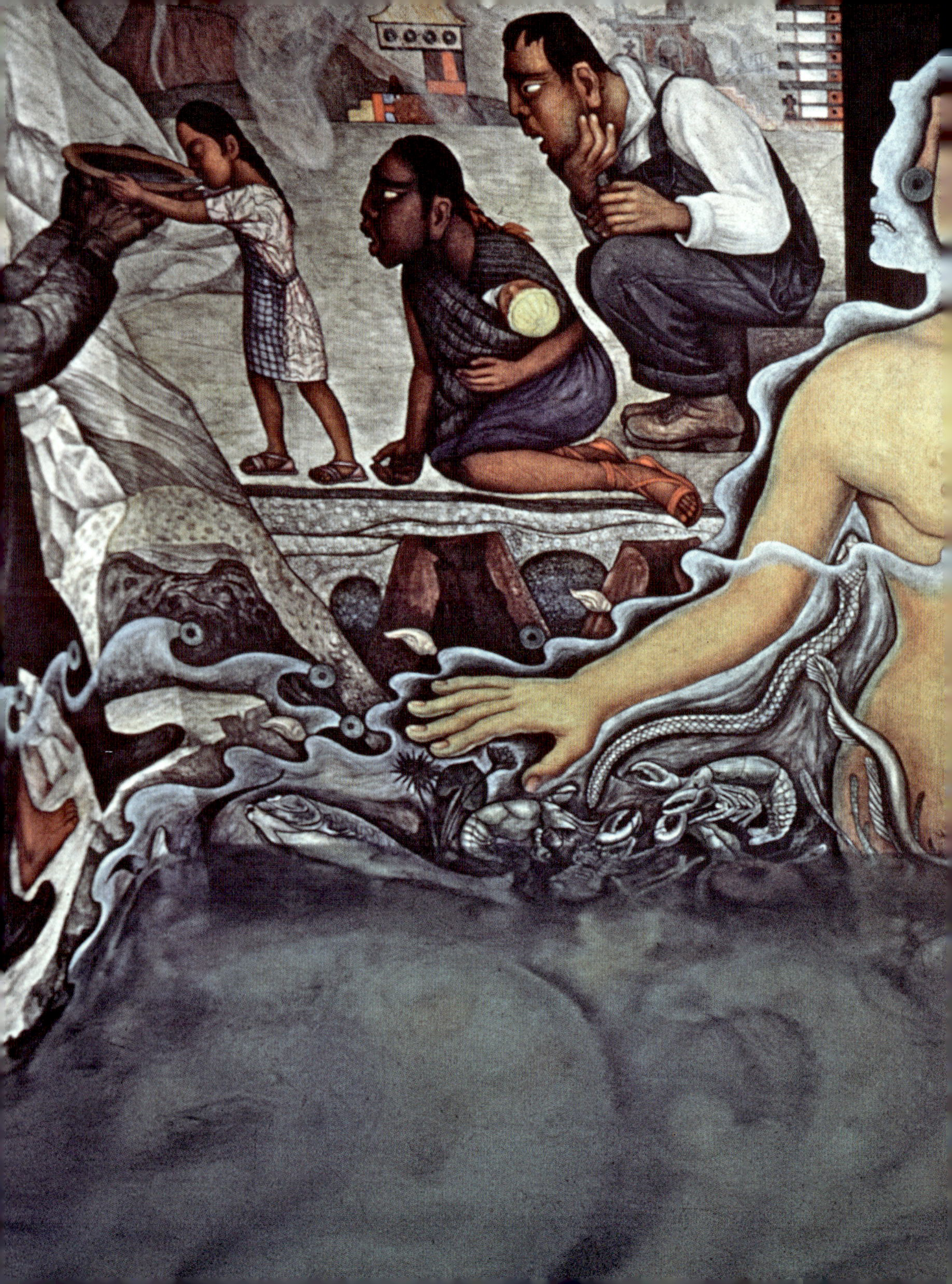

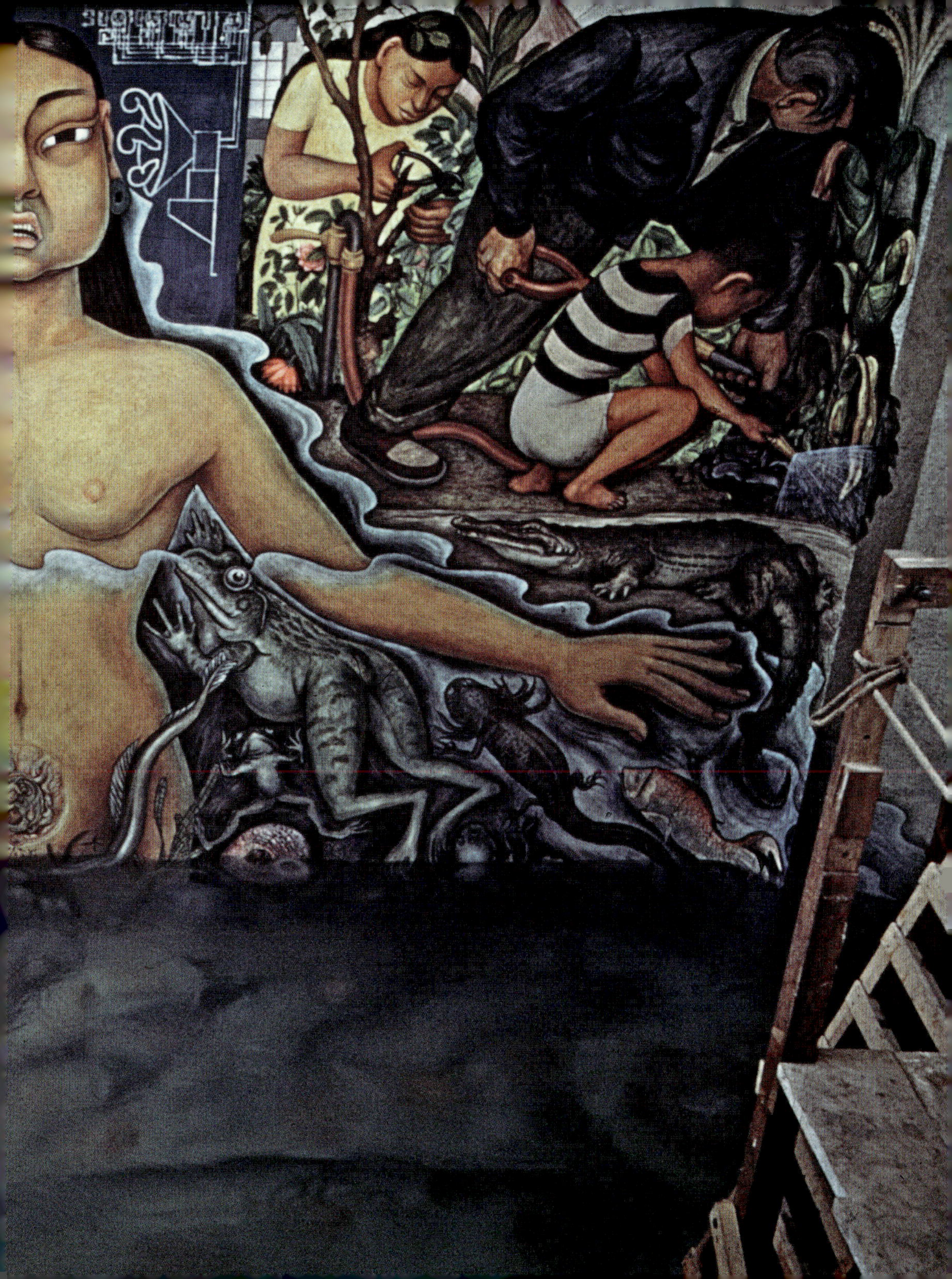

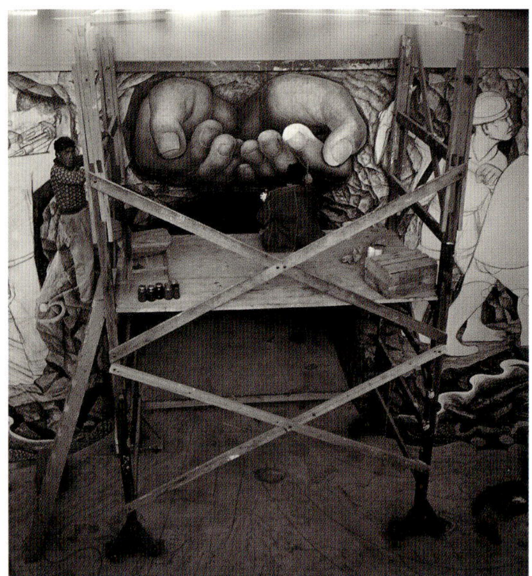

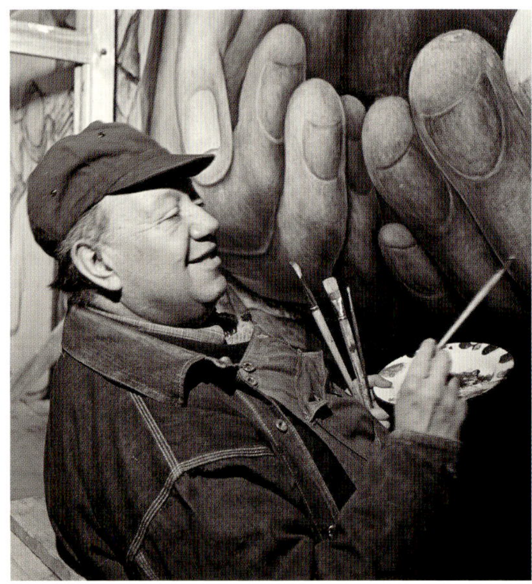

Diego at work on his fresco *Water, Origin of Life*, 1951.

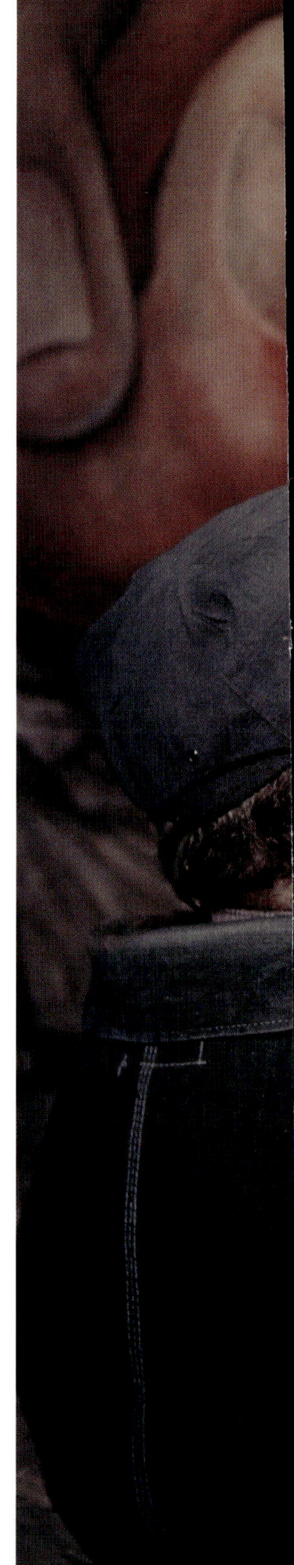

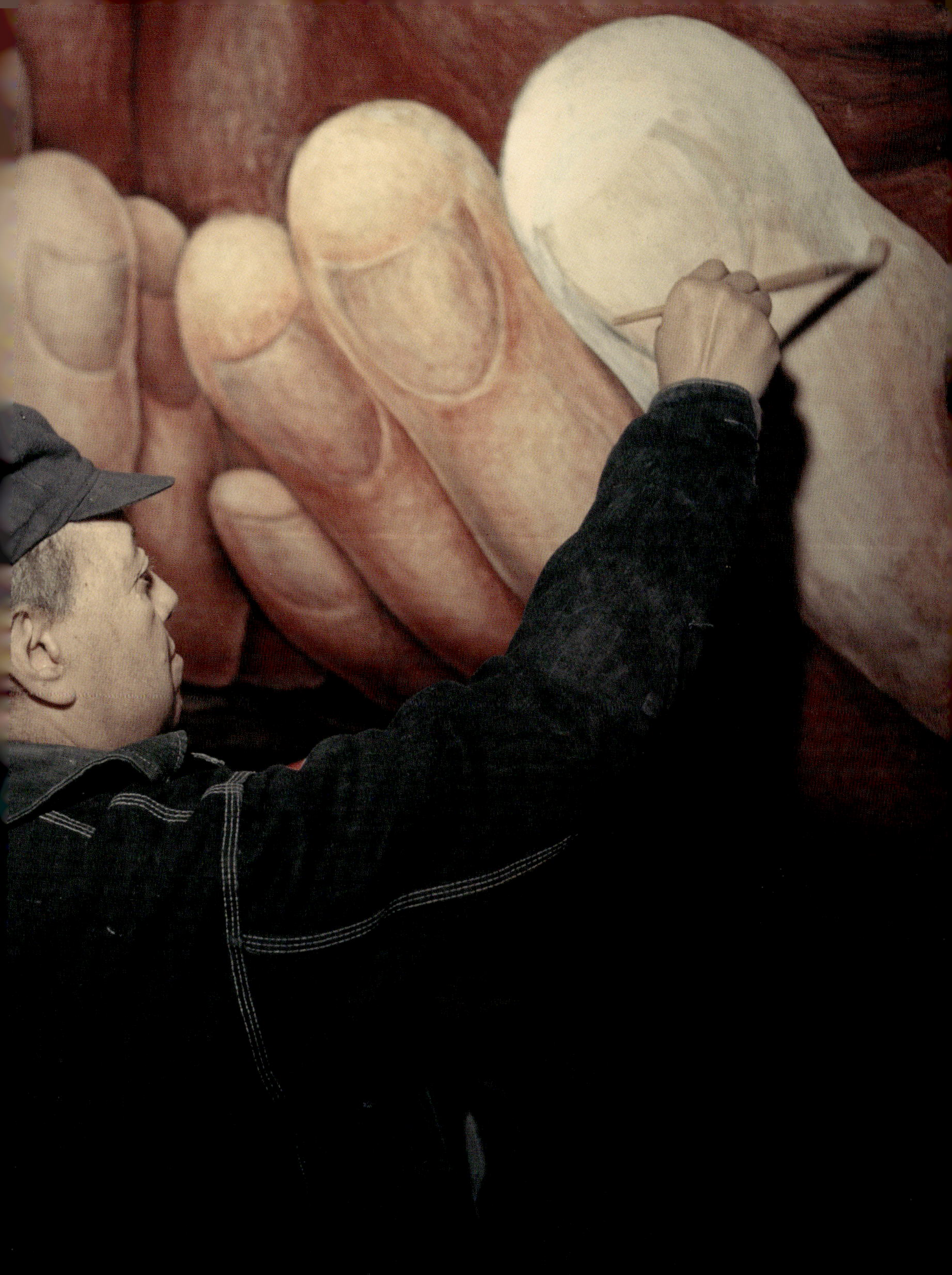

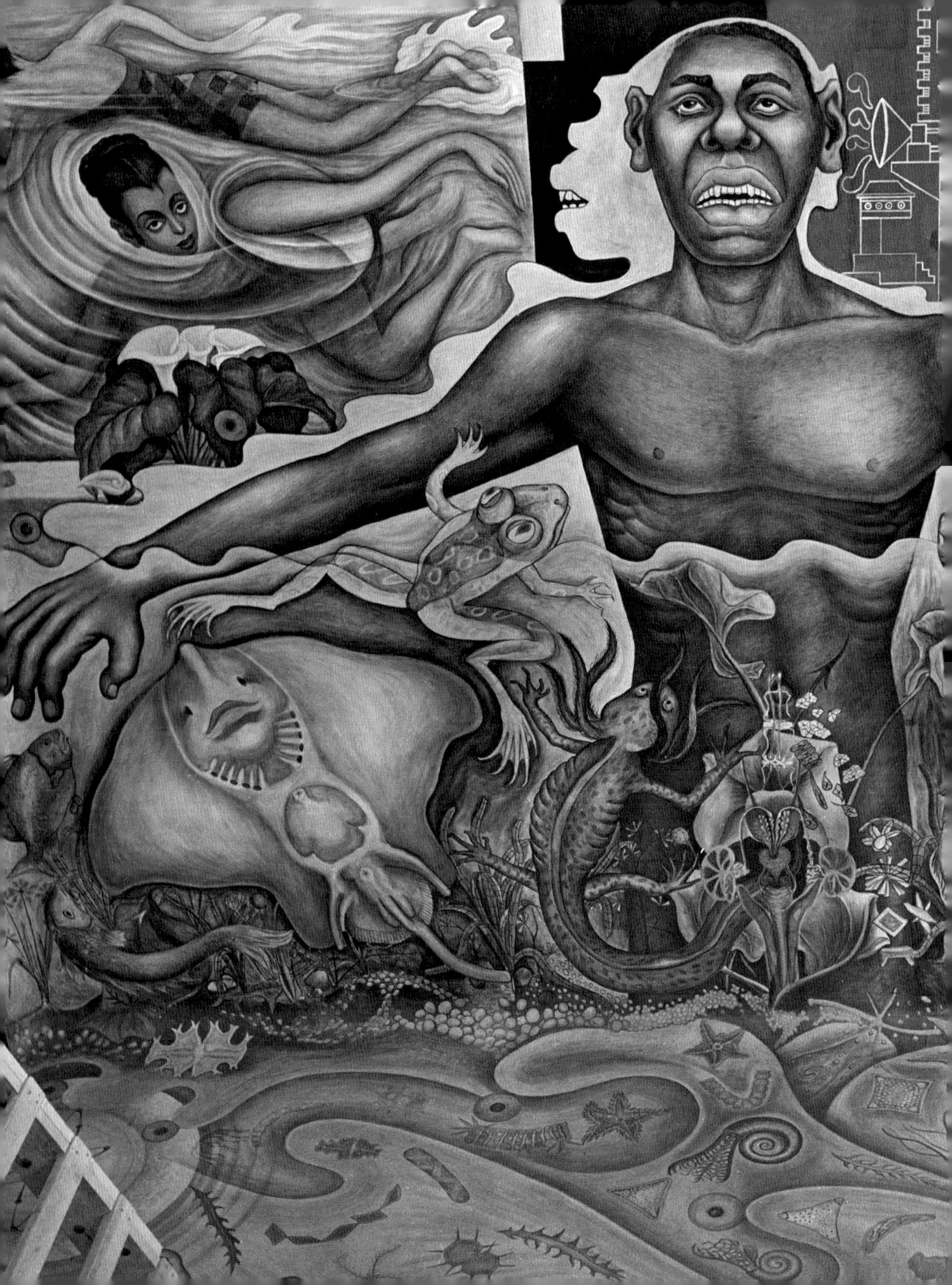

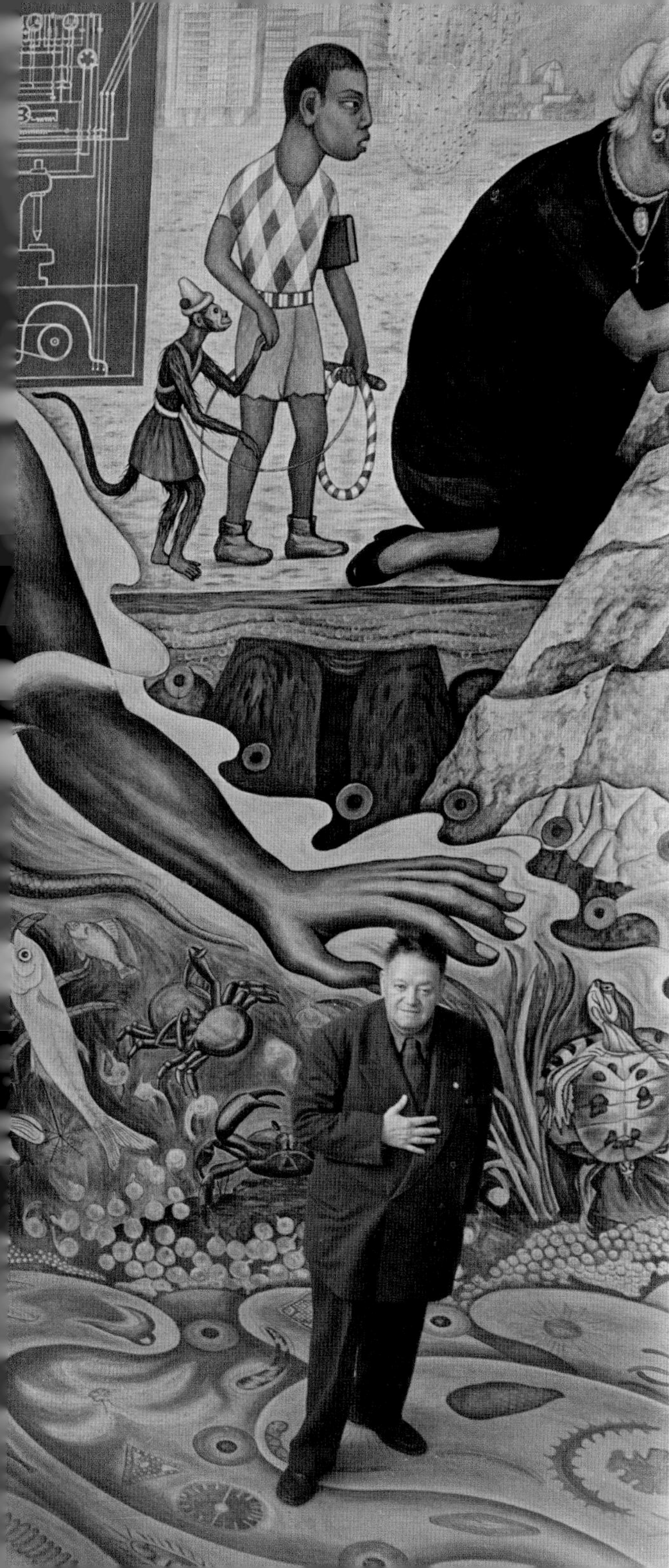

Diego Rivera in front of his fresco *Water, Origin of Life,* Chapultepec Park, Mexico City, 1951.

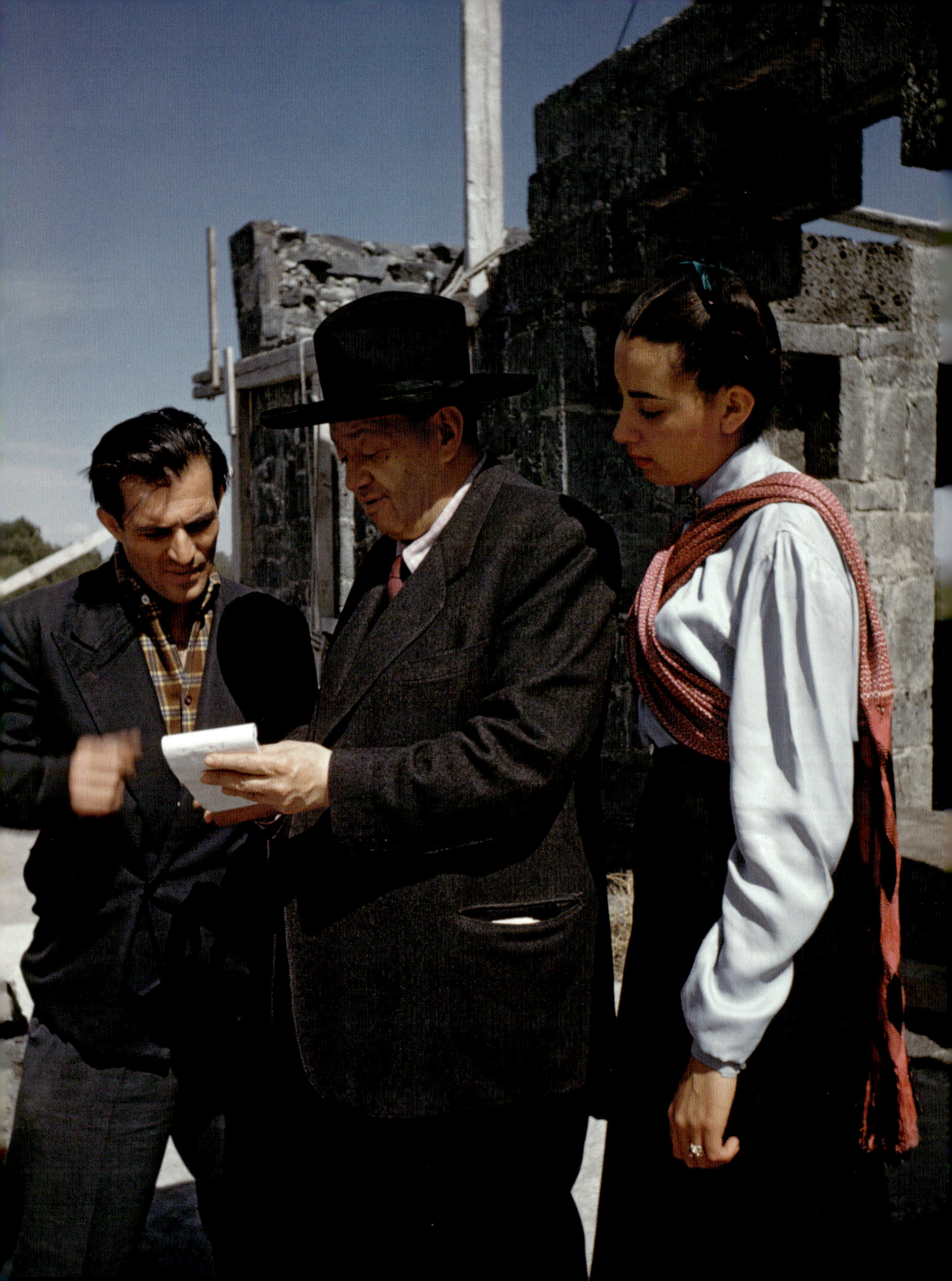

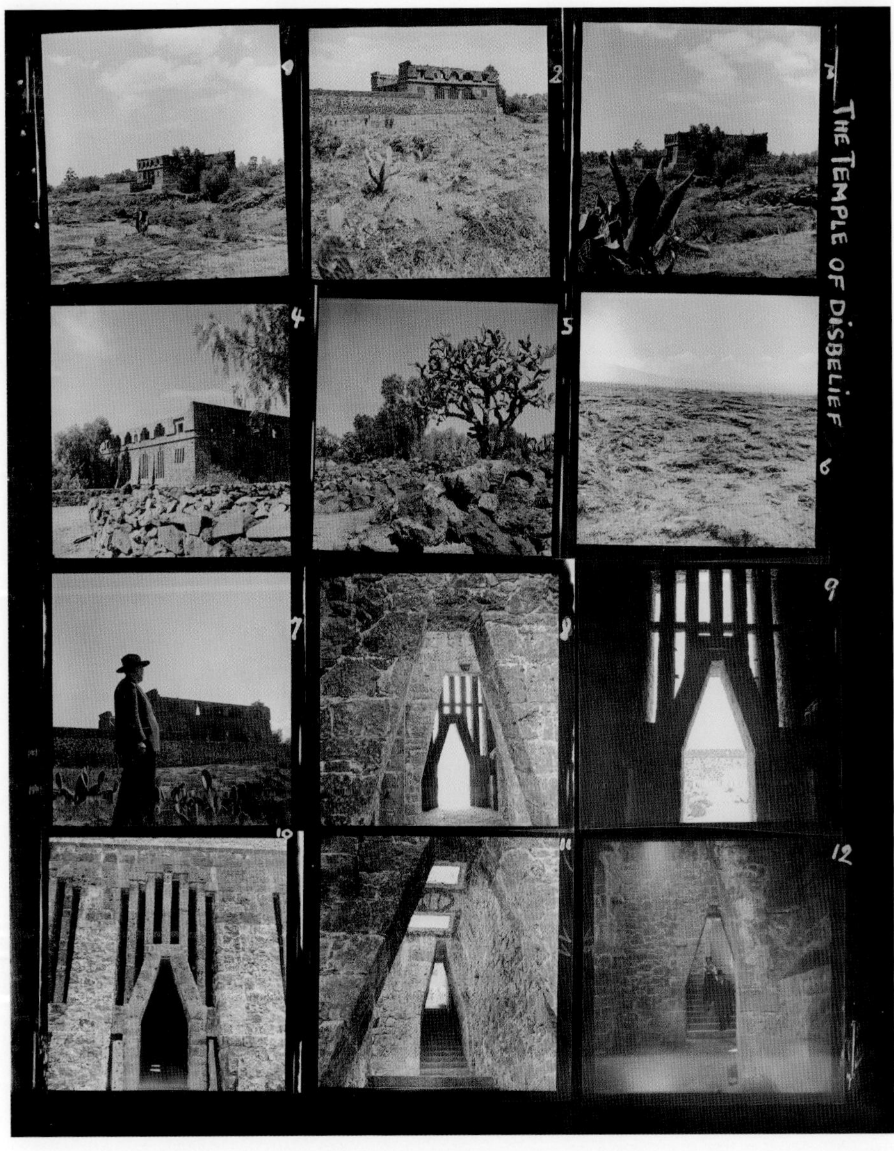

Diego Rivera in front of his temple under construction (now the Anahuacalli Museum), San Pablo Tepetlapa, Mexico, 1951, and contact print of photographs of the temple, 1951. Following double-page spread: Exterior view of the temple, 1951.

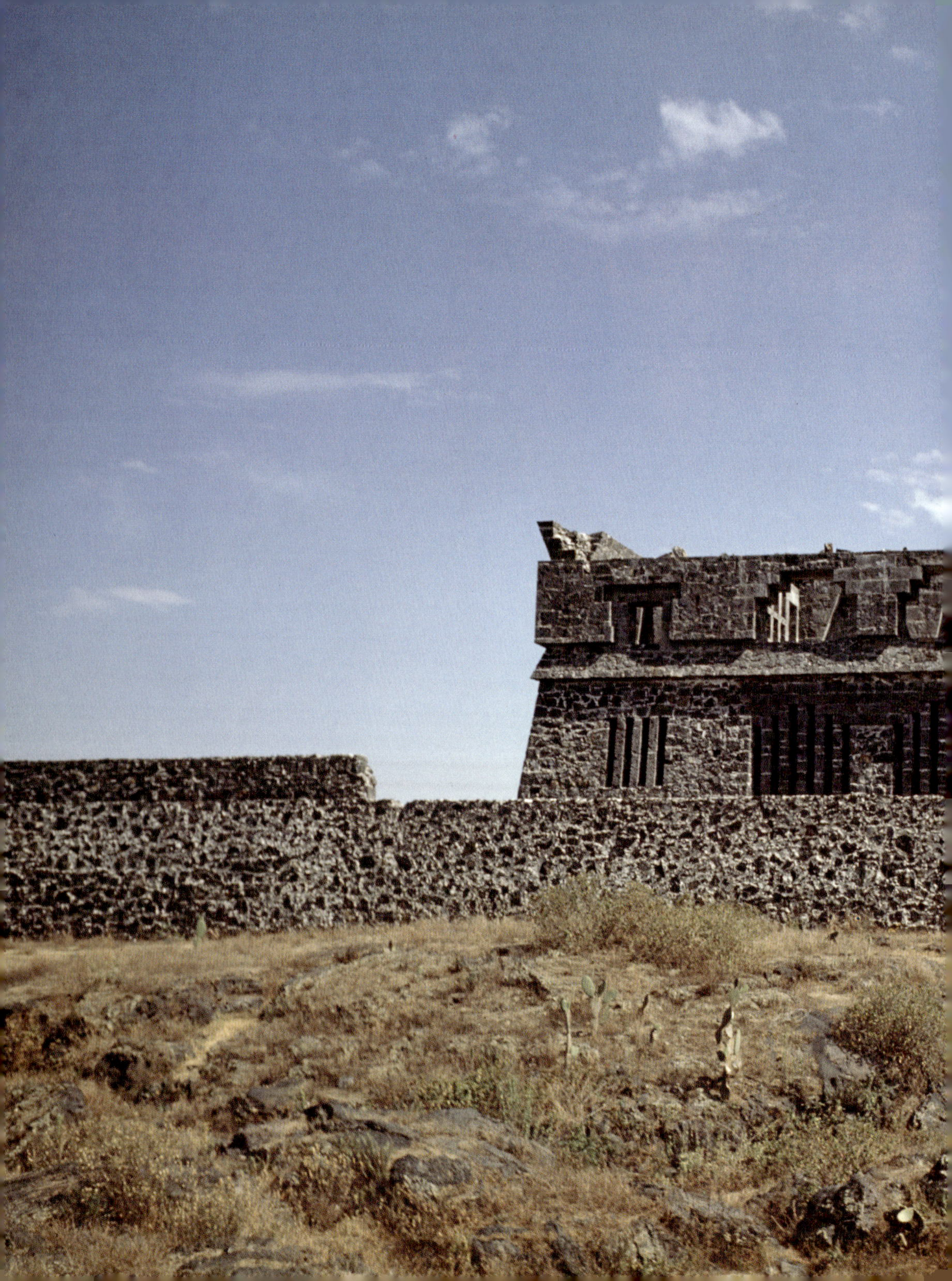

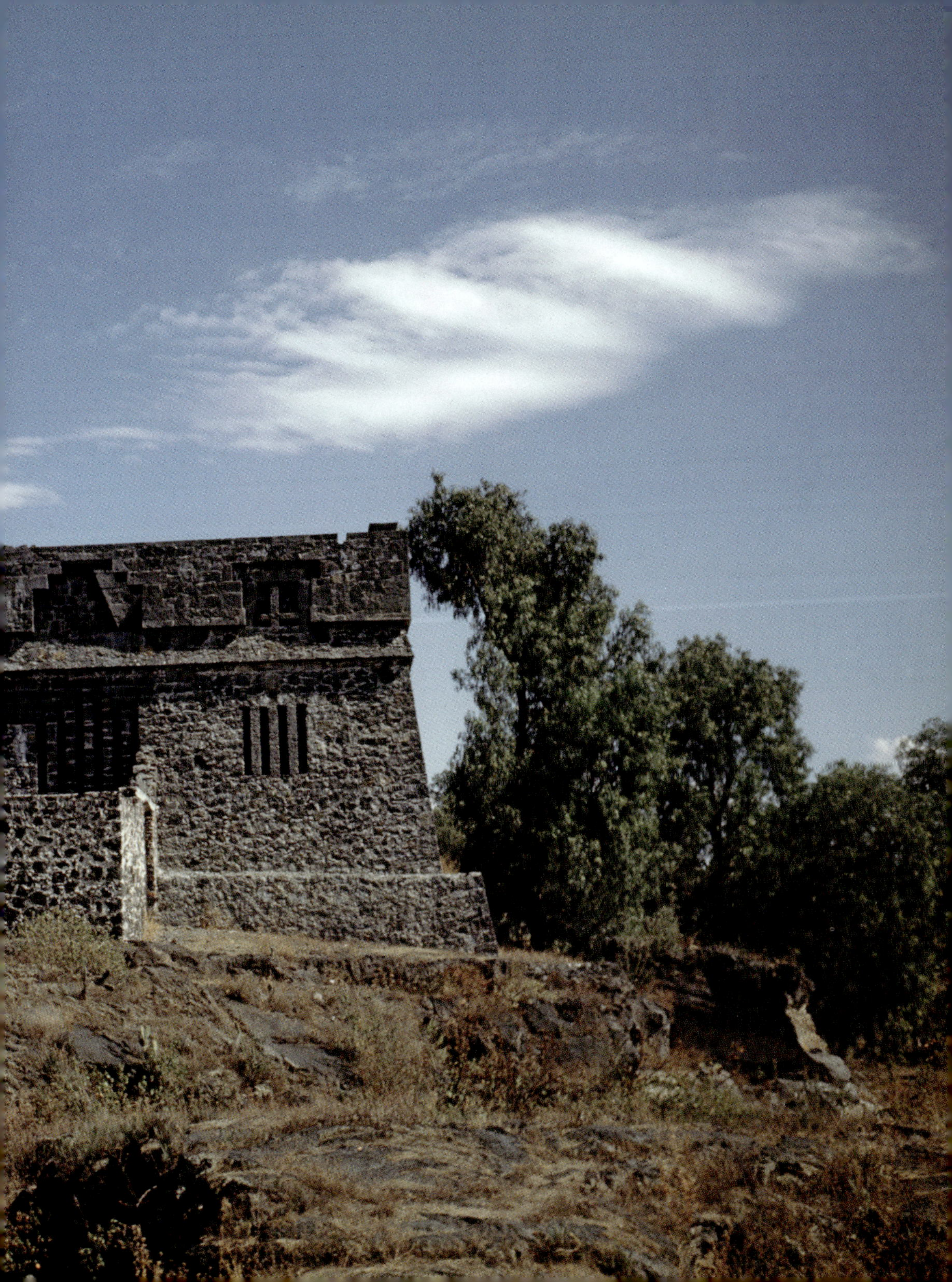

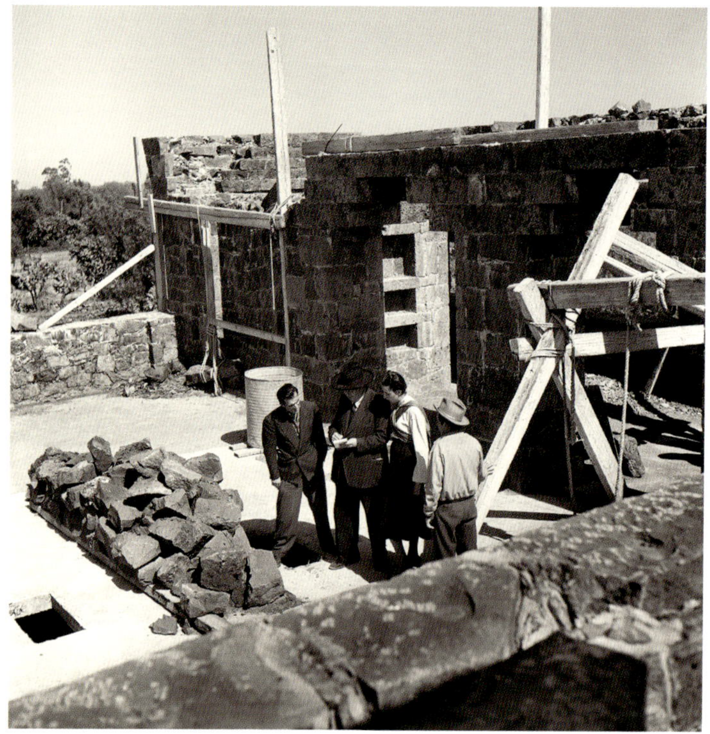

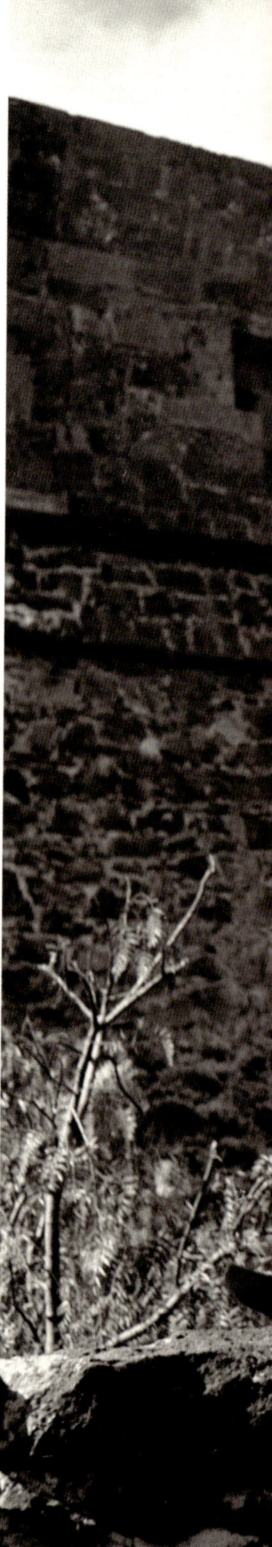

Diego Rivera in front of his temple, 1951.

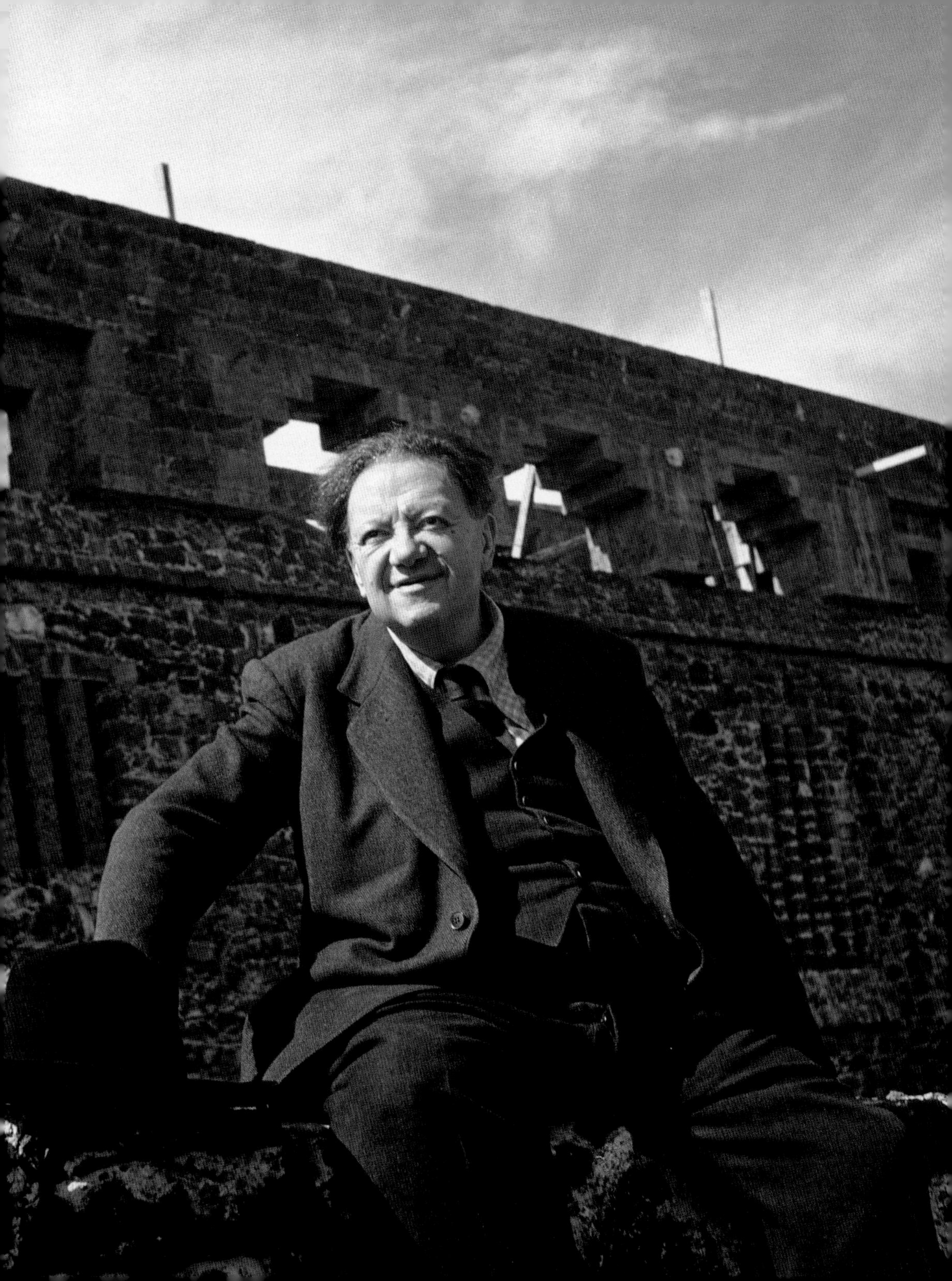

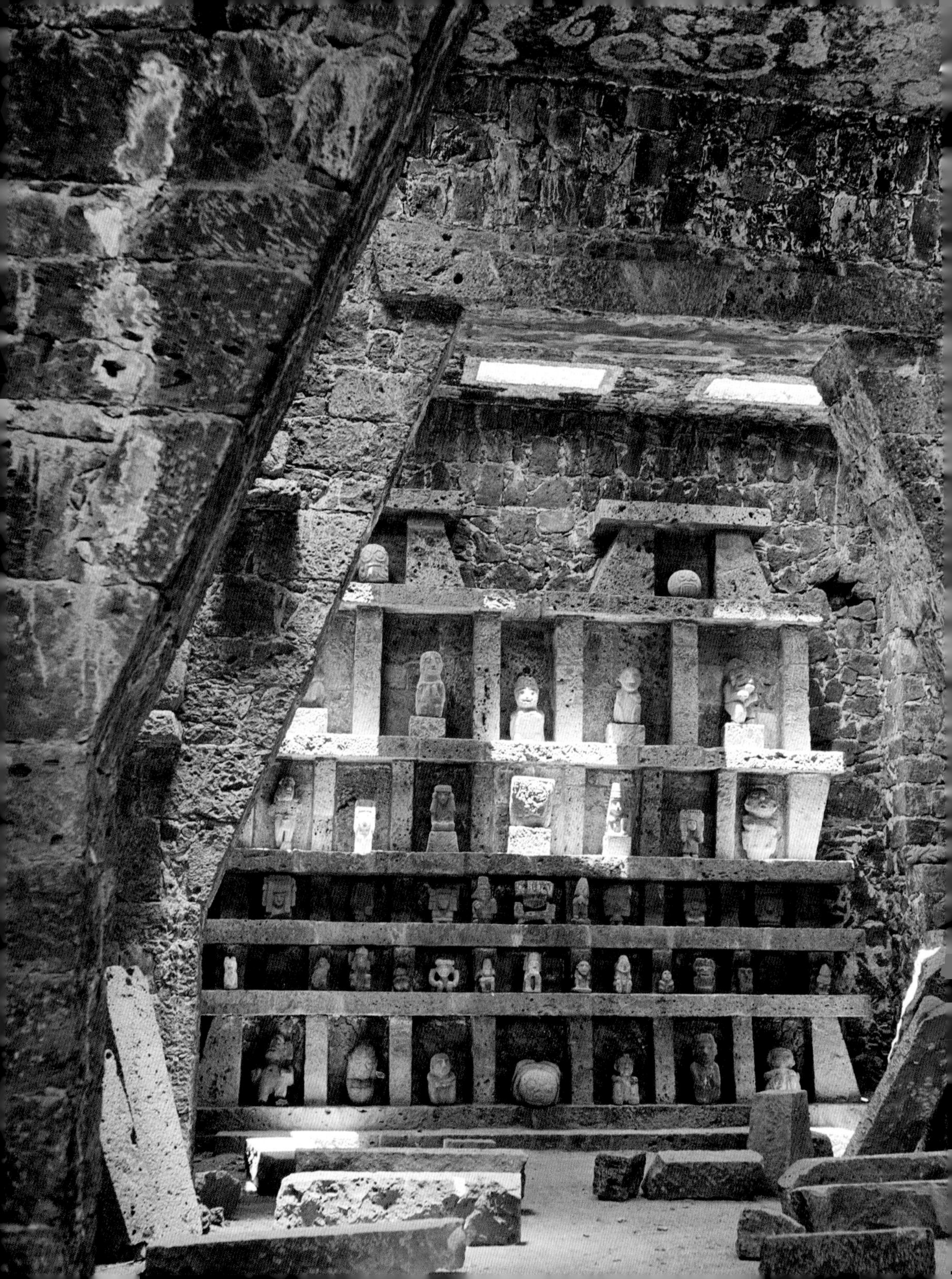

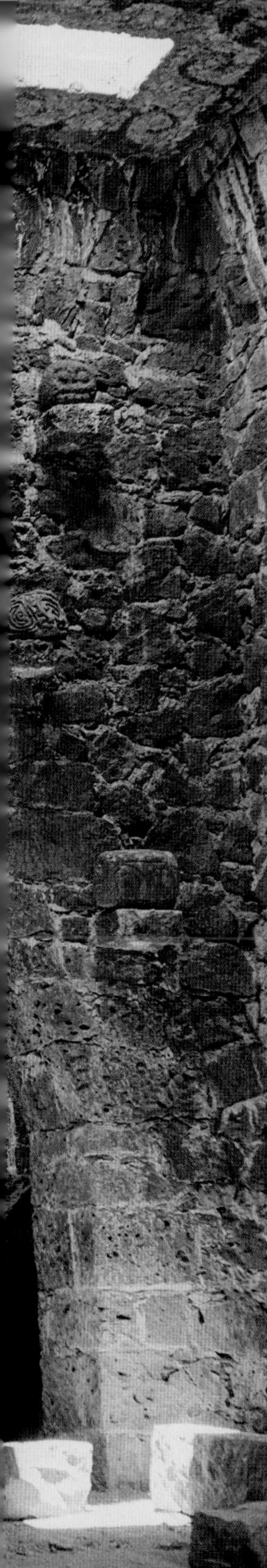

Interior view of the temple, 1951. “The principal altar of the temple Rivera realized by marrying ancient and modern styles. A great number of the most representative elements of his collection . . . are shown here” (Gisèle Freund caption found on the back of a press print).

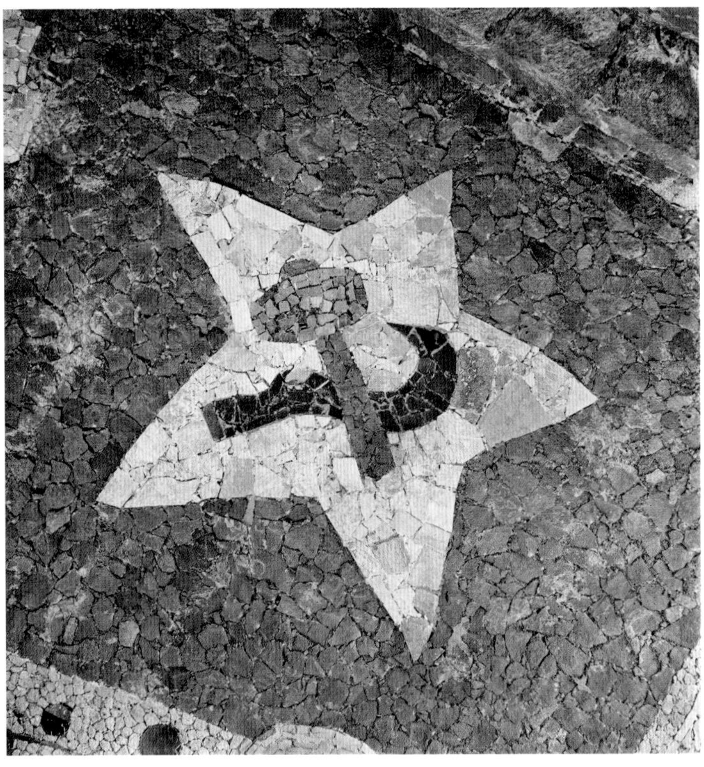

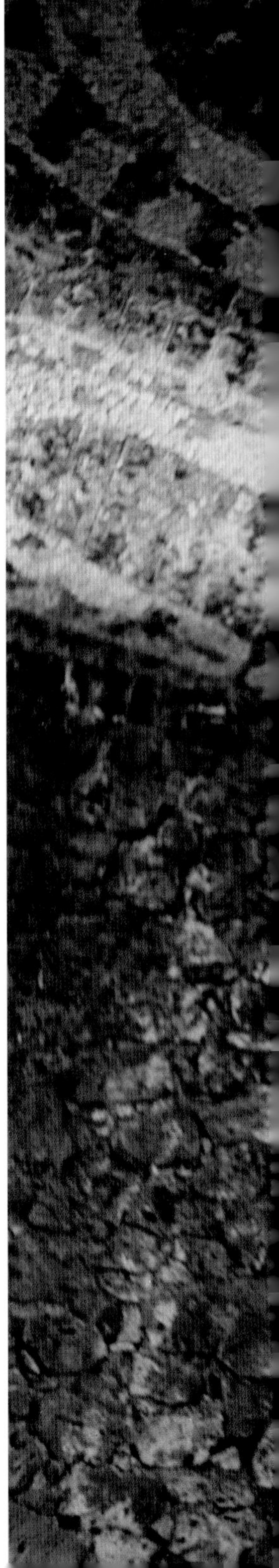

Details of the temple's interior, 1951. "The infiltration of light amplifies this curious structure's magic. Beams of sunlight pass through the narrow but tall gaps in the walls, spreading a uniform light throughout the rooms" (Gisèle Freund, from the photo story "Découverte d'une ville précortésienne près de Mexico City").

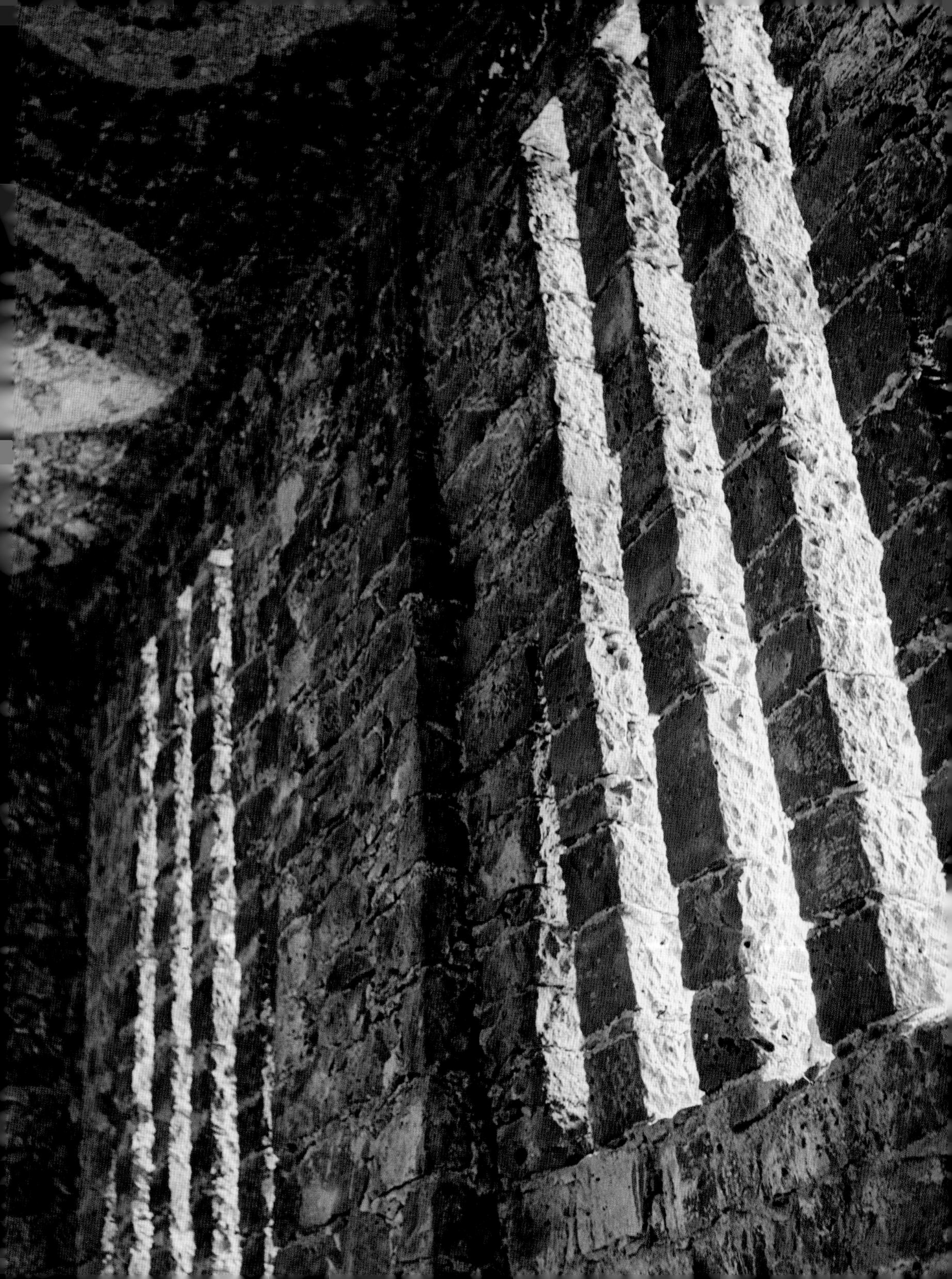

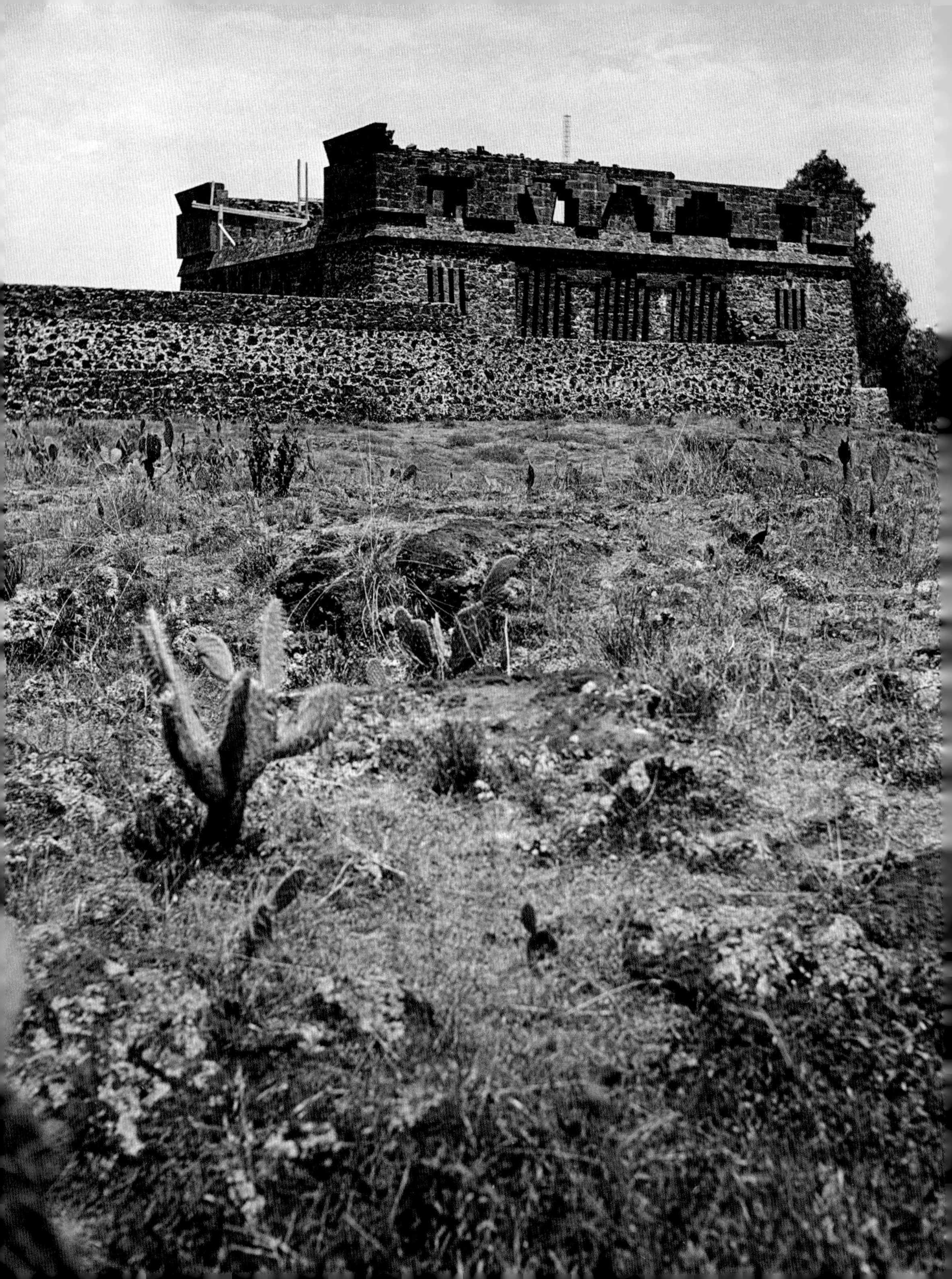

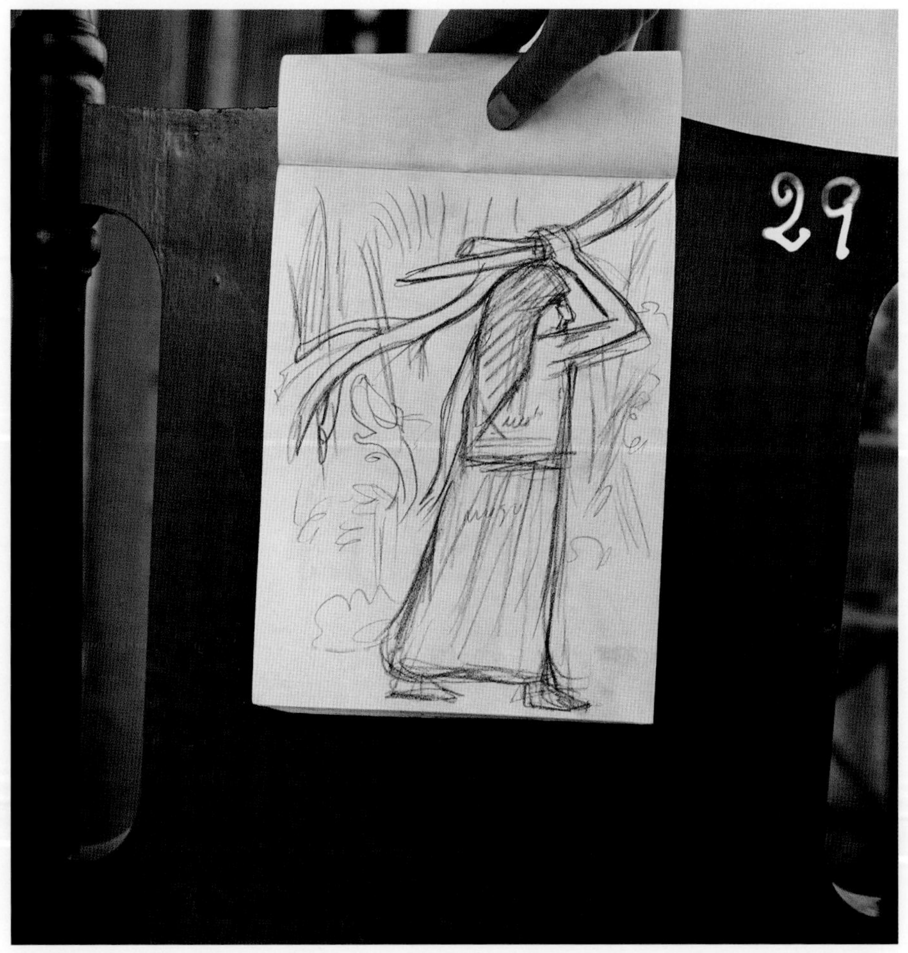

The temple and its surroundings, and a sketch by Diego Rivera, 1951.

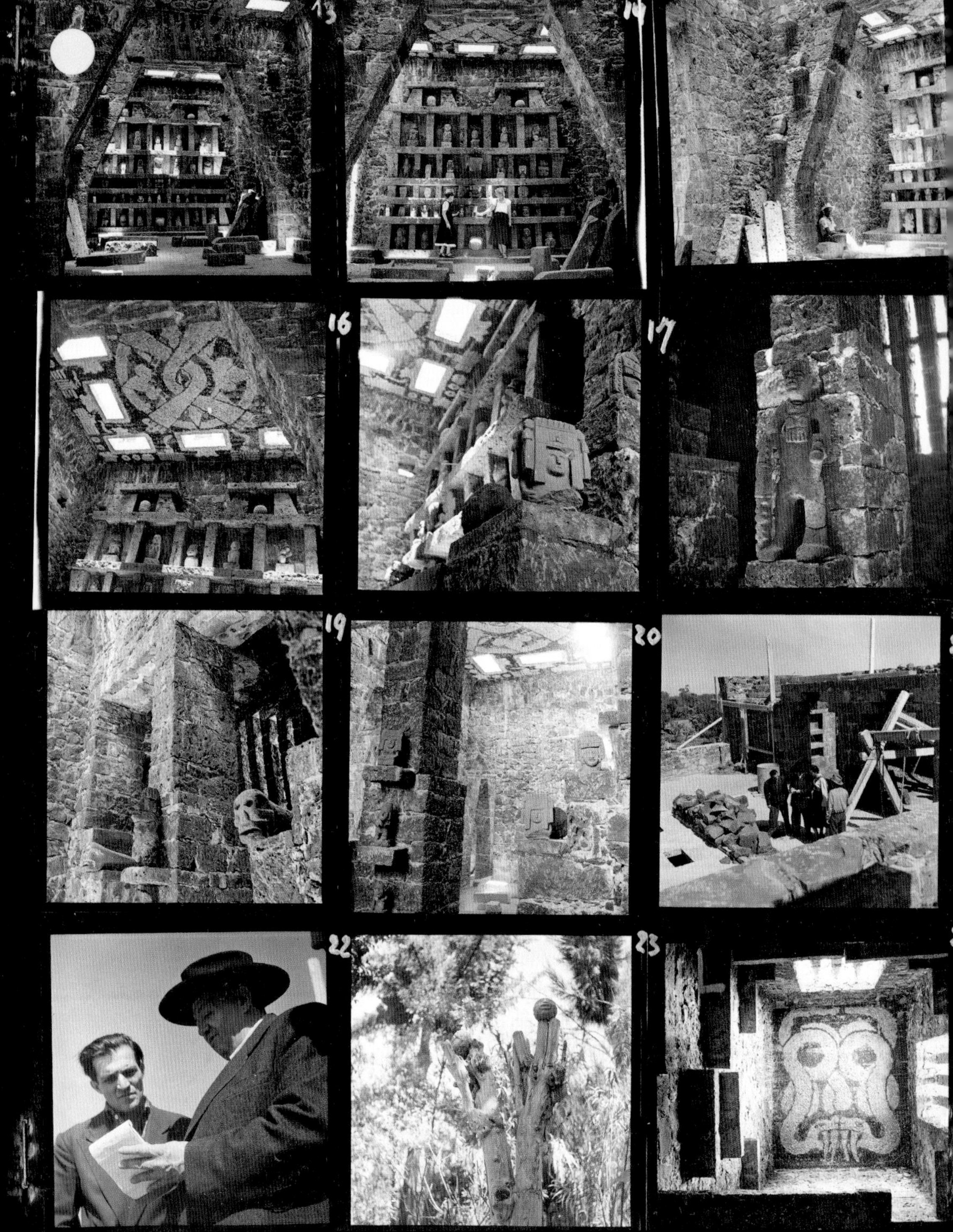

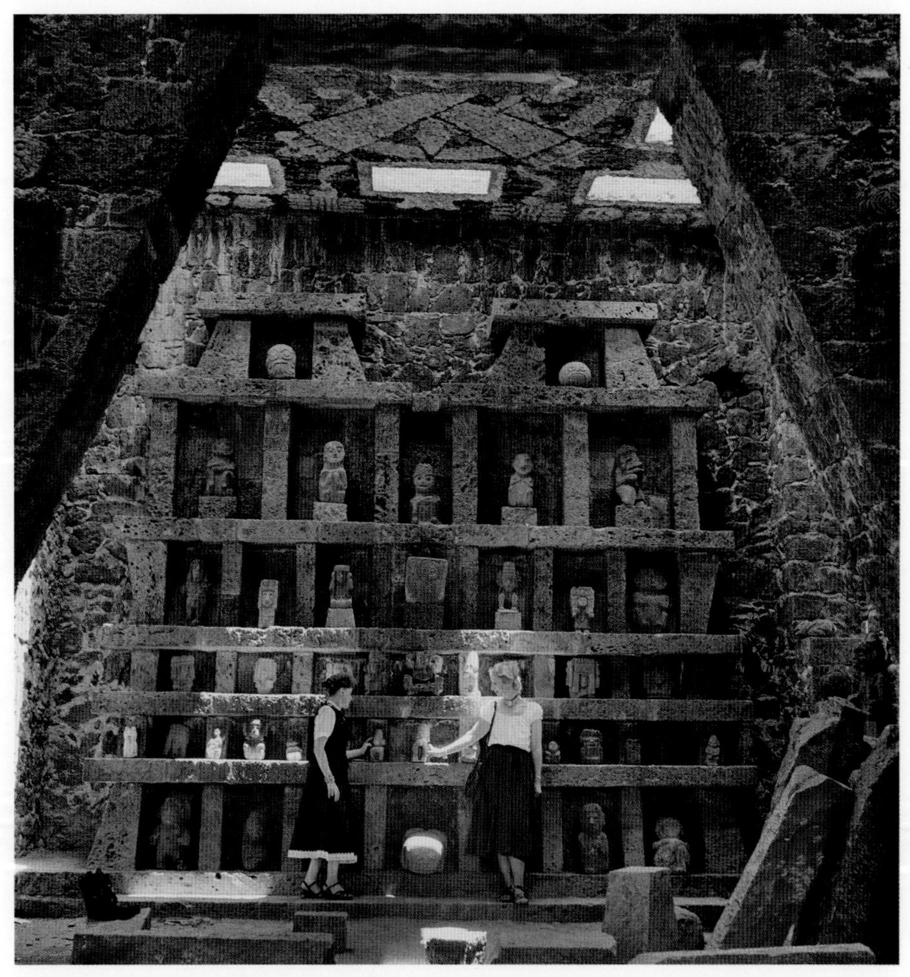

Contact print of photographs of Diego Rivera's temple (now the Anahuacalli Museum), 1951, and visitors to the temple, San Pablo Tepetlapa, Mexico, 1951.

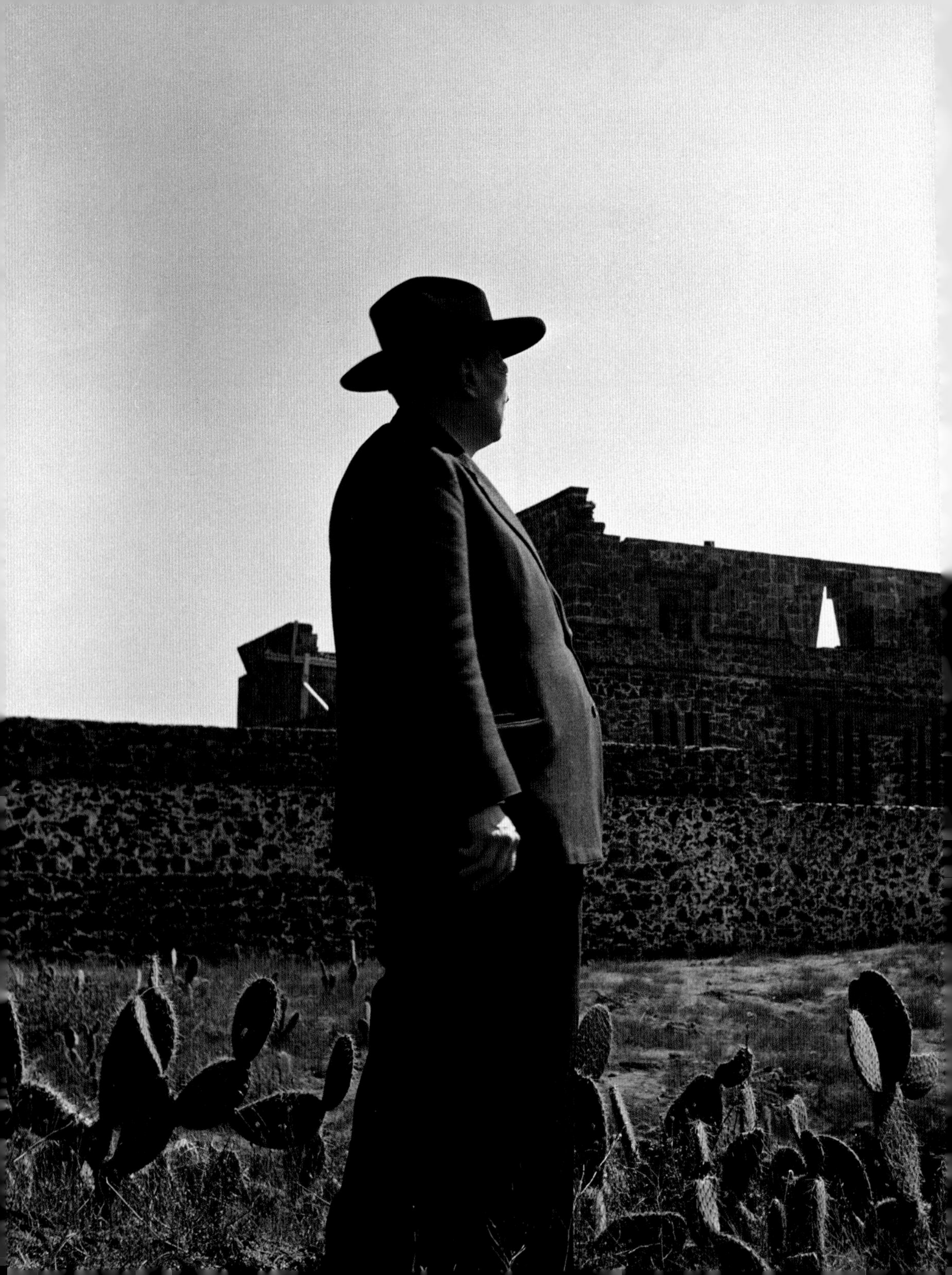

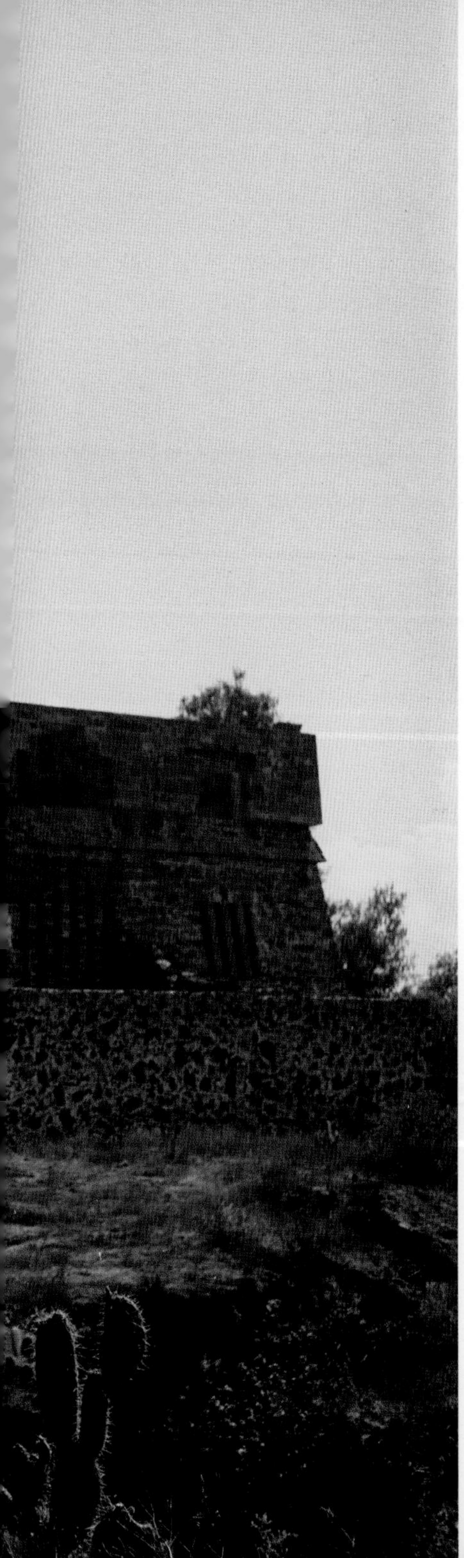

Diego Rivera looking at his temple. "The Mexican painter Diego Rivera before the 'sun temple' he is secretly building near Mexico City in the style of a Mayan pyramid. This monument is intended to house the artist's extraordinary collection of pre-Columbian art" (Gisèle Freund caption found on the back of a press print).

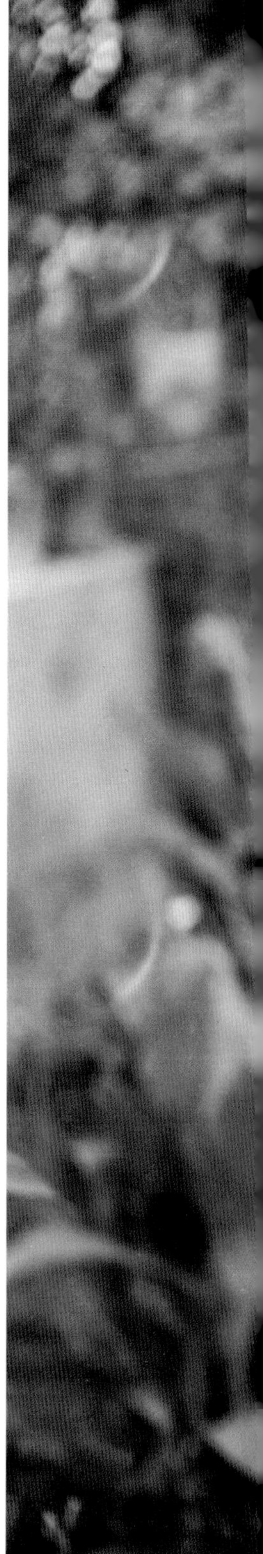

View of La Casa Azul's garden populated with pre-Cortesian sculptures, 1951.

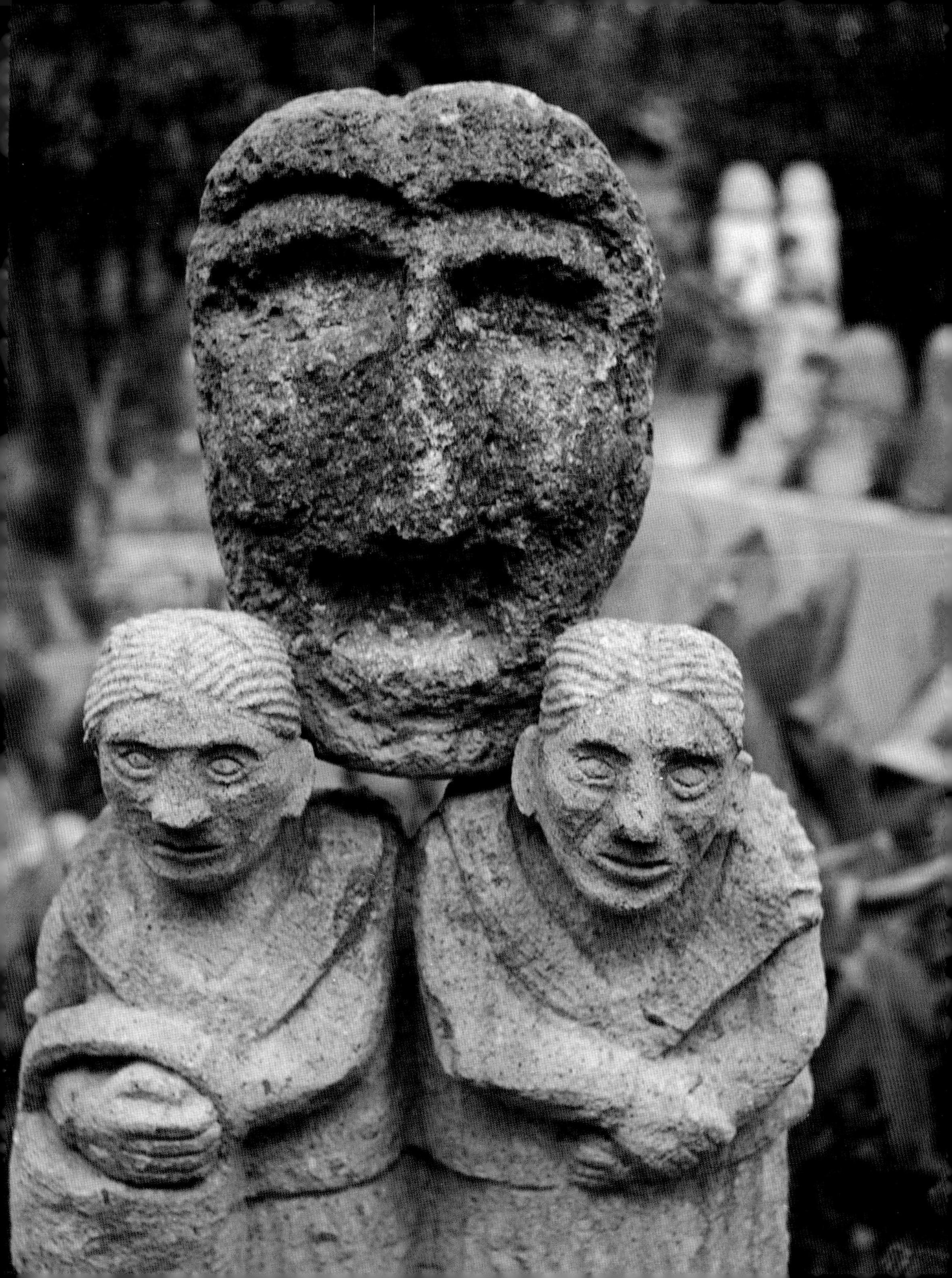

4

THE "UNSEEN" PHOTOGRAPHS

BY LORRAINE AUDRIC

A trip to Mexico that stretched on and on, two long years spent crisscrossing the nation with a small Leica and a Rolleiflex, and a fascination for the country that would last her entire life. Given all this, it comes as no surprise that the selection of Gisèle Freund's photographs revealed in this volume makes up only a fragment of a far vaster body of work, with many photographs remaining to be discovered. The Mexican muralists occupy pride of place in her work, as do writers, poets, and intellectuals, all additions to her already famous collection of portraits. But that is not all: One also finds the tortilla vendor from the local market and the itinerant photographer with his colorful open-air studio—in short, the everyday people of Mexico whom she sought out with an anthropologist's appetite. She was encouraged by her friends Diego and Frida, who also introduced her to Mexican folklore and the pre-Cortesian art she so admired.[1]

Yet Mexico was only one trip among so many others, as evidenced by her archives containing images gathered in over fifty years of work as a portraitist and photojournalist. In total, there are about 12,000 color slides,[2] 1,600 rolls of original black-and-white negatives with their contact sheets, 1,200 original color and black-and-white prints, 1,000 duplicates, and more than 8,000 press prints, all kept in the collections of the Institut Mémoires de l'édition contemporaine (IMEC) [Institute for the Memory of Contemporary Publishing] archives since 2009. There are also unclassifiable items such as a metal case full of short 16-mm films, each meticulously wrapped in a yellowing piece of paper held in place by a bit of string and carefully identified in pencil. Among these, two little filmstrips document a unique moment: Diego Rivera at work helping his photographer friend try her hand at filmmaking (see page 158).

1. She devoted dozens of rolls of film to photographing pre-Columbian art, which would form the material for a book: Paul Rivet and Gisèle Freund, *Mexique précolombien [Pre-Columbian Mexico]*, éditions Ides et Calendes, Neuchâtel, 1954.
2. Including both originals and duplicates.

The Gisèle Freund collection at IMEC also contains all her literary archives, which include a mix of invoices, correspondence, typescripts, publications, her library, and much more. This is a significant part of the collection, given that Gisèle Freund's contribution to the field of photography is not limited to her portraits but is also found–in a sense primarily, for it is where she started[3]–in her sociological writings, in which she provides a very early analysis of the mechanisms implicit in the use of photography, notably in the media. These archives were used to glean information to guide the ongoing digitization of the photographic collection begun by IMEC and the Réunion des musées nationaux [Consortium of National Museums] in 2012.

This volume features images that were largely previously unpublished and needed to be reproduced from the archives to be made visible. This apparently simple, banal operation involves a number of choices that, having unfortunately not been made while the artist was alive, must be thoughtfully weighed.[4] Additionally, digital technology has now reached a point where nearly anything is possible.[5] The only limits are set by an ethic embodied in a single question: To what point can we modify an image without being disrespectful to the work of art? Each photographic print is always and inevitably an interpretation, an unavoidably subjective stage, and, given the artist's absence, the possibilities are infinite. So it is necessary to establish a rigorous framework to be defined based on the objectives and uses pursued, the available archives, and in-depth historical research.

The Gisèle Freund collection includes many originals, slides, and negatives, which can offer an unrivaled reproduction quality when digitized. Those documents marked by time were restored, both to conserve the documents and to aid in their dissemination.[6] Since the prints available in the archives are, unfortunately, too disparate and patchy to serve as references, and in order to avoid the trap of trying to imitate the artist's approach, the

3. She published her thesis *(La Photographie en France au xixe siècle [Photography in France in the Nineteenth Century],* Paris: La Maison des Amis des livres) in 1936, having defended it at the Sorbonne the previous year. She had begun her work at the department of sociology at the University of Frankfurt under the direction of Karl Mannheim. 4. Which images to select? What to do with previously unpublished photos? What medium to choose? Since the photograph is a multiple, the same image can be found in numerous different forms (negative, press print, collection print, duplicate, and internegative, to name a few). What framing to use? Which caption to print: the one found on the back of a print, the one published, the one written on the mount of the slide? The decisions to be made are numerous. 5. The stains soiling a negative or the folds slashing a print can be eliminated, the lost colors of an old slide can be re-created, and all of this can be done while leaving any visual manipulation completely undetectable to the human eye. 6. A "digital negative" (raw scan) is conserved for each document in order to allow easy reversal of the choices made.

decision was made to stick as closely as possible to the other documents left in the collection by using technical analysis and various clues[7] to bring out colors and densities that are still present in the original and through always working on the image uniformly. It is, therefore, more accurate to speak of a "restitution," one that allows certain images to appear as they have never been seen before.

So are these images truly previously "unseen"? Technically speaking, perhaps not. They are simply being made available for viewing through a digitization project that seeks a balance between the idealization of a return to the original and the overestimation of an inherited document. But in this volume, they find new life and return Gisèle Freund's work to the vigor of its original moment.

7. For example, by establishing the black point (lying outside the frame) and the white point (the flash reflection off pupils), the tonal range of the image can be determined, and any fading that may have occurred due to time can be counteracted.

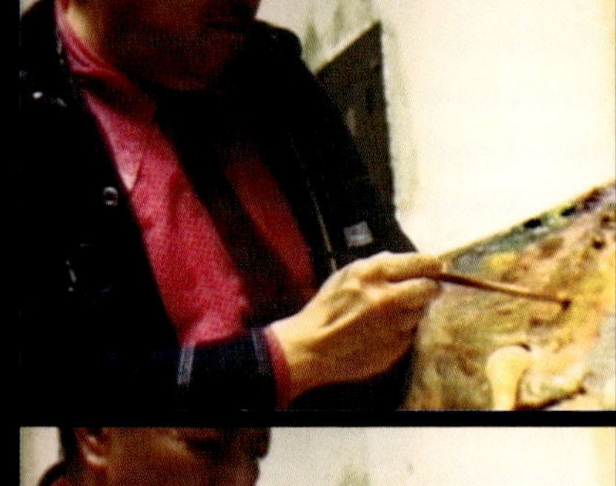
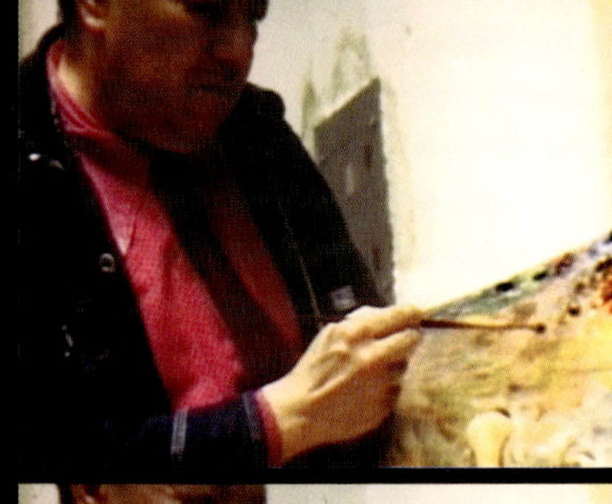
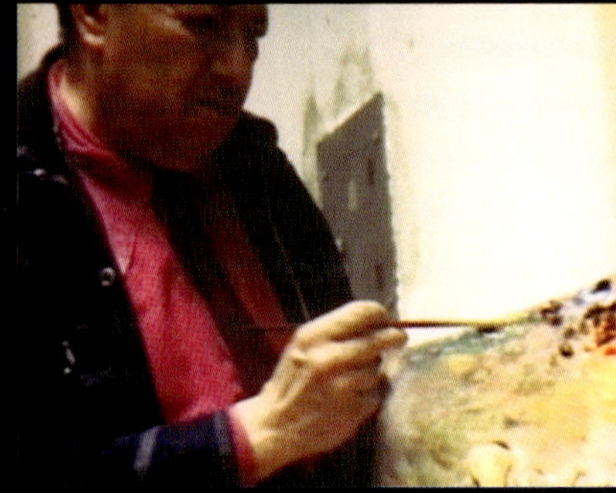
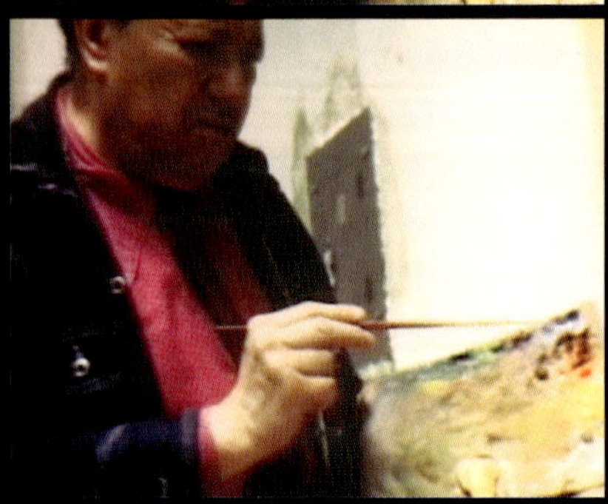
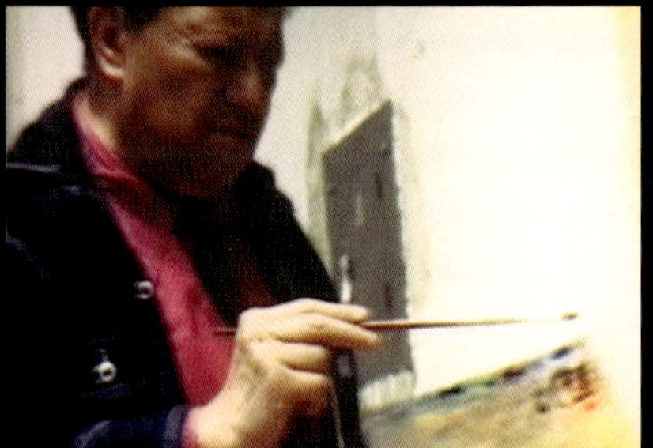

5

THE UNRELEASED FILM

DIEGO RIVERA AT WORK

Exclusively for readers of this volume:
Discover Gisèle Freund's previously unreleased color film showing Diego Rivera painting in 1951.

Visit www.abramsbooks.com/fridakahlo and enter access code 1951.

CREDITS

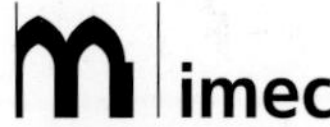

Founded at the initiative of publishing researchers and professionals, the Institut Mémoires de l'édition contemporaine (IMEC) [Institute for the Memory of Contemporary Publishing] gathers, preserves, and showcases archive collections and studies dedicated to the major publishing houses, periodicals, and various participants in the world of books and art.

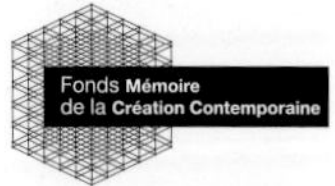

Founded in 2011 by a group of patrons from the publishing, conservation, research, and art worlds, the endowment fund Fonds Mémoire de la création contemporaine (Fonds MCC) [Memory of Contemporary Art Collection] received all of Gisèle Freund's archives as a donation in March 2011 and entrusted them to the IMEC.

TECHNIQUES AND DIMENSIONS

From original color slides, 24 x 36 mm (0.94 x 1.41 inches): pages 2, 4, 16-17, 33, 37, 40, 44, 50, 65, 66, 68-69, 71, 78, 89, 108, 110-111, 112, 114-115, 124-125, 130-131, 133, 136, 138-139.
From original black-and-white negatives, 6 x 6 cm (2.36 x 2.36 inches): pages 11, 13, 14, 15, 25, 31, 32, 35, 36, 38, 39, 41, 42, 43, 45, 46, 47, 48, 49, 51, 52, 53, 54, 55, 57, 59, 60, 61, 62, 72, 73, 75, 76, 79, 80, 82, 83, 84, 85, 86, 87, 88, 90, 92, 93, 94, 95, 96, 97, 99, 100, 101, 102, 109, 113, 117, 118, 119, 120, 121, 122, 123, 126, 127, 129, 132, 134, 140, 141, 142, 144, 145, 146, 147, 149, 150, 153.
Black-and-white contact sheet (detail), 227 x 35 mm (8.93 x 1.37 inches): pages 28-29.
Contact sheet stapled to cardboard, 23.5 x 26 cm (9.25 x 10.23 inches): pages 56, 67, 98, 103, 128, 137, 148.
Black-and-white press print, 16.7 x 12 cm (6.57 x 4.72 inches): page 74.
Black-and-white press print, 25 x 24.8 cm (9.84 x 9.76 inches): page 77.
Black-and-white press print, 11.6 x 10 cm (4.56 x 3.93 inches): page 91.
Black-and-white contact print, 6 x 6 cm (2.36 x 2.36 inches): pages 104, 105, 106, 107.

COPYRIGHTS

ADDITIONAL COPYRIGHTS FOR WORKS OF ART REPRODUCED

FRENCH EDITION

Editorial Director: Nicolas de Cointet
Artistic Director: Franklin Labbé
Layout: Caroline Dauvois
Production Management: Alix Willaert
Photo-Engraving: Les artisans du Regard

ABRAMS EDITION

Translated from the French
by Nicholas Elliott

Editor: Laura Dozier
Designer: Sebit Min
Production Manager: Erin Vandeveer

Library of Congress Control Number: 2014932111

ISBN: 978-1-4197-1423-8

Éditions Albin Michel, 22 rue Huyghens, 75014 Paris, www.albin-michel.fr

Originally published in 2013 Albin Michel / IMEC

Printed and bound in China
10 9 8 7 6 5 4 3

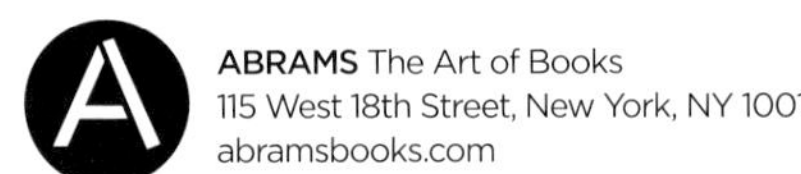
ABRAMS The Art of Books
115 West 18th Street, New York, NY 10011
abramsbooks.com